DULWICH PICTURE GALLERY—A CATALOGUE

A view of Dulwich Picture Gallery by Joseph Michael Gandy, after a design by Sir John Soane, 1811 (reproduced by permission of the Trustees of Sir John Soane's Museum)

DULWICH PICTURE GALLERY

A Catalogue

PETER MURRAY

Sotheby Parke Bernet

Text © Peter Murray 1980

Illustrations © The Governors of Dulwich College 1980

First published in 1980 for Sotheby Parke Bernet Publications
in association with the Governors of Dulwich College by
Philip Wilson Publishers Ltd
Russell Chambers, Covent Garden, London WC2E 8AA

and

Biblio Distribution Centre
81 Adams Drive
Totowa, New Jersey 07512, U.S.A.

ISBN 0 85667 071 5

Designed by Paul Sharp

Filmset and printed by
BAS Printers Limited, Over Wallop, Hampshire
and bound by
Mansell (Bookbinders) Limited, Witham, Essex

Jacket illustration: *The Triumph of David* by Nicolas Poussin

Foreword

The publication of a new catalogue of the Dulwich Picture Gallery is long overdue. This is one of the two or three most important collections of paintings in Britain, in range and quality matched only by the national museums and the greatest private collections.

The Governors are greatly indebted to Professor Peter Murray for the research and scholarship which he has contributed to the preparation of this most important work. Its publication has been made possible by the generous financial support of Sotheby Parke Bernet.

BASIL GREENHILL
Chairman
Dulwich Picture Gallery Committee
College Governors of Alleyn's College of God's Gift

Chronological List of Dulwich Catalogues

1813	Inventory of Bourgeois Bequest
(1814	Gallery opened to the public)
c 1816	Pamphlet compiled by R. Cockburn, the first curator of the Gallery—with modifications this lasted for sixty years
1858/9	Partial new catalogue, in manuscript only
1876	*Descriptive Catalogue* by J. C. L. Sparkes
1880	Catalogue by J. P. Richter, the German art historian, in which non-British entries were rewritten
1890	Catalogue of the Cartwright Bequest and other non-Bourgeois pictures by Sparkes and Canon Carver
1892	1876, 1880 and 1890 catalogues were amalgamated and the pictures were given new numbers
1914	1892 catalogue revised by Sir E. Cook
1926	Further revisions to the 1914 catalogue were made to incorporate the Fairfax Murray pictures
1953	*Brief Catalogue* was published, a list of artists' names and picture titles

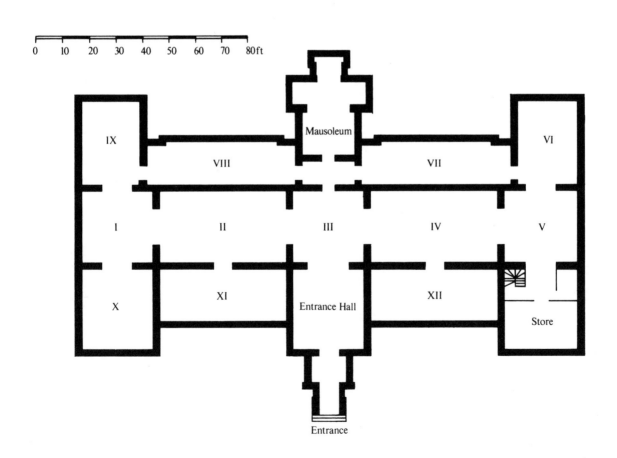

Contents

PLATE I

Guido Reni (1575–1642) 262 *S. John the Baptist in the Wilderness*

PLATE II

Rembrandt van Ryn (1606–69)   221   *A Young Man, perhaps the Artist's Son Titus*

PLATE II

PLATE III

Sir Anthony van Dyck (1599–1641)   173   *Emmanuel Philibert of Savoy, Prince of Oneglia*

PLATE IV

Meindert Hobbema (1638–1709)   87 *Wooded Landscape with Water-mill*

PLATE V

Aelbert Cuyp (1620–91)   124   *A Road near a River*

PLATE VI

Sir Peter Paul Rubens (1577–1640)   131   *Hagar in the Desert*

PLATE VII

Thomas Gainsborough, RA (1727–88)   588   *An Unknown Couple in a Landscape*

PLATE VIII

Nicolas Poussin (1594–1665)   236 *The Triumph of David*

Introduction

1 It mentions the 'Duke of Yorke' (146), who became James II in February 1685. The Inventory is said to be in Cartwright's own illegible hand.

British School
443 *Edward Alleyn*

John Greenhill
393 *William Cartwright*

The collection of pictures at Dulwich came into being more or less by accident. When he died, in 1626, Edward Alleyn naturally left his pictures to his Foundation, including the portraits of his wife (British School, 444) and himself (British School, 443). There were probably 39 pictures in all, but only those two are now exhibited, most of the others being mere furniture-pictures of kings, queens and sibyls. The next important bequest followed only 60 years later, when William Cartwright (*d* 1686: *see* Greenhill, 393), who like Alleyn was connected with the stage and the book trade, left his large and miscellaneous collection of pictures to the College. Fortunately, the Inventory of his pictures, drawn up in or before 1686,[1] and preserved in the Gallery archives, is a document of great art-historical importance, as well as a record of late 17th-century taste. Less fortunately, it contains no fewer than 239 items, of which only 80 can now be identified with certainty: it seems that Cartwright's servants—and perhaps others—were less scrupulous than they should have been, since it is clear that many (perhaps most) of the 239 never reached Dulwich. It is not possible to be entirely certain about a few of these Cartwright pictures, since one leaf (containing items 186–209) is missing from the Inventory. The most interesting example of a possible Cartwright picture is the view of the Thames in the late 17th century by Cornelis Bol (360), which may have been one of the missing items. The other great significance of the Cartwright Inventory lies in the rarity of such documents and their importance in identifying painters who might otherwise have remained obscure—for example, the three portraits (374, 416, 418) at Dulwich recorded in the Cartwright Inventory as by John Greenhill (who died in 1676), together with a signed one (399), now form the principal corpus of his work, and must be used as a basis for any further attributions. The two pictures by the mysterious Adam Colonia (371, 431)—about one-fifth of his entire known output—demonstrate another aspect of such inventories; the mere survival of the Cartwright Collection, even after its heavy losses, provides an historical context more important than the sum of the individual pictures. Because the two Colonias have been kept together with a group of copies after Bassano (386, 398, 412, 422) it is possible to attribute them to him, thus increasing his known works by some 40 per cent. The seapieces by the even more obscure Castro (359, 361, 428, 436, 437, 517) are another case in point.

Historically important, and indeed fascinating, as the Alleyn and Cartwright pictures are, they are artistically no more important than such similar collections as the Tradescant pictures at Oxford. What transformed the Dulwich College collections into a major picture gallery, ranking with many of the great European collections, and ante-dating the National Gallery itself by a decade, was the splendid donation, in 1811, by Sir Peter Francis Bourgeois, of the collection built up by his friend Noel Desenfans and himself.

The history of the Desenfans–Bourgeois Bequest of some 371 paintings, including many of the very highest quality—works by Rembrandt, Rubens, van Dyck, Murillo, Poussin, Claude, Cuyp, Reni, Guercino, Veronese and others—is worth considering in detail. The collection was begun about 1780, certainly before 1785, since a few of the pictures now in the Gallery (*eg* Gelder, 126; R. Wilson, 171) can be shown to have belonged to Desenfans at that date, and Bourgeois seems to have continued to collect until his sudden death in 1811. These years were, perhaps, the most favourable in the whole history of collecting for the acquisition of great works of art. The French Revolution, followed by the Napoleonic Wars, led to the dispersal of many of the great French private collections. For example, Calonne, a friend of

Paintings

A detail from a page from the Cartwright Inventory, *c* 1686

James Northcote, RA
28 *Noel Joseph Desenfans*

Desenfans, who had been Prime Minister of France, brought his collection to London, where it was sold in 1795. Two fine pictures came from his collection to Dulwich: the Teniers *Sow and Litter* (146) and the Murillo *Flower Girl* (199). The Napoleonic campaigns of plunder spread across Europe and, especially in Italy, caused further waves of selling, not to mention looting from churches and suppressed religious houses. Some of the finest pictures in the Gallery were acquired as a result of Napoleon's depredations, including the Reni (262) and the Rubens sketch (148); while others, such as the portrait of Archibald Hope (Sanders, 577), came indirectly, a century later, because of the flight of refugees from the French invasions.

Noel Desenfans was born in Douai, in Northern France, in 1745 and died in London in 1807. He was educated at the University of Paris and made some stir with a defence of Fénelon against Lord Chesterfield, as well as a Rousseauish essay, *L'Élève de la Nature*, written as early as 1763. He came to London as a teacher of languages, and there met and married Miss Margaret Morris (627), the sister of Sir John Morris of Clasemont, Glamorgan, who brought him a dowry of £5000, with which he began to buy and sell pictures at the London auctions. By 1785 he was in a position to hold a sale of his own collection; and in that year on 11 May and three following days, Mr Christie advertised 'A Catalogue of The First Part of the Truly Superb Collection . . . being the Sole and Genuine Property of Monsieur DESENFANS, Going Abroad'. There seems to have been no second part of the collection, which is hardly surprising since the existing catalogue lists 333 items, only five of which, including the Horst (214: then called Rembrandt), can be identified with reasonable certainty. They remained in Desenfans' possession until his death, and thus passed to Bourgeois and so to Dulwich. In all, there are six known catalogues of Desenfans' sales, including the one in 1802, although Lugt records[2] four others, which do not appear to be traceable. All these sale catalogues have been used in the compilation of the present catalogue; but the identifications can rarely be absolutely certain, so words like 'perhaps', 'possibly', 'probably', have been used to indicate the degree of dubiety in the compiler's mind. In the case of the 1802 Catalogue, however, the identification is usually rendered simple by the descriptions given.

Probably during the 1780s Desenfans became friendly with the French painter and dealer J. B. P. Lebrun, the very unsatisfactory husband of the celebrated portrait painter, Mme Vigée-Lebrun. A group of letters from him to Desenfans is preserved in Dulwich College Library, containing interesting

2 F. Lugt, *Répertoire des catalogues de ventes* (The Hague, 1938), I, nos 3341, 3814, 4370 and 4503. The information came from notes made by Hofstede de Groot, but the Rijksbureau voor Kunsthistorische Documentatie at The Hague can find no trace of them. The catalogue of 28 February 1795, now in the Victoria and Albert Museum, was previously unknown.

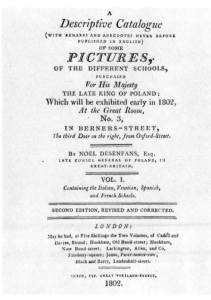

Title page from the Desenfans Descriptive Catalogue, 1802

3 The second edition, revised and corrected, is in the Gallery archives.

4 Probably only 123, since 66 and 67 seem to be the same picture (Reynolds, *A Little Girl* for both numbers: no such picture is now in the Gallery). The *Lord Ligonier* (Insurance List no 59), previously said to be the picture in the Tate Gallery, is in fact Dulwich Reynolds, 333.

5 It is clear from the records of Messrs Christie, Manson & Woods and other sources that Desenfans and Bourgeois had been engaged in a dealing partnership for many years, from at least as early as 1780.

Sir William Beechey, RA
17 *Sir Peter Francis Bourgeois*

details of some of his purchases and offers to Desenfans. In 1790, according to his own account, Desenfans was commissioned by Michael Poniatowski, Prince Primate of Poland (Kucharski, 489) to collect paintings for his brother, Stanislas Augustus, King of Poland (Kucharski, 490), as a nucleus for a projected Polish National Gallery. Stanislas, however, was forced to abdicate in 1795 and went to Russia, where he died in 1798; and Desenfans found himself with a collection of masterpieces on his hands. After vain attempts to persuade the Russian government to take over Stanislas's debts, he proposed, in 1799, a plan by which the British government should acquire the pictures on very good terms, as a British National Gallery. The government of the day, however, like its successor in 1830, when the fabulous collection of drawings assembled by Sir Thomas Lawrence was offered to it at a derisory price, took no action. Later British governments have had to pay far more for parts of these collections than would have been needed to purchase the whole.

Desenfans, therefore, organised a private exhibition and sale of his collection in 1802: 'A Descriptive Catalogue ... of some pictures ... purchased for His Majesty The Late King of Poland; which will be exhibited early in 1802 ... by Noel Desenfans, Esq. Late Consul General of Poland, in Great-Britain ...',[3] contains detailed notes on 187 pictures (including nine by Bourgeois), and a long introduction giving the history of the collection. Many of the ex-Polish pictures must have been sold then, and it is clear that Desenfans had managed to dispose of some of them before 1802, since the Rubens *Venus, Mars and Cupid* (285) was sold in London in 1798 and again in Amsterdam in 1803, when it was described as coming from the ex-King of Poland's collection: it must, however, have been bought back, as it came to Dulwich with the Bourgeois Bequest. Other pictures in the 1802 Sale can be identified in other collections, and not more than 56 of the 187 items can be positively identified with pictures now at Dulwich. In addition, there is the Insurance List of 6 July 1804, when Desenfans drew up a list of 124[4] pictures which he valued at £37,370. Only one of these, the *Annunciation* by Zuccarelli, can definitely be excluded from the number now in the Gallery, since almost all the rest can reasonably be identified with pictures in the Bourgeois Bequest.

Desenfans died in 1807, leaving his collection to his wife, and, after her, to his life-long friend Peter Francis Bourgeois (1756–1811: see Beechey, 17). Unfortunately, we do not know exactly which pictures he left, since he had doubtless continued to buy and sell between 1804 and 1807 and no posthumous inventory seems to have been drawn up. A letter of March 1807 (see Reni, 262) estimates the total then at about 300, but as the writer records meeting Bourgeois he may have seen their joint collection. There is no doubt that Bourgeois already had a collection of his own, and he certainly added to—and perhaps sold from—his newly augmented collection up to the time of his death. It has become the established myth that Desenfans collected the pictures and Bourgeois merely kept them until they passed to Dulwich on his death, but it now seems clear that, of the 371 items in the official Inventory of the Bourgeois Bequest, drawn up in 1813, not more than about 100 can be proved to have been in Desenfans' possession, leaving 248 (apart from 23 paintings by Bourgeois himself) which were either acquired by Bourgeois or are of doubtful provenance, having possibly belonged to Desenfans.[5]

In any case, the 371 pictures in the 1813 Inventory came to the Gallery because Mrs Desenfans, who survived both her husband and Bourgeois—she died in 1814, and was buried in the new Mausoleum which is part of the Gallery—waived her life-interest and gave the pictures to Dulwich. Sir John

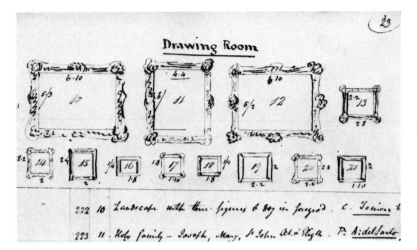

Soane, the greatest architect of the age, had been a friend and fellow-Academician of Bourgeois, and undertook to design and build a Mausoleum for the three benefactors and a Gallery for the pictures. This rather unusual combination arose from Desenfans' express desire not to be buried underground, and, in 1807, Soane had already built 'a Mausoleum, or Chapel . . . adjacent to Sir Francis' house in Charlotte Street, Portland Place, for the reception of the remains of Mr. and Mrs. Desenfans, and for divine service'. Bourgeois had originally intended to build his gallery in Charlotte Street, but the ground-landlord, the Duke of Portland, was very unhelpful and so Bourgeois decided to leave the pictures to Dulwich, not trusting either the British Museum or Royal Academy to maintain the collection intact. Soane therefore designed a new Mausoleum for the three benefactors, similar to the earlier one,[6] together with one of the first (and still one of the best) purpose-built galleries, with carefully thought-out top-lighting and typically Soanic economy of detailing. Soane's estimate, submitted in July 1811, immediately after Bourgeois' death, amounted to £11,270. Bourgeois had bequeathed £12,000 and the residue of his estate towards the cost of building and maintaining the Mausoleum and Gallery, but the new building contained, in addition, apartments for six of the poor women from the Foundation Almshouses, and so the actual cost was £14,222. 15s. 8d.

When the Gallery was opened to the public, late in 1814, the collection was transformed, and the College became responsible for the most important public gallery in the country. The National Gallery was not opened until 1824, and the Ashmolean Museum in Oxford did not then possess pictures of the same quality: the British Museum had been founded in 1753, but it was not a picture gallery. The other great gallery at Cambridge did not come into existence until Lord Fitzwilliam's bequest of 1816 enabled the Fitzwilliam Museum to be built. Only the University of Glasgow has a clear priority, with the small but choice collection of pictures bequeathed by the great anatomist William Hunter in 1783.

Perhaps as a result of the interest aroused, several bequests and gifts came in, the most important being the group of portraits of the Linley family of musicians (*see* Gainsborough, 140 for details). A little later, in 1831, Captain Moody gave another fine Gainsborough portrait (316). All these were works by recent British painters and they joined one or two others, such as the Romney (440) of Dr Joseph Allen, Warden of the College, which had been commissioned by the College in 1775, but, on the whole, the Desenfans–Bourgeois Bequest contained very few 'modern' paintings (Reynolds's *Mrs Siddons* (318) and R. Wilson's *Tivoli* (171) being notable exceptions) since modern British works were not generally thought suitable for a public picture gallery.

It was probably this rather poor representation of the British School which brought about the next great donation. In 1911, exactly a century after

6 The Charlotte Street Mausoleum is known from the original drawings in the Soane Museum, Lincoln's Inn Fields, and the details given here are based on papers and drawings in the Soane Museum; *see* A. T. Bolton, *The Works of Soane* (1924), Ch VI.

Charles Fairfax Murray
A self-portrait
(Fitzwilliam Museum, Cambridge)

Bourgeois' death, Charles Fairfax Murray gave a group of pictures anonymously. They included outstanding examples of the work of Lely (555, 563), Hogarth (580) and Gainsborough (588), and were followed by further gifts before his death in 1919. Fairfax Murray was an unusual man: he had a fine head, but it was set on the body of a dwarf, which may account for his retiring, not to say secretive, life. He remained 'The Anonymous Donor' until after his death; and indeed even now it is hard to find out much about him, since—apparently by his own desire—there are no more than the briefest obituaries and he is not included in the *Dictionary of National Biography*, although he was a well-known art expert for many years and formed a notable collection of Old Master drawings. He was trained as a painter under Rossetti and was an assistant to Burne-Jones—an example of his work belongs to the Gallery—but he soon became an authority on early Italian painting. As early as 1877 he bought in Venice the *Madonna*, now in the National Gallery of Scotland, which he sold to Ruskin and which has been attributed to Leonardo as well as to Verrocchio, and for the rest of his life he was actively engaged in buying and selling pictures, often in conjunction with Colnaghi's or Agnew's. Early in the present century he became convinced that British painting was under-estimated and that more examples should be acquired by public collections; in particular, he realised that signed examples by lesser-known painters provide the only sure basis for the attribution of unsigned works, and he set himself to obtain such paintings, usually buying them at auctions. He presented them to more than one gallery, but Dulwich has by far the largest number of his benefactions (46 in all), although he had no connection with either the school or the district. Henry Yates Thompson, a fellow-collector and for long an active member of the Picture Gallery Committee, probably influenced his decision.

Unfortunately, Fairfax Murray's anonymity was transferred to his pictures in that he seems to have been unaware how important it is, historically, that a picture should not only be signed, but should also, if at all possible, have a known provenance—that is, its history should be traceable from the day it was finished. In a few cases, such as the Lely (563), which once belonged to Horace Walpole, we know where Fairfax Murray acquired his pictures, but in many other cases it has proved difficult to find anything about their provenance— the other Fairfax Murray Lely, *Nymphs by a Fountain* (555), which is said once to have borne a signature and an (improbable) date now has neither, and all we know is that Murray bought it in Paris before 1911. The lovely early Gainsborough (588) also presents problems of provenance, so there is still work to be done on several of the paintings in his Gift, which must rank second in importance only to the Bourgeois Bequest.

During the course of the 19th century various alterations and additions to the Gallery were made and extra rooms were added in the 1920s, but almost everything was destroyed by a flying bomb in July 1944. Because the original drawings are preserved in the Soane Museum it was possible to rebuild from them, and, with minor alterations, the present building is closer to Soane's design than it has been in living memory. The rebuilding was done under the direction of Arthur Davis and Sir Edward Maufe and with the help of a most generous grant from the Pilgrim Trust. The Gallery was re-opened by H.M. Queen Elizabeth, The Queen Mother, on 27 April 1953. The finest pictures had been in Wales, with the National Gallery's paintings, throughout the war, and the opportunity was taken to clean and restore many of them, as a result of which several discoveries were made.[7] Before the re-opening of the Gallery

7 Unfortunately about a dozen of the pictures left in London were destroyed or badly damaged.

many paintings were lent to Leeds Art Gallery, and in 1947 a special exhibition of 54 pictures was held at the National Gallery, with a catalogue incorporating much new material,[8] mostly due to Professor A. F. Blunt, Sir E. K. Waterhouse and the late Dr L. Burchard.

8 In the present catalogue references are given to the National Gallery exhibition catalogue, but not to the Leeds exhibition.

> J. Britton submits this as a very concise and imperfect Catalogue. . . . J.B. however thinks it will be expedient to have a more correct and *particular* Catalogue made hereafter; to define the Subjects, and identify the Names of the respective Painters . . . it will be desirable to explain the Subjects, and animadvert on their peculiarities of composition, execution, colouring and other characteristics. . . .
>
> John Britton, FSA, in his preface to the
> Inventory of the Bourgeois Bequest, 24 May 1813

The Bourgeois pictures were moved into the Gallery in 1814 and the public was admitted soon afterwards. By 1816 it was evident that a catalogue was desirable and the first one was compiled by the first Curator, Ralph Cockburn (1816–20). This was a small pamphlet of 20 pages, several copies of which have survived, two in the Gallery's own archives and others in the British Library and elsewhere. It lists 360 items, but it is not really a catalogue at all, since it gives no more than the number, title, and painter's name. Curiously, the attributions do not always follow those in the 1813 Inventory, and, where they differ, they are often wrong. The great Dr Waagen, Director of the Berlin Gallery, observed sharply in 1854: 'In none of the galleries which I have hitherto seen in England do the pictures agree so little with the names given to them, nor is so much that is excellent mixed with much that is indifferent and quite worthless. . . . The catalogue is composed, not only with insufficient knowledge, but with great carelessness, since pictures which are inscribed with the name of the real master are quite arbitrarily ascribed to others'.[9] This inadequate handlist survived for about 60 years; most of the existing copies, including the two in the Gallery, can be dated after 1831, since they include the Gainsborough *Mrs Moody* (316), given in that year, and were issued from an address known to have been occupied by the printer *c* 1837–47. Far more important than this first handlist was the combination of a series of engravings by Cockburn of 50 of the principal pictures, and a long article by William Hazlitt (who was a painter as well as a writer). This appeared in *The London Magazine* for January 1823, and is included in his Collected Works, so that the combination of essay and engravings must have made the Gallery very well known in the 1820s and later, when the National Gallery itself (opened in 1824) was still a very small collection of some 38 pictures. The evident need for a proper catalogue, highlighted by the criticisms of Waagen and Mrs Jameson, in her influential *Handbook to Public Galleries* (1842), was recognised as early as the 1850s. S. P. Denning (*see* 304) succeeded Cockburn as Curator in 1821 and began a descriptive and historical catalogue. The first draft was completed in 1858, and a partial fair copy, dated 1859, dealt with the first 202 items. This was never printed, and it was not until 1876 that a real catalogue was published. It was the work of J. C. L. Sparkes, of the Art Department at Dulwich College, and it was soon superseded by the remarkable new catalogue commissioned by the Governors from the brilliant young German art historian, J. P. Richter, on the advice of the Royal Academy (which almost certainly means Charles Eastlake, later Director of the National Gallery). Richter confined himself to the non-British schools, so the 1880 Catalogue is

9 G. F. Waagen, *Treasures of Art in Gt Britain* (1854), II, 342.

10 It seems worth recording, if only as an historical curiosity, that Richter, whose monumental work on Leonardo was first published in 1883, died in 1937 in his 90th year. His two daughters, Gisela and Irma, were themselves distinguished art historians and edited the correspondence (1876–91) between their father and Morelli, although Irma died before it was finished. The present writer was able to assist Dr Gisela Richter with it. References to Dulwich occur on pp 70, 73 and 123 (*Italienische Malerei der Renaissance*, Baden-Baden, 1960).

11 The most striking instance is Richter's apparently arbitrary division of the Teniers pictures into two.

really a collaboration between him and Sparkes, but the result is a major work of scholarship—the great Italian critic, Giovanni Morelli, writing to Richter on 26 June 1880, acknowledging receipt of a copy sent him by his friend, described it as the best gallery catalogue known to him.[10] It certainly provides more information than ever before and gives reasons for changes of attribution (although not all of these have been ratified by later generations).[11] It may be observed that, in cases where the present catalogue rejects a Richter attribution the 'new' one is frequently the traditional one recorded by Britton in the 1813 Inventory. Nevertheless, the 1880 Richter Catalogue deserves Morelli's praise and compares well with contemporary catalogues of the National Gallery, the Louvre, and other major museums.

One of the most important features of the Richter Catalogue is the facsimile given of every signature, and the great care taken to examine every picture minutely for traces of a signature or other inscription. These have been checked in the preparation of the present catalogue and almost all have been confirmed, but in a very few cases recent cleaning has revealed a signature invisible a century ago (*see* Gelder, 126), or the facsimile has provided evidence of a signature no longer legible, or, perhaps a falsification (*see* Horst, 214). The edition of 1880 was revised in 1892, when it was amalgamated with a catalogue, by Sparkes and Canon Carver, of the Cartwright and other pictures. In 1905, and, rather more completely, in 1914, the Richter Catalogue was again revised. The 1914 version was the work of Sir Edward Cook, to which further notes were added in 1926, bringing the number of entries up to 608. The 1926 catalogue was current until the Second World War, and is still usually quoted; but unfortunately it omitted the facsimile signatures, and introduced much new biographical and anecdotal material, not all of it relevant. It also included new entries on the Fairfax Murray pictures and other gifts and bequests, but the opportunity was missed to obtain the details of provenance at a time when it would have been much easier than it is half a century later. The 1953 *Brief Catalogue* was issued as a temporary measure and is no more than a handlist, recording a few of the changes of attribution and new acquisitions (609–615).

The present catalogue is intended to replace Richter's and endeavours to follow its spirit, but in one respect it must fall short of its predecessor of a century ago. Richter's Catalogue included every picture in the Gallery and later editions included those elsewhere: the present one includes only those actually on exhibition, or which might be exhibited on occasion; a total of some 300, or just under half the entire collection (*see* p 299 for further details). Entries on the paintings stored in the depot are being prepared, and an up-to-date typescript will be kept in the Gallery for reference. (It is hoped that it will be possible to publish this catalogue at a later date.) Most of these pictures are kept in the Gallery store-rooms and may be seen on application to the staff.

All the pictures have been re-measured for the present catalogue, and dimensions are given in both inches and centimetres, height first. The work of measurement has been done by Mr E. C. Shaw and Mr G. Pidgeon of the Gallery staff. It should be noted that the 1880 measurements were sight-size, *ie* inside the frames, whereas the present ones are of the actual size of the canvas, panel, etc, to the nearest $\frac{1}{8}$ inch. In all cases, pictures are in oil, unless otherwise stated: the support—canvas, panel, copper and so on—is given, but no attempt has been made to distinguish the various woods in the case of panel paintings. Most are on oak.

Mr Shaw and Mr Pidgeon have also checked the backs of all the pictures for labels, inscriptions, seals and other useful material, all of which is recorded in the catalogue where relevant. Messrs Christie, Manson & Woods have helped greatly by identifying their own code-marks on the backs of many of the Murray pictures and others which have passed through their hands, as have Messrs Agnew, who frequently collaborated with Fairfax Murray. Acknowledgements are also due, and gratefully rendered, to many friends and colleagues for much help over a period of years. In 1880 Richter thanked Scharf, Frizzoni, Bode, Justi, Curtis, and Weale, and I take pleasure in thanking their successors: Mr K. K. Andrews, of the National Gallery of Scotland, Dr W. Bernt, Professor A. F. Blunt, Mr H. Brigstocke, of the National Gallery of Scotland, Mr C. Brown, of the National Gallery, London, Professor M. Jaffé of the Fitzwilliam Museum, Mr J. Kerslake, of the National Portrait Gallery, London, Sir Oliver Millar, Surveyor of Her Majesty's Pictures, Mr M. Robinson, formerly of the National Maritime Museum, Mr F. Simpson, formerly of the Mellon Centre in London, Miss Mildred Steinbach of the Frick Art Reference Library, New York, Dr D. Thomson, of the Scottish National Portrait Gallery, Sir Ellis Waterhouse, and Mrs Clare Ford Wille.

To the late Sir Harold Hartley, CH, FRS, who initiated this catalogue, but did not live to see it completed; to my colleagues and friends in the Witt Library; and to the staff of the Picture Gallery itself, who have borne with my endless questions and insatiable desire to look at the backs of pictures, I owe a special debt of gratitude.

References to literature have been restricted to those which seemed essential, and much of the older literature—Hazlitt, Waagen, and many old monographs—has been omitted. References to such sources as *The Dictionary of National Biography*, Thieme-Becker, G.E.C.'s *Complete Peerage*, Redford's and Graves's compilations of Sale Catalogues and Exhibitions, and Blanc's *Trésor de la Curiosité* have, for the most part, been omitted: where, for example, Thieme-Becker is specifically cited, it makes a significant contribution.

In addition to such usual abbreviations as *c, ibid, id* the following have been employed: BI—British Institution; BM—British Museum; NG—National Gallery (London unless indicated); NPG—National Portrait Gallery; RA—Royal Academy. The following books and periodicals are referred to in abbreviated form: *Burl.Mag.*—*The Burlington Magazine*; W. Buchanan, *Memoirs* . . .—W. Buchanan, *Memoirs of Painting, with a Chronological History of the Importation of Pictures by the Great Masters into England since the French Revolution* (1824) 2 vols; HdG—Hofstede de Groot, *A Catalogue raisonné of the works of . . . Dutch Painters of the Seventeenth Century, based on the Work of John Smith* (1907–27), vols 1–8 (London), vols 9–10 (in German) (Esslingen and Paris, 1926, 1928); KdK—the *Klassiker der Kunst* series; Sm—John Smith, *A Catalogue Raisonné of the Works of the most Eminent Dutch, Flemish, and French Painters* . . . (1829–42) 9 vols; Vertue, *Note books* . . .—*The Notebooks of George Vertue* (Walpole Society, 1929–55), vols 1–5 and Index vol, and vol 6.

Birkbeck College,
University of London

PETER MURRAY
September 1977

Catalogue

ANONYMOUS *see* Circle of MABUSE (505)

ANTWERP MASTER (second quarter of the 16th century)

250 *The Crucifixion*

This type of *Crucifixion*, with a very high cross which is embraced by the kneeling Magdalen, and with a panoramic view of Jerusalem including the Temple (the large round building) is traceable to the workshop of Quentin Metsys (*d* 1530). This picture was probably produced in Antwerp, under the influence of Metsys, about 1520/50. There is a smaller version of the subject, possibly the prototype, by Metsys in the National Gallery of Canada, Ottawa.

Panel, $47\frac{3}{4} \times 35\frac{3}{4}$in (121.3 × 90.8cm)

PROVENANCE Dr G. Webster of Dulwich; bequeathed by him, 1875

Sisto **BADALOCCHIO** *see* After Annibale CARRACCI (265)

Ludolf **BAKHUIZEN** (1631–1708)
Bakhuizen was born in Germany, at Emden, where his father was town clerk, but soon moved to Amsterdam, where he died. He specialised in seapieces, and was reckoned to excel in storm scenes such as this, which may have influenced English artists like Turner (*cf Calais Pier* in the National Gallery). His harbour scenes were imitated by Abraham Storck (*cf* 608 in this collection).

327 *Boats in a Storm*

Signed: *LBAKHUZEN* (or *L.BAKHUZYN*) and dated: *1696* (on a plank)

Canvas, $25 \times 31\frac{1}{4}$in (63 × 79cm)

PROVENANCE Probably Desenfans Sale, Christie's, 14.v.1785 (21); Desenfans Private Sale, 8ff.iv.1786 (89); and 8.vi.1786 (65); and Christie's, 15.vii.1786 (71); Desenfans Sale, Skinner & Dyke, 27.ii.1795 (59); Bourgeois Bequest, 1811

LITERATURE HdG, VII, no 235; W. Bernt, *Die Niederlaendischen Maler des 17. Jahrhunderts* (Munich, 1948), I, no 36, rep.

Mary **BEALE** (1633–99)
Mrs Beale was the daughter of a Suffolk rector and married Charles Beale, an artist's colourman and Deputy Clerk of the Patents. 'Great numbers of persons of good rank sat to her, especially the greatest part of the dignified clergy of her time; an acquaintance she got by her husband, who was much in favour with that robe.' She learned by copying Lely's works—he was a customer of her husband and helped her by his criticisms, becoming a

friend of the family. She became a professional portrait painter about 1654, but nothing is known for certain before 1671, when her husband began to keep notes of his 'deare heart's' works: he recorded about 140 rather tame Lely-style portraits in ten years.

574   *Young Man, perhaps one of the Painter's Sons*

Signed: *Mary Beale*

Like 563, this was formerly regarded as a portrait of the poet, Abraham Cowley (1618–67), who was a guest of the Beales in 1664. He was then 46, and, as this picture dates from the 1660s on style, it can hardly represent him: the few authentic portraits of Cowley also show markedly different lips. Mrs Beale painted her sons more than once, and this may well represent one of them.

Canvas, $30\frac{1}{8} \times 25\frac{1}{8}$in (76.5 × 63.8cm)

PROVENANCE Perhaps Dr Mead (*d* 1754) and Sir Henry Wilmot in 1857 (as Cowley, by an unknown painter); anon. sale, Christie's, 19.xi.1910 (40: as Cowley, unknown painter), bt Agnew; Fairfax Murray Gift, 1911

EXHIBITED Possibly Manchester, Art Treasures, 1857 (143: lent by Sir H. Wilmot, as *Abraham Cowley, young*, by an unknown painter)

LITERATURE B. Buckeridge, *Essay towards an English School* in R. de Piles, *Art of Painting*, 3rd edn (*c* 1744), 358 (for Mary Beale); E. Walsh in *Connoisseur* (1953), CXXXI, 3ff.

Sir William **BEECHEY**, RA (1753–1839)
Beechey became an ARA in 1793 and was made Portrait Painter to the Queen. In 1798 his huge picture of *George III and the Prince of Wales reviewing Troops* (in the Royal Collection) brought him a knighthood as well as full membership of the RA. Less dazzling than Lawrence's, his portraits are probably more truthful.

17   *Sir Peter Francis Bourgeois*, RA

(466)   The Bourgeois Bequest of 1811 was the principal benefaction to this Gallery (*see* Introduction, p 17). He was born of Swiss descent in London in 1756 and became friendly with Desenfans as a young man. He trained as a painter under Loutherbourg (*see* Loutherbourg, 297, 339), travelled in Italy, France, and Holland, and began exhibiting at the Royal Academy from 1776, becoming ARA in 1798 and RA in 1793. He visited Poland and was appointed Painter to King Stanislas (for whom Desenfans originally bought many of the pictures now in Dulwich). Stanislas conferred on him the Order Merentibus which he is shown wearing (the actual medal now belongs to Dulwich College); on 12 April 1791 George III allowed him to rank as a Knight, and appointed him his Landscape Painter in 1794. After the death of Desenfans in 1807 Bourgeois retired and devoted himself to the collection which he inherited and built up. He died, after a fall from his horse, in 1811, leaving some 370 pictures to Dulwich, thus forming a major gallery open to the public more than a decade earlier than the National Gallery. Another portrait of him, when younger, is 172, by Northcote.
      There are two copies of 17 at Dulwich, both by Bourgeois himself (465, 466): 466 is exhibited in place of 17 for two reasons—it is in very much better condition than the original, and 17 is painted on the back of a sketch by Reynolds (17a) which can therefore be exhibited: indeed, Beechey is said to have painted the portrait as a means of preserving the Reynolds. Since Bourgeois made two copies the original by Beechey must date from before 1811, but the age of the sitter makes a date *c* 1810 likely.

Panel (17), $29\frac{1}{2} \times 24\frac{1}{2}$in (74.9 × 62.2cm);
Canvas (466), $30\frac{1}{8} \times 24\frac{1}{4}$in (76.5 × 64.1cm)

PROVENANCE 17 was given by Beechey himself, 1836; 466 came with the Bourgeois Bequest, 1811, though not included in the 1813 Inventory

EXHIBITED Probably RA 1813 (221), but this might have been one of the versions listed below

ENGRAVED J. Vendramini for Cadell's *British Gallery of Contemporary Portraits*, 1811

VERSIONS Two, by Beechey himself, are in the National Portrait Gallery and the Soane Museum, London

LITERATURE W. Roberts, *Beechey* (1907), 125–6 (the Dulwich picture 'probably' that in the Royal Academy, 1813)

111 *John Philip Kemble*

The celebrated actor, brother of Mrs Siddons (Reynolds, 318) and Charles Kemble (Briggs, 291), was born in 1757 in Lancashire and educated at the English Catholic College in Douai, Desenfans' home town. Thinking his father intended him for the priesthood, he ran away and joined a travelling company of actors. He made his London debut as Hamlet in 1783 and played all the great Shakespearean roles, often with his sister. He was manager of Covent Garden Theatre from 1802 until he retired in 1817, after which he lived mostly abroad. He died at Lausanne in 1823. He is said to have been instrumental in suggesting Dulwich to Bourgeois as a home for his collection. Desenfans wrote to Beechey in 1798 to congratulate him on his knighthood and mentions this picture: 'I hope as soon as you are at leisure you will go on with the Kemble portrait, so that I may have to boast I possess *the first picture* of Sir William Beechey . . .'.

Canvas, $30\frac{1}{4} \times 25\frac{1}{4}$in (76.8 × 64.1cm)

PROVENANCE Commissioned by Desenfans, *c* 1798; Bourgeois Bequest, 1811

EXHIBITED RA 1799 (174); International Exhibition, 1862 (225)

VERSION Garrick Club, London

LITERATURE W. Roberts, *Beechey* (1907), 66–7; J. Kerslake (ed.), *Catalogue of Theatrical Portraits in London Public Collections* (Society for Theatre Research, 1961), no 373

169 *Charles Small Pybus,* MP

C. S. Pybus was MP for Dover and was Commissioner for the Lord High Admiral 1791–5. He was a friend of Noel Desenfans.

Canvas, $30\frac{5}{8} \times 25\frac{1}{2}$in (77.7 × 64.8cm)

PROVENANCE Presumably Desenfans, but not recorded; Bourgeois Bequest, 1811

LITERATURE W. Roberts, *Beechey* (1907), 83 n

Nicolaes **BERCHEM** (1620–83)
Nicolaes, born in Haarlem, was the son of a still-life painter, Pieter Claesz. He changed his name to Berchem and was one of the most successful of the Italianate landscape painters, influencing Both and Pynacker as well as his own pupil Du Jardin (all of whom are represented at Dulwich). The evidence for his journey or journeys to Italy is inconclusive: he may have gone in 1642/5 and again in 1653/5.

88   *A Farrier and Peasants near Roman Ruins*

Signed: *Ber . . . f* (recorded in the early catalogues as *Berchem f*)

Canvas, 27 × 32¾in (68.5 × 83.1cm)

PROVENANCE Apparently sold in Amsterdam, 21.viii.1799 (15*), bt J. P. van der Schley; Bourgeois Bequest, 1811

LITERATURE HdG, IX, no 174

122   *A Road through a Wood*

Signed: *C Berghem* (*C* [for Claesz.] *B* in monogram)

Probably an early work, and of the type which influenced Gainsborough (*cf* the National Gallery's *Cornard Wood*, or, to a lesser extent, 588 in this collection).

Canvas, 46⅞ × 35⅜in (119.1 × 89.4cm)

PROVENANCE Desenfans Insurance List, 1804 (87); Bourgeois Bequest, 1811

EXHIBITED NG 1947 (I)

LITERATURE HdG, IX, no 345

157   *Travelling Peasants* ('*Le Soir*') and *Roman Fountain with Cattle and Figures* ('*Le Midi*')
166
Signed: (157) *Berchem f*; (166) *Berchem*

These two paintings have been regarded as a pair since the 18th century, but they are not the same size and are first recorded together in the Gaignat Sale in 1768.

Panel, (157) 13½ × 18in (34.4 × 45.6cm);
(166) 14½ × 19⅛in (36.8 × 48.4cm)

PROVENANCE (157) van Kretschmar Sale, Amsterdam, 29.iii.1757 (40); (both) Gaignat Sale, Paris, xii.1768; Bourgeois Bequest, 1811

EXHIBITED (166) BI 1815 (69); 1843 (93)

ENGRAVING F. Dequevauviller, as '*Le Soir*' and '*Le Midi*', presumably while in the Gaignat Collection

VERSION HdG no 241 'from an old French collection' is a version of 166

LITERATURE Sm nos 17, 18; HdG, IX, nos 192, 380

196   *Peasants at a Ford*

Formerly signed: *Berchem f*

The signature was recorded by Richter in 1880, but is not now legible. In the early catalogues (1816 and later) the picture was attributed to Du Jardin, though it is said to be signed in the 1876 Catalogue, and was attributed to Berchem in the 1813 Inventory.

Panel, 17¾ × 21⅝in (44 × 55cm)

PROVENANCE Bourgeois Bequest, 1811

LITERATURE HdG, IX, no 381

Dirk van **BERGEN** *see* Jan LAPP (330)

Simon Du **BOIS** (Dubois) (1632–1708)
Du Bois was born in Antwerp, spent some years in Italy, returned to Holland, and finally
settled in London in 1681, where he enjoyed the patronage of Lord Somers (*see* Riley, 565).
Vertue described him as 'a grate mimick of Italien Masters. especialy their small easel
pictures abundance of which were sold by him during his Life for capital Italian paintings
... He painted Portraits Curiously tho' not very successful that way'. He also worked for—and
in the style of—Wouwerman and Willem van de Velde, whose daughter he married in 1708,
when he was 75.

584 *Sir William Jones* and *Lady Jones*
585
Both signed: *S. du Bois fecit*; *Sir William* is also inscribed: *A.D. 1682* and *AEt 77*. and, in a
different hand, *Sr Wm Jones/Father to Ly/Pelham*; *Lady Jones* is dated *1682* after the signature
and also inscribed: *Ly Jones/Mother to Ly/Pelham*

These are the earliest dated pictures painted by Du Bois in London. Sir William Jones
(1631–82)—the age given, 77, is thus impossible—was Solicitor-General (1673–5) and
Attorney-General (1675–9). He directed the prosecution of the victims of Titus Oates's
plot, resulting in the judicial murder of some 35 people. Dryden, who hated him,
characterised him in *Absalom and Achitopel* as 'Bull-faced Jonas, who could statutes draw/To
mean rebellion, and make treason law'. He died in the year in which this portrait was
painted, and Lady Jones is shown in mourning. She died in 1700.

Canvas, both 29⅞ × 24⅞in (75.9 × 63.2cm)

PROVENANCE Presumably Pelham family, passed to Townshend; Townshend Heirlooms Sale,
Christie's, 7.iii.1904 (172–3), bt Agnew; Fairfax Murray Gift, 1911

LITERATURE C. H. Collins-Baker, *Lely and the Stuart Portrait Painters* (1912), II, 66–9 and reps;
id in *Onze Kunst* (1915), 101ff. and both rep.; E. Croft-Murray and P. Hulton, *Catalogue of
British Drawings ... in the British Museum* (1960), I, 299–300 (for Du Bois)

Cornelis **BOL** (?1589–1666 or later?)
Cornelis Bol, a mysterious Flemish artist, was born probably in Antwerp, but was
recorded as a member of the Dutch Church in London in 1636. He is said to have painted the
Great Fire of London in 1666.

360 *Westminster and the Thames*

Signed: *CB*

This is the only known signed work by Bol and the identification of the initials as his
depends upon the early 18th-century writer George Vertue, who recorded 'at Sr John
Evelyns. at Wootton. ... three views of London from the River side Arundel house
Somersett house Tower lond. painted before the fire of Lond. by Cornelius Boll. a good free
Taste'. These views—presumably painted for the diarist Evelyn in the 1660s—still exist in
the family collection. One of them is almost identical with 360 in view-point, and clearly is
by the same hand. In our painting the principal buildings are, starting from the right, where
a man walks down old Strand Lane to the ferry: Old Somerset House, destroyed in the 18th
century to make way for the present building shown here before the alterations of *c* 1662;
the Savoy Chapel; the four towers of Old Northumberland House, formerly standing where
Whitehall now meets Northumberland Avenue; the Banqueting House; Westminster
Abbey (without the western towers added in the 18th century); and Westminster Hall.
Across the river, at the extreme left, is Lambeth Palace.

Canvas, $25 \times 42\frac{7}{8}$in (63.5×108.7cm)

PROVENANCE Unknown, but probably one of the missing items in the Cartwright Inventory and therefore bequeathed to the College *c* 1686 (*cf* Introduction, p 17)

LITERATURE Vertue *Notebooks . . .*, IV, 53; M. D. Whinney and O. Millar, *English Art, 1625–1714* (Oxford, 1957), 263, n 1; E. Croft-Murray and P. Hulton, *Catalogue of British Drawings . . . in the British Museum* (1960), I, 250–51; *Age of Charles II* (exhibition catalogue), RA, 1960/61, no 224 (the Evelyn version)

Jan **BOTH** (*c* 1618–52)
Jan and his brother, Andries (*c* 1608–41/9) were Utrecht painters who worked together until Andries's death (he fell into a canal in Venice). Jan was one of the best Dutch painters of Italianate landscapes in imitation of Claude: Dulwich is rich in works of this school—*cf* Cuyp, Berghem, Miel, Du Jardin, Pynacker.

10 *Italian Landscape with an Ox-cart*

Canvas, $19\frac{3}{8} \times 16\frac{1}{8}$in ($49.1 \times 40.8$cm)

PROVENANCE Bourgeois Bequest, 1811

VERSION There is a replica in the Galleria Nazionale, Rome (HdG no 132)

LITERATURE Sm no 114; HdG, IX, no 131; J. Burke, *Both* (New York, 1976), no 61 (as a copy, possibly by Both, of the painting in Rome)

12 *Banks of a Brook*

Canvas, $21\frac{3}{4} \times 27\frac{1}{8}$in ($55.2 \times 68.9$cm)

PROVENANCE Bourgeois Bequest, 1811

VERSIONS Two similar paintings are in Antwerp and Schwerin

LITERATURE Sm no 113; HdG, IX, no 234; J. Burke, *Both* (New York, 1976), no 62 (as a copy, *c* 1641/5, possibly by Both, of the painting in Antwerp)

15 *Road by the Edge of a Lake*

It has been suggested that Moucheron and Adriaen van de Velde may have collaborated with Both on this picture, but there is no reason to believe this.

Panel, $22\frac{1}{2} \times 20\frac{1}{4}$in ($57.2 \times 51.3$cm)

PROVENANCE Poullain Collection, Paris, 1781 (62: as by Both and Moucheron); Bourgeois Bequest, 1811

ENGRAVING Barns, 1781 (as in Poullain Collection)

LITERATURE Sm no 115; HdG, IX, no 142; J. Burke, *Both* (New York, 1976), no 63 (as painted in Jan's Roman period, *c* 1638–41)

208 *A Mountain Path*

Signed: *J Both·f* (*JB* in monogram)

Possibly an early work, but dated 1645–50 by Burke.

Canvas, $27\frac{7}{8} \times 43\frac{7}{8}$in ($70.8 \times 111.4$cm)

PROVENANCE Bourgeois Bequest, 1811

LITERATURE Sm no 116; HdG, IX, no 235; J. Burke, *Both* (New York, 1976), no 64

Sébastien **BOURDON** (1616–71)
Bourdon served in the French army until 1634, when he was discharged and went to Rome. Here he was influenced by the 'Bamboccianti'—Dutch and Flemish painters of low-life subjects—although he subsequently came more under the influence of Claude and Poussin. He returned to Paris in 1637, but spent 1652–4 in Sweden as Court Painter to Queen Christina.

557 *A Brawl in a Guard-room*

This type of military picture, known as a *koortegardje*, was popular among the Northern painters working in Italy: Bourdon's are mostly datable 1640/50.

Canvas, $29\frac{1}{2} \times 23\frac{7}{8}$in ($74.9 \times 60.6$cm)

PROVENANCE Anon. Sale, Christie's, 12.v.1906 (100: as Le Nain), bt Agnew; Fairfax Murray by 1907; Fairfax Murray Gift, 1911

EXHIBITED RA 1908 (51: as Le Nain); Burlington Fine Arts Club, 1910 (39: as Le Nain, but catalogue mentions Bourdon, on evidence of similar Kassel picture)

VERSION Lent by Wildenstein to Réalité Exhibition, Paris, 1934

LITERATURE A. F. Blunt, *Art and Architecture in France*, 2nd edn (1970), 186 and n 140

Sir Peter Francis **BOURGEOIS**, RA (466) *see* Sir William BEECHEY (17)

Bartholomeus **BREENBERGH** (1599/1600–57)
Breenbergh was born in Deventer. He went to Rome at the age of 20, where he was influenced by Elsheimer and Bril, but mainly by the slightly older Poelenburgh (*cf* 25 of this Gallery). He stayed in Rome for ten years, making many drawings of the antiquities which he could use as a basis for imaginary landscapes with ruins, such as ours. He also made very fine etchings.

23 *A Ruined Temple* and *Landscape with a Roman Ruin*
26

The temple in 23 is based on that of the Sibyl at Tivoli, while 26 may be based on the central part of the Ponte Nomentana in Rome. Both are examples of the imaginary Italianate landscapes influenced by Poelenburgh.

Panel, both $6\frac{3}{8} \times 9\frac{3}{8}$in ($16.2 \times 23.7$cm)

PROVENANCE Bourgeois Bequest, 1811

VERSION/DRAWING Several paintings by Breenbergh show similar subject-matter, but Apsley House (V & A) has a version of 26. It appears to be based on drawings, formerly Sir R. Witt Collection, and Budapest Museum

LITERATURE M. Roethlisberger, *Breenbergh Handzeichnungen* (Berlin, 1969), no 62 (remarking that the Dulwich pair are not certainly attributable to Breenbergh, wrongly relating 26 to the Witt drawing, suggesting an attribution to K. de Hooch)

338   *Valley with Ruins and Figures*

Panel (elliptical), $13\frac{5}{8} \times 17\frac{1}{2}$in ($34.5 \times 44.5$cm)

PROVENANCE An inscription on the back records it as in the Duc de Valentinois Collection, 1725; Bourgeois Bequest, 1811

Henry Perronet **BRIGGS**, RA (1791–1844)
Briggs was the friend of Margaret Gainsborough, who left him some of her father's works. He was elected RA in 1832 and exhibited many portraits there.

291   *Charles Kemble*

Charles was the brother of John Kemble (Beechey, 111) and Mrs Siddons (Reynolds, 318). He was best known as a comic actor, and became manager of Covent Garden Theatre in 1822. He died in 1854, and the portrait was presumably presented to the College on his death.

Canvas, $30\frac{1}{8} \times 25\frac{1}{8}$in ($76.5 \times 63.8$cm)

PROVENANCE Probably H. P. Briggs Sale, Christie's, 27.iv.1844 (565); given by George Bartley, stage manager of Covent Garden, 1854

LITERATURE J. Kerslake (ed.), *Catalogue of Theatrical Portraits in London* (Society for Theatre Research, 1961), no 370

BRITISH SCHOOL

375   *Called Sir Martin Frobisher*

This portrait has been identified with 174 in the Cartwright Inventory of 1686: 'Sr Martin Furbushers pictur in a white dubblet & a grand Ruff, with a goulde Chaine . . .', but the sitter bears no resemblance to the 1577 documented portrait of Frobisher, in the Bodleian Library, Oxford. Frobisher received his gold chain from Elizabeth I in recognition of his Arctic explorations. He took a leading part in the defeat of the Spanish Armada, 1588, and was knighted for his valour. He died in 1594. This is probably a 17th-century copy of a 16th-century image, which would explain the lack of likeness.

Canvas, $32\frac{1}{4} \times 23\frac{3}{8}$in ($81.9 \times 59.4$cm)

PROVENANCE Presumably Cartwright Bequest, 1686

LITERATURE D. Lysons, *Environs of London* (1796), I, 108ff. (on Dulwich pictures); R. Strong, *The English Icon* (1969), fig 100 (for Bodley portrait)

385 *Nathan Field*

Nathan Field (1587–in or before 1634) was the son of a Puritan minister who was bitterly opposed to the stage. Nathan was seized and pressed into service, about 1600, by the Master of the Children of the Chapel Royal, although a subsequent court case revealed that he had no singing voice. He seems, however, to have been made an actor and is recorded as such in the First Folio of Shakespeare (1623). He also wrote two plays. The Cartwright Inventory of 1686 lists '167 master feilds pictur in his Shurt on a bourd . . . an Actour'.

Panel, $22\frac{1}{4} \times 16\frac{5}{8}$in ($56.5 \times 42.2$cm)

PROVENANCE Cartwright Bequest, 1686

EXHIBITED Manchester, Art Treasures, 1857 (88); National Portrait Exhibition, 1866 (534)

ENGRAVING W. Gardner, 1790, in S. Harding, *Shakespeare Illustrated*, 1793

LITERATURE D. Lysons, *Environs of London* (1796), I, 108ff.; E. K. Chambers, *Elizabethan Stage* (1923), II, 316–18; W. Leon in *The Pauline* (March, 1974), XCII, 9–11, with rep.

390 *Tom Bond*

Bond was an actor in the reign of Charles I, who was a member of the Prince's Company in 1632. The Cartwright Inventory of 1686 (148) has 'Tom bonds pictur, an Actour, in a band Rought with Ambrodery bared neck on a bourd, in a black frame, very ould'. The last phrase, if it does not refer to the frame, may be intended to mean that the painting was of the early 17th century and not a modern copy made for Cartwright.

Panel, $15\frac{3}{8} \times 12\frac{1}{4}$in ($39 \times 31$cm)

PROVENANCE Cartwright Bequest, 1686

LITERATURE D. Lysons, *Environs of London* (1796), I, 108ff.

391 *Head of a Man, called William Sly*

Traditionally identified with *Mr Slys picture y^e Actour*, 109 in Cartwright's Catalogue of 1686, but there is reason to doubt this. Sly was a well-known actor and contemporary of Alleyn, who was mentioned as an actor in 1588 and died in 1608. It is difficult to imagine this picture painted before 1608, but the sitter is a relatively young man; there is an inscription on the back which has been read (wrongly) as *by Dobson* (which would be stylistically conceivable), but there is also said to have been the number 196 (not now legible). If 196 is correct, it must refer to Cartwright's Catalogue, but the missing page of the Catalogue (*see* Introduction p 17) includes that number. There seems, however, no compelling reason to identify this man with the Mr Sly who was 109.

Canvas on panel, $15\frac{1}{4} \times 11$in (38.8×27.8cm)

PROVENANCE Presumably Cartwright Bequest, 1686

LITERATURE D. Lysons, *Environs of London* (1796), I, 108ff. (as Sly)

395 *Richard Burbage*

Richard Burbage (?1567–1619) inherited an interest in the Blackfriars and Globe Theatres and was himself a distinguished actor. He excelled in tragic parts and played in many of the great Shakespeare tragedies, 1595–1618. He was closely associated with Shakespeare and probably with Alleyn as well. The Chandos portrait of Shakespeare (National Portrait Gallery) was once attributed to him, and this has also been called a self-portrait, but there is no evidence for either, and the Cartwright Inventory of 1686 does not attribute it to him—

'105 Mr Burbig his head . . . a small closit pece' (although 103 in Cartwright's Catalogue is ascribed to him). The picture appears to have been cut down, but the description makes it clear that, if so, it must have been before 1686.

Canvas, $12 \times 10\frac{1}{4}$in (30.3×26.2cm)

PROVENANCE Cartwright Bequest, 1686

EXHIBITED Manchester, Art Treasures, 1857 (87: as Anon); National Portrait Exhibition, 1866 (377: as by Burbage)

ENGRAVING S. Harding, 1790, in his *Shakespeare Illustrated*, 1793 (enlarged)

LITERATURE D. Lysons, *Environs of London* (1796), I, 108ff.

400 'Old Mr Cartwright'

Inscribed: *AETATIS SV[AE]/59*

This portrait is described in the 1686 Cartwright Inventory (168) as: 'oul mr Cartwright Actour', to distinguish him from 'young mr Cartwright' (411). Since he is described as 59 years old and is wearing a type of lace collar which can be dated between about 1605 and 1615 he was probably born about 1550, which means that he may have been the grandfather of William Cartwright (Greenhill, 393), the donor of the pictures, who was probably born *c* 1620. The sitter is usually identified with the William Cartwright who was a well-known actor in the early 17th century and was associated with Alleyn—he is recorded as dining with Alleyn on 9 April 1620, when he would have been about 70.

Panel, $30\frac{7}{8} \times 24\frac{5}{8}$in ($78.5 \times 62.5$cm)

PROVENANCE Cartwright Bequest, 1686

LITERATURE D. Lysons, *Environs of London* (1796), I, 108ff.

411 'Young Mr Cartwright'

This is 169 in the Cartwright Inventory of 1686, described as 'young mr Cartwright Actour' to distinguish the sitter from 'oul mr Cartwright Actour' (400). The picture dates from the decade 1630–40, when the lace collar depicted was fashionable, so the sitter must have been born 1605/20, which would make it possible for him to be William Cartwright, the donor of the picture (*see* Greenhill, 393), who was born in 1606/7. However, he describes 393 as 'my pictur', and is hardly likely to have referred to himself as 'Young Mr Cartwright' in his own Inventory, so the probability is that this Mr Cartwright was his brother, cousin, or even uncle. Nothing seems to be known of such an actor, and he may have died young. The authorship of the picture is equally unclear: it has always been ascribed to an anonymous English painter, but the quality of the painting is much higher than that of most of the Cartwright pictures, and the dress allows us to date it fairly closely. Cornelius Johnson (1593–1661) painted at least five very similar portraits between 1631 and *c* 1640. Mytens, the only other likely candidate, does not seem to have produced anything comparable, so an attribution to Johnson seems worth consideration.

Canvas, $26\frac{1}{4} \times 23$in (66.7×58.1cm)

PROVENANCE Cartwright Bequest, 1686

VERSION What seems to have been a very similar portrait was sold in Vienna in 1928 as by Johnson (rep. from the sale catalogue in the Witt Library)

LITERATURE D. Lysons, *Environs of London* (1796), I, 108ff. (as 'Cartwright the Younger in Vandyke dress')

423   *Richard Perkins*

Richard Perkins was a successful actor during the reigns of James I and Charles I. In 1602 he was under Henslowe's management and he seems to have continued to act until the suppression of stage plays in 1647, when he is said to have retired to Clerkenwell. The allusion to van Dyck's portraits of Charles I—especially the *Charles I in Three Positions* made for Bernini to work from—makes it likely that this portrait dates from the later 1630s.

Canvas, $27\frac{1}{2} \times 24\frac{3}{8}$in (69.8 × 61.9cm)

PROVENANCE Cartwright Bequest, 1686 (166: *Mr pirkines y^e actour*)

ENGRAVING R. Clamp for S. Harding, *Shakespeare Illustrated*, 1793

LITERATURE D. Lysons, *Environs of London* (1796), I, 108ff.

430   *Michael Drayton*

Michael Drayton (1563–1631) wrote *Polyolbion* and several plays. He was a friend of Shakespeare and his claim to have been Poet Laureate is apparently substantiated by the laurel wreath he wears. This is one of only three authentic portraits and is dated *An^o 1628*.

Canvas, $21\frac{1}{2} \times 16\frac{1}{2}$in (54.5 × 41.9cm)

PROVENANCE Cartwright Bequest, 1686 (108: *Mickill Darayton y^e poet*)

EXHIBITED National Portrait Exhibition, 1866 (338); Paris, Bibliothèque Nationale, 1951/2 (472); Manchester, Coronation Exhibition, 1953 (54)

LITERATURE D. Lysons, *Environs of London* (1796), I, 108ff.; R. Strong, *Tudor and Jacobean Portraits* (NPG Catalogue, 1969), I, 72; II, pl. 130

443   *Edward Alleyn, Founder of the College of God's Gift at Dulwich*

Inscribed: *1626*

Edward Alleyn (1566–1626), actor, theatrical manager, and bear-garden proprietor became owner of the manor of Dulwich 1605–14 and began to found the College in 1613. It was formally opened in 1619. In 1592 he married Joan Woodward (British School, 444) and when she died in 1623 he married, in the same year, Constance, daughter of John Donne the poet and divine. The date presumably refers to Alleyn's bequest rather than to the date of the picture. It has been damaged and repainted, and some alterations were made in the late 18th century (*see* Engraving below), but there is a general resemblance to the style associated with the shop of Marcus Gheeraerts II (*d* 1635).

Canvas, $80\frac{1}{4} \times 44\frac{7}{8}$in (203.8 × 114cm)

PROVENANCE Presumably bequeathed by Alleyn, 1626

ENGRAVING A drawing of 1790 by Sylvester Harding, belonging to the College, is a preparation for his engraving of 1792: this shows differences in the gloves, cuffs, and position of the ring, perhaps indicating the extent of the 'repair' known to have been carried out in 1790 by George Paterson

LITERATURE J. Aubrey, *Natural History and Antiquities of Surrey* (1719), I, 195; R. Seymour, *A Survey of the Cities of London and Westminster . . .* (1733), I, 209; D. Lysons, *Environs of London* (1796), I, 108ff.

444   *Joan Alleyn*

Inscribed: [A]*ETS 22* [*ie* Aetatis 22]/*1596*

Traditionally regarded as a portrait of Joan Woodward, first wife of Edward Alleyn. She was the step-daughter of Phillip Henslowe the theatrical manager and was born c 1573/4. She married in 1592 and died in 1623. She is buried in the College Chapel. The portrait has been much damaged and overpainted, so that no attribution is possible.

Panel, 31¼ × 24⅞in (79.1 × 63.2cm)

PROVENANCE Presumably Alleyn Bequest, 1626

EXHIBITION Manchester, Coronation Exhibition, 1953 (26)

LITERATURE J. Aubrey, *Natural History and Antiquities of Surrey* (1719), I, 195; R. Seymour, *A Survey of the Cities of London and Westminster . . .* (1733), I, 209; D. Lysons, *Environs of London* (1796), I, 108ff.

445 *Francis Bacon, 1st Baron Verulam and Viscount St Alban*

Francis Bacon (1561–1626), first Baron Verulam and Viscount St Alban, was admitted to Gray's Inn in 1575 and became Lord Chancellor in 1618; in 1622 he was charged with bribery and confessed to corruption and neglect. He is best remembered for his *Essays*, first published in 1597 and enlarged in 1625, and for his philosophical and scientific works, the *Novum Organum*, 1620, and the *Advancement of Learning*, 1605, which advocate a more scientific conception of nature than the prevailing Aristotelianism. Aubrey records that 'Dr Harvey told me it was like the eie of a viper'. This portrait was formerly ascribed to van Somer, but it seems to be a rather poor version of the full-length ascribed to Blyenberch, though it is closest to the anonymous portrait in the National Portrait Gallery (1288). The condition of the picture makes it difficult to judge whether the history given—which takes it back to c 1622—can be entirely correct.

Canvas, 24 × 18½in (61 × 47cm)

PROVENANCE Traditionally given by Bacon himself to the Andrew family of Wandsworth, relations by marriage, c 1622; passed by descent to John Acworth and by descent to Marian Sedgwick; her cousin, Admiral Love; given by Miss Love, his sister, 1873

LITERATURE R. Strong, *Tudor and Jacobean Portraits* (NPG Catalogue, 1969), I, 10ff. (on portraits of Bacon); II, pls 21–4

569 *Nathaniel Lee*

Lee (?1653–92) failed as an actor and became a playwright. He collaborated with Dryden in 1679 and 1682, but went mad in 1684 and was in Bedlam until 1689. He died mad. What is said to be the only authentic portrait of him, by Dobson, is in the Garrick Club—and is a manifest impossibility, since Dobson died in 1646, seven years before Lee was born. The sitter, however, is probably the same, so 569 may well represent Lee, presumably c 1680, although there is some doubt whether the Garrick Club picture actually represents him.

Canvas, 24¾ × 19½in (62.8 × 49.5cm)

PROVENANCE Fairfax Murray Gift, 1911

VERSION Apart from the Garrick Club picture, another, more Romantic, version was sold at Christie's in 1954. It was an 18th-century pastiche, and 569 may well be a similar Romantic interpretation

604   *John Dive*

Inscribed: *IOHN eldest son, of IOHN DIVE/Esqᵉ: married DOROTHY Daughtʳ,/of WALTER ASTON Esqᵉ: of/Millwich, com̄: Staffordshire*

In the top left corner a coat of arms, of Dive of Millwich, Staffs, charged with Aston of Staffs. Dorothy was presumably a daughter of the Walter Aston, who claimed to be Lord Aston of Forfar, 1712–63. Dorothy was therefore born in or after 1733, and apparently married John Dive not much earlier than 1753. The style of the portrait is not easily identifiable as that of a British painter active around the middle of the 18th century, but the nearest comparable portrait seems to be Francis Cotes's *Taylor White*, a signed and dated pastel of 1758, in the Coram Foundation, London.

Canvas, 25¼ × 20⅛in (64.1 × 51.1cm)

PROVENANCE   Unknown; Fairfax Murray Gift, 1917

Adriaen **BROUWER** (1605/6–38)
Brouwer was the link between Flemish and Dutch genre painting of the 17th century. He was born in Oudenaarde and died in Antwerp, but may have been trained in Haarlem under Frans Hals. He was a Master in the Antwerp Guild in 1631/2 and was imprisoned there for a political offence in 1633 (the prison baker, J. van Craesbeck, became his pupil and imitator). The squalor of his subject-matter is often offset by the beauty of his colour, and Rubens is known to have admired his work.

108   *Interior of a Tavern*

The pipes being smoked probably contained a mixture of belladonna and hemp, illegally obtainable in Flemish 17th-century taverns of the more disreputable sort. A replica of this picture, formerly in the Duc D'Arenberg Collection, may be the original or both may be copies of a lost original, but opinion seems to be against accepting 108 as entirely by Brouwer himself.

Panel, 12¾ × 17in (32.4 × 43.2cm)

PROVENANCE   Perhaps the *Conversation* in Desenfans Sale, 8ff.iv.1786 (50); Bourgeois Bequest, 1811

EXHIBITED   RA, Flemish, 1953/4 (340)

VERSIONS   Copies are in the Hermitage, Leningrad, and Valenciennes. The Arenberg version was sold at Lempertz, Cologne, 26.xi.1970 (32)

LITERATURE   HdG, III, no 111; G. Knuttel, *Brouwer* (English) (The Hague, 1962), 59, 114, 115 n and fig 34 (as replica of the Arenberg picture, without determining which, if either, is the original); W. Bernt, *Netherlandish Painters of the 17th Century* (1970), I, fig 199 (as Brouwer)

Richard **BURBAGE** *see* BRITISH SCHOOL (395)

Abraham van **CALRAET** (1642–1722)
Little is known about Calraet except that he worked in Dordrecht and had the same initials as the most famous painter of that town, Aelbert Cuyp. Calraet may have been a pupil of Cuyp's, but he also painted figures and fruit pieces. The initials *AC*, usually very small, are now thought to be Calraet's, rather than Cuyp's, and all five of the Dulwich pictures, now attributed to Calraet, were formerly regarded as by Cuyp. The position is not made any clearer by another *AC* who is identified as A. Coosemans, a painter of still-life. There are three *AC* pictures in the National Gallery, all now attributed to Calraet.

65   *White Horse in a Riding School*

Signed: *AC*

This picture and 71 are characteristic examples of the Calraet/Cuyps.

Panel, $13\frac{3}{4} \times 20\frac{1}{2}$in (34.9 × 52cm)

PROVENANCE Desenfans Insurance List, 1804 (either 102 or 103, as Cuyp); Bourgeois Bequest, 1811

EXHIBITED NG 1947 (9: attributed to Cuyp, but suggesting Calraet)

LITERATURE HdG, II, no 604 (as Cuyp)

71   *Two Horses*

Signed: AC

The very small initials, at lower left, have not previously been noted: they seem to be those of Abraham van Calraet (*see* 65) rather than of Aelbert Cuyp, to whom the picture was formerly attributed.

Panel, $11\frac{3}{8} \times 15\frac{7}{8}$in (29 × 40.4cm)

PROVENANCE As 65

EXHIBITED NG 1947 (10: 'hitherto called Cuyp, but perhaps by Calraet')

LITERATURE HdG, II, no 551 (as Cuyp); A. Bredius in *Burl.Mag.* (1919), XXXV, 120 (as Calraet)

181   *Fishing on the Ice*

This picture, which is unsigned, was attributed to Cuyp until recently. In 1947, when 65 and 71 were exhibited at the National Gallery as by Calraet this was still attributed to Cuyp, but stylistically it belongs with 65, 71 and 296.

Panel, $15\frac{3}{4} \times 20\frac{1}{4}$in (40 × 51cm)

PROVENANCE Probably Desenfans (1804 Insurance List, ?78); Bourgeois Bequest, 1811

EXHIBITED NG 1947 (7: as Cuyp)

LITERATURE HdG, II, no 734 (as Cuyp)

296   *A Riding School in the Open Air*

Signed: *A.C*

The initials, previously unrecorded, are very small and obscured by the lower edge of the frame. The style shows Calraet's affinity with that of Wouwerman (*cf* National Gallery, 1851)

Panel, $15\frac{3}{8} \times 20\frac{3}{8}$in (39 × 51.6cm)

PROVENANCE Probably J. van der Linden van Slingeland, Dordrecht, Sale 22.viii.1785(88), bt Roos; Sale, Amsterdam, 11.vii.1798 (24), bt Gruyter; Bourgeois Bequest, 1811

LITERATURE Sm no 28; HdG, II, no 605 (both as Cuyp)

Govaert **CAMPHUYSEN** (1623/4–72)

Govaert was probably the pupil of his elder brother, but he worked in the style of Paulus Potter (1625–54), as may be seen from the forged signature on 64. He worked mainly in Amsterdam, except for 11 years in Stockholm. His masterpiece is in the Wallace Collection, London.

64 *Two Peasants with Cows*

Forged signature: *P. Potter*

The attribution to Camphuysen was made by Richter in the 1880 Catalogue and can be confirmed by comparison with signed works, notably those in Montreal and the Wallace Collection.

Panel, $18\frac{5}{8} \times 24\frac{3}{4}$in (47.3 × 62.8cm)

PROVENANCE Bourgeois Bequest, 1811

CANALETTO (1697–1768)

Giovanni Antonio Canale, called Canaletto, was one of the three great Venetian painters in the 18th century who specialised in *vedute*—views of their native city, mainly for the Grand Tourist trade. By 1726 he was already working for the English market, and in 1746 he settled in London for nearly ten years (*see* 600). Most of his Venetian views were painted from drawings, sometimes made with the help of a *camera obscura*, but in spite of their limited subject-matter they are rarely repetitive. The Royal Collection has by far the largest and best selection of his paintings, drawings and etchings.

599 *The Bucentaur at the Molo on Ascension Day*

The Bucentaur, or 'Bucintoro', was the great State vessel in which, every year on Ascension Day, the Doge left the Molo and put out into the Adriatic to perform the ceremony of the Wedding of Venice and the Sea by casting a gold ring into the water. The vessel shown here was the last Bucintoro, built in 1724 and destroyed when Napoleon overthrew the Venetian Republic. Canaletto painted a number of versions of the scene, all based on a drawing by him now at Windsor Castle. Windsor also has a painting of *c* 1734, made for his early patron, Consul Smith. Our version is much later, and has been dated to 1755 or later on the evidence of alterations to the Torre dell' Orologio in the background. An odd feature is the presence of two domes on S. Mark's, where only one would actually be visible. This may be due to a *pentimento*, but it has also been suggested that the picture was painted in England and is the result of a slip; however, if it is up-to-date with the Torre dell' Orologio it is hardly likely that Canaletto would have made such a blunder.

Canvas, $23 \times 40\frac{1}{8}$in (58.3 × 101.8cm)

PROVENANCE An old label on the back has '51 . . . From the collection of Mr [illegible] . . . sold in Manchester 1838 [*or* 6]'; H. Yates Thompson; given by him, 1915

ENGRAVING Visentini, *Prospectus Magni Canalis* (from the Windsor painting)

LITERATURE K. T. Parker, *Canaletto Drawings at Windsor* (1948), no 7; W. G. Constable, *Canaletto* (Oxford, 1962), II, no 339 and pl 64; 2nd edn, ed. J. Links (Oxford, 1976), suggesting date after 1755 and perhaps *c* 1763; M. Levey, *Later Italian Pictures in the Collection of H.M. the Queen* (1964), no 397; P. Rosenberg and L. Puppi, *Tout l'oeuvre peint de Canaletto* (Paris, 1975) (from Italian edn, 1968), no 232

600 *Old Walton Bridge over the Thames*

There was originally an inscription by Canaletto himself on the back, saying that the picture was painted in London in 1754, for 'the first and last time', for his patron Thomas Hollis, the Republican and benefactor of Harvard University. The inscription read: *Fatto nel anno 1754 in Londra per la prima ed ultima volta con ogni maggior attenzione ad instanza del Signior Cavaliere Hollis padrone mio stimatissimo/Antonio Canal detto il Canaletto.* A label on the back, signed by John Disney and dated 1850 records this. Another version, now in the Paul Mellon Collection, U.S.A., has a similar inscription, but with the date 1755. The two pictures are, however, quite different, and in an old catalogue of the Hollis pictures we are told that the foreground figures are Thomas Hollis himself, his friend Thomas Brand (to whom he bequeathed the picture), and his servant, Francesco Giovannini, with his dog, Malta. These figures are not in the Mellon version, but both show the house on the left, which belonged to Samuel Dicker MP, who built the bridge in 1750, and commissioned the Mellon version. The bridge was rebuilt in 1780. Canaletto painted six pictures in London for Hollis, and at least three of them had similar inscriptions on the back. The *Ranelagh* (now National Gallery, 1429) has almost exactly the same inscription as our picture.

Canvas, 19¼ × 30¼in (48.8 × 76.7cm)

PROVENANCE Painted for T. Hollis, 1754; bequeathed by him to T. Brand (Hollis) in 1774; bequeathed by him to Rev. J. Disney, 1804; passed by descent to Edgar Disney; Anon. (Mrs E. Disney) Sale, Christie's, 3.v.1884 (130), bt Denison; C. Becket Denison; sold Christie's, 13.vi.1885 (858), bt H. Yates Thompson; presented by Miss E. Murray Smith, 1917

EXHIBITED BI 1864 (158); NG 1947 (2); RA 1954/5 (24); London, Somerset House, 1977 (15)

VERSION/DRAWING A drawing in the Paul Mellon Collection and an engraving by A. Walker both seem to relate to the Mellon painting of 1755

LITERATURE H. Finberg in *Walpole Society* (1920/21), IX, 66 and rep.; W. T. Whitley, *Artists and their Friends* ... (1928), I, 118–19 (quoting Hollis catalogue); F. Watson, *Canaletto* (1949), 17 and rep.; W. G. Constable, *Canaletto* (Oxford, 1962), II, no 441 (no 442 is the Mellon version); and 2nd edn, ed. J. Links (Oxford, 1976); P. Rosenberg and L. Puppi, *Tout l'oeuvre peint de Canaletto* (Paris, 1975) (from Italian edn, 1968), no 302

Lodovico **CARRACCI** (1555–1619)
Agostino **CARRACCI** (1557–1602)
Annibale **CARRACCI** (1560–1609)

Lodovico and his cousins, Agostino and Annibale, were the founders of the Bolognese School. Lodovico, as the eldest, was the leading member of their teaching Academy and worked for most of his life in Bologna. Agostino was principally an engraver, but he worked with his brother Annibale, the greatest artist of the Bolognese School, in Rome. Annibale's frescoes in the Farnese Palace in Rome (1595–1604) are, with Caravaggio's easel paintings, the major works produced in Rome at the beginning of the 17th century.

Agostino **CARRACCI**

255 *The Last Communion of S. Francis*

Formerly called the *Death of S. Francis*, but clearly his last Communion, since he died in the evening of 3 October 1226, lying on the bare ground in a hut near the Portiuncula at Assisi. This picture probably dates from *c* 1590.

Canvas, 26¾ × 22in (67 × 55.9cm)

PROVENANCE Desenfans Private Sale, 8ff.iv.1786 (124: as L. Carracci); his Sale, Skinner & Dyke, 27.ii.1795 (36: Carrache); Insurance List, 1804 (76: L. Carracci); Bourgeois Bequest, 1811

ENGRAVING/DRAWING Engraved with minor variations by T. Galle, presumably before 1596. Jaffé published a drawing in a private collection, London (*see* below)

LITERATURE M. Jaffé in *Paragone*, 83 (1956), 12ff. and rep. figs 10, 11 (the painting and drawing); A. Boschloo, *Annibale Carracci in Bologna* (The Hague, 1974), I, 179, n 5

After Annibale **CARRACCI**

265 *The Entombment of Christ*

This is one of a group of paintings, some of which (including 265) have been more or less positively attributed to Sisto Badalocchio (1585–after 1621), who was Annibale Carracci's favourite assistant. The main versions are in Cremona, Christ Church Gallery, Oxford, and the National Gallery (which is slightly different in composition). Our picture seems likely to be by Badalocchio, but is probably dependent upon a Carracci design.

Canvas, 18¾ × 15⅛in (47.6 × 38.4cm)

PROVENANCE Perhaps Desenfans Sale, Skinner & Dyke, 24ff.ii.1795 (3rd day, 6: but this may have been Dulwich 162); Bourgeois Bequest, 1811 (as Lodovico Carracci)

LITERATURE M. V. Brugnoli in *Bolletino d' Arte* (1956), 359 and rep. (as by Badalocchio); J. Byam Shaw, *Catalogue of Paintings at Christ Church Oxford* (1967), no 185; M. Levey, *Catalogue of 17th & 18th Century Italian Schools* (NG, 1971) (*s.v.* Badalocchio)

Attributed to Lodovico **CARRACCI**

232 *SS. Peter and Francis of Assisi*

This little picture, which, as Richter observed in 1880, shows the influence of Schedone and Correggio, is probably a product of the Carracci shop.

Copper, 9⅜ × 7⅜in (23.7 × 18.7cm)

PROVENANCE Desenfans, Insurance List, 1804 (107: as 'Carracci'); Bourgeois Bequest, 1811 (1813 Inventory as Agostino)

LITERATURE H. Bodmer, *L. Carracci* (Burg bei Magdeburg, 1939), 142 (as attributed to Lodovico)

Studio of Lodovico **CARRACCI**

269   *S. Francis in Meditation*

Formerly called *A Franciscan Monk*, but there can be no doubt that it represents the familiar subject of S. Francis of Assisi with a skull. In the Bourgeois Inventory of 1813 it is attributed merely to 'Carracci', but it has been given to Lodovico since it entered the Gallery.

Copper, $13\frac{3}{4} \times 10\frac{1}{8}$in (34.9 × 25.7cm)

PROVENANCE Desenfans owned a picture of this subject, but his Sale Catalogue of 8ff.iv.1786 (417) describes it as a canvas, 48 × 42in, and it was this which, presumably, was in his Sale of 26.ii.1795—the present picture was probably in the J. Reynolds Sale, Christie's, 14.iii.1795 (55: as Annibale Carracci, S. Francis at Devotion, small, on copper), bt Champernowne (?); Bourgeois Bequest, 1811

LITERATURE H. Bodmer, *L. Carracci* (Burg bei Magdeburg, 1939), 142 (as Studio of Lodovico)

L. A. **CASTRO** (active last quarter of the 17th century)
There are several seapieces recorded in the Cartwright Inventory as by 'Castro', so he must have been active in the 1670s and early 1680s, presumably in London, where he was still working *c* 1700. It is tempting to identify him with Leonardo Antonio de Castro (1655–1745), a Spanish painter, but his style is Northern and there is no reason to suppose the Spaniard ever painted seapieces: in any case Laureys a Castro, recorded in the Antwerp Guild in 1664/5, would fit better for style and date, and the two can hardly be identical. Our Castro uses Mediterranean settings, so he may have been Portuguese or even Maltese by origin. The six pictures in Dulwich are by far the largest collection of his works in one gallery: others are in Ipswich Museum, Parham Park, Sussex (*The Sovereign of the Seas*), and the National Maritime Museum.

359, 361, 428, 436, 437, 517   *Seapieces*

All six pictures are inscribed *L. A. Castro* or *Castro*, and all but one are identifiable with paintings in the Cartwright Inventory (*c* 1686) attributed to him.

359 is cartwright 225: 'A Galley of Malta . . . Castro'; 361 is 224: 'A large Seascift . . . Ruff watter . . . Castro'; 428 is 227: 'A Large peece of a sea fight . . . Castro'; 436 is probably 216: 'A calme with ships and a wharfe . . . Castro'; 437 might be one of several Cartwright pictures, *eg* 216, 218, 219; and 517 is probably 219: 'A Sea Scift ruffe watters', which is not specified as by Castro, though it is inscribed with his name.

Canvas, (359) $30 \times 52\frac{7}{8}$in (76.2 × 134.3cm);
    (361) $37\frac{1}{2} \times 70\frac{3}{8}$in (95.3 × 178.7cm);
    (428) $42\frac{1}{8} \times 36\frac{1}{2}$in (107 × 92.7cm);
    (436) $24\frac{7}{8} \times 30$in (63.2 × 76.2cm);
    (437) $25 \times 30\frac{1}{8}$in (63.5 × 76.5cm);
    (517) $18\frac{5}{8} \times 25\frac{1}{8}$in (47.3 × 63.8cm)

PROVENANCE Cartwright Bequest, 1686

CLAUDE Gellée, called Claude Lorrain (1600–82)
Born near Nancy, Claude went to Italy at the age of about 13 and spent nearly all the rest of his long life in Rome, where, with Poussin, he became the leader of the French artists settled

in Italy. He was the most important landscape painter of the 17th century, and his vision of Italy affected all artists of the later 17th, 18th and early 19th centuries—Turner, for example. His *Liber Veritatis* ('The Book of Truth') contains 195 drawings after his own paintings, as a record of his work and a safeguard against forgeries. The *Liber* is now in the British Museum. Most of his pictures are based on the Roman Campagna and his infinite distances, melting into a haze of light, have been perhaps the most influential landscapes ever painted.

205   *Jacob with Laban and his Daughters*

Signed (or inscribed) and dated: *CLADIO IVF ROMAE. 1676*

The subject is from *Genesis*, xxix, but does not have any specific reference. An earlier version (1654) of the same subject is at Petworth House, Sussex (National Trust). The present composition is based on Claude's own etching of 1663, and his drawing of it in the *Liber Veritatis* (188) is inscribed: *quadro facto per ill^{mo} sig^{re} francesco Mayer di otto^{bre} 12 1676 Roma Claudio Gillee fecit I.V.* This was the third picture Claude painted for Mayer, an Imperial Councillor.

Canvas, $28\frac{1}{2} \times 37\frac{1}{4}$in ($72 \times 94.5$cm)

PROVENANCE F. Mayer, Regensburg; Earl of Halifax; his Sale, 10.iii.1739 (80); Duke of St Albans; his (Anon.) Sale, Phillips, 8.vi.1798 (78), bt Bourgeois (there seems no reason to suppose it ever belonged to Desenfans); Bourgeois Bequest, 1811

EXHIBITED RA 1902 (50); NG 1947 (3); RA, Landscape in French Art, 1949/50 (77)

DRAWINGS Preparatory drawings are in the Louvre (dated 1676) and the Morgan Library, New York; *Liber Veritatis* 188 is in the British Museum

LITERATURE *Liber Veritatis* no 188; Sm no 188; A. Blum, *Les eauxfortes de Claude . . .* (Paris, 1923), no 40; M. Röthlisberger, *Claude: The Paintings* (New Haven, 1961), I, 442–3; II, fig 308; *id, The Drawings* (Berkeley, Calif., 1968), nos 1094–5; *id* and D. Cecchi, *L'opera completa di Claude* (Milan, 1975), no 266; M. Kitson, *Claude Lorrain: Liber Veritatis* (1978), no 188

Circle of **CLAUDE**

174   *The Campo Vaccino, Rome*

The ancient Forum was often known as the Campo Vaccino—the cow pasture—in the 17th and 18th centuries. There are several variants on this composition: the earliest seems to be the one by Swanevelt (*cf* 11), now in the Fitzwilliam Museum, Cambridge, which is signed and dated 16(31?). It must date from before 1632 when the façade of the smaller church in the middle distance was altered. What is generally held to be Claude's own version of Swanevelt's theme is a painting in the Louvre (*c* 1636), with an etching of 1636 and two drawings. Our picture differs from the painting in Paris mainly by the transformation of a group of six figures at the bottom right into the four men playing cards. Both these paintings show the church in its post-1632 state. Our painting is not accepted as a work of either Claude or Swanevelt, but seems to be by an artist influenced by both.

Canvas, $30\frac{3}{4} \times 41\frac{3}{4}$in ($78.1 \times 106.1$cm)

PROVENANCE Bourgeois Bequest, 1811

LITERATURE Sm no 10 (for the Louvre picture—no mention of 174); M. Kitson in *Revue des Arts*, (1958), VIII, nos 5 and 6, 215ff. and 259ff.; M. Röthlisberger, *Claude: The Paintings* (New Haven, 1961), I, 114 (good contemporary copy); II, fig 428

Imitator of **CLAUDE**

215   *Classical Seaport at Sunset*

This type of composition, with the setting sun on water, was a favourite with Claude. There are three examples in the National Gallery, one of which (5), may have been the prototype (in reverse) for our picture. Röthlisberger calls it an imitation but knows no other by the same hand, which he thinks may be Italian, 17th or 18th century.

Canvas, $29\frac{1}{4} \times 39$in (74.3×99.1cm)

PROVENANCE Perhaps one of the two *Seaports* in Desenfans Insurance List, 1804 (70, 72); Bourgeois Bequest, 1811

EXHIBITION RA 1902 (52)

LITERATURE Sm no 306; M. Röthlisberger, *Claude: The Paintings* (New Haven, 1961), I, 515ff., no 255 and II, fig 365

School of **CLAUDE**

53   *Landscape with a Column and Figures*

There are very faint traces of what may have been a monogram (?*P*), followed by an *F*, but they have never been recorded. The picture was attributed to Claude in the Bourgeois Inventory of 1813, but this attribution is no longer accepted. A landscape of about the same size, by Pierre Patel (*c* 1605–76), who is known to have worked in the manner of Claude, certainly belonged to Desenfans before 1795.

Canvas, $41\frac{1}{4} \times 55\frac{1}{8}$in ($104.8 \times 140$cm)

PROVENANCE Perhaps the picture recorded in Desenfans Sale, 8.iv.1786 (385) as 'Patel, Landscape engraved by Vivares and the figures by Bartolozzi', 42×52in, including frame; Desenfans Sale, Skinner & Dyke, 24.ii.1795 (1st day, 85: Pattel, *Landscape with Ruins and Figures*, no size given); Bourgeois Bequest, 1811

Copy after **CLAUDE**

312   *The Rest on the Flight into Egypt*

A copy of the original by Claude, signed and dated 1676, in the collection of the Earl of Leicester, Holkham Hall, Norfolk. Mrs Jameson (1842) thought it was a copy of a Claude belonging to the Emperor of Russia, but that picture (now in the Hermitage, Leningrad) is a variant on the same theme.

Canvas, $15\frac{1}{4} \times 19\frac{5}{8}$in ($38.7 \times 49.8$cm)

PROVENANCE Bourgeois Bequest, 1811

LITERATURE A. Jameson, *Handbook to the Public Galleries . . .* (1842), 477, no 211; M. Röthlisberger, *Claude: The Paintings* (New Haven, 1961), I, 442 ('rather poor copy'); *id* and D. Cecchi, *L'opera completa di Claude* (Milan, 1975), no 265

Attributed to John Baptist **CLOSTERMAN** (*c* 1660–1711)

611   *A Physician, formerly called Boerhaave, but perhaps Blackmore*

This portrait raises a number of problems. It was presented to the Gallery in 1934 and has no known history; it was attributed to Kneller, and was said to represent Dr Herman Boerhaave (1668–1738), the greatest medical teacher of the 18th century. It is certainly not of him (*see* G. Lindeboom, *Iconographia Boerhaavii*, Leyden, 1963); nor is it by Kneller, though it is probably a work of the Closterman/Kneller circle, dating from the period before 1700. The anatomical drawings make it clear that an anatomist is represented, but it seems to date from before 1701, when Boerhaave began his enormously successful career, so it can hardly represent him, let alone any of his hundreds of pupils. Richard Blackmore, however, graduated MD at Padua in 1687 and became Physician to William and Mary. He was knighted and was also known as a writer. He died in 1729, and a portrait of him, attributed to Closterman, in the Royal College of Physicians, London, shows strong similarities in the shape of the nose and drooping left eye-lid, but the mouth is rather different.

Canvas, $29\frac{7}{8} \times 25$ in (75.9 × 63.5 cm)

PROVENANCE   Possibly Fairfax Murray Collection; given by Miss H. M. Spanton, whose father had been a friend of Fairfax Murray, 1934

Adam **COLONIA** (1634–85)

Colonia, born in Rotterdam, was the son of a painter and the grandson of Adam Louisz. Colonia (1574–1651) who is almost certainly the Adam de Colone, one of the founders of Scottish portraiture active in Edinburgh in the 1620s. The younger Colonia settled in London around 1670 and spent the rest of his life there. An almost contemporary biography says that he 'resided a great while in England, and became especially eminent for his small figures in rural pieces, for his cattle, country-wakes, fire-pieces &c. He also copied many pictures of beasts after Bassan, particularly those of the royal collection, which are esteemed his best performances'. The four copies after Bassano (386, 398, 412 and 422) from the Cartwright Collection are probably his work, but 431 shows him in a more Dutch mood, close to Berchem. There are very few paintings known to be by him, but there is one in Rotterdam signed and dated 1662. Both the Dulwich pictures were presumably painted in London and therefore date 1670/85.

371   *Sheep Shearing*

Signed: *A* (perhaps monogram *AD*) *Colonia*

A pastoral in the manner of Bassano: there are four copies of Bassanesque *Seasons* (386, 398, 412 and 422) which may be attributed to Colonia and which contain, for example, the figures of the shearer and the woman with the yoke. Colonia may have known the Bassanos in the Royal Collection as well as the engravings by Teniers from the *Seasons* in Vienna (which differ slightly).

Canvas, $39\frac{1}{8} \times 58\frac{1}{4}$ in (99.4 × 147.9 cm)

PROVENANCE   Presumably bought from the painter by Cartwright; his Inventory (83, without attribution); his Bequest, 1686

LITERATURE   B. Buckeridge, *Essay towards an English School*, in R. de Piles, *Art of Painting*, 3rd edn (*c* 1750), 362 (for Colonia); W. Bernt, *Netherlandish Painters of the 17th Century* (1970), I, p 25 (for form of signature)

431 *The Flight into Egypt*

Signed: *A* (perhaps monogram *AD*) *Colonia*

This shows Colonia working in a style much closer to Berchem than in 371.

Canvas, $27\frac{1}{4} \times 18\frac{3}{4}$in (69.2 × 47.7cm)

PROVENANCE Presumably bought from the painter by Cartwright; his Inventory (82); his Bequest, 1686

LITERATURE As 371

Samuel **COOPER** *see* Gerard SOEST (573)

John De **CRITZ**(?) (1555–1641)

De Critz was a Flemish painter who came to England as a boy and was made joint Serjeant-Painter in 1605. There are no certainly documented works by him, but he was paid for a full-length portrait of James I in 1606, and other payments make it likely that he originated this type of portrait. His sisters married Marcus Gheeraerts I and II, and it is hardly possible to distinguish between these family workshops. This, like most of the other versions of *James I*, was formerly attributed to Gheeraerts the Younger, but the documents of payment make it more likely that the pattern originated with De Critz.

548 *James I and VI*

King James (1566–1625), the son of Mary, Queen of Scots, became James VI of Scotland on his mother's abdication in 1567. He united the Kingdoms of England and Scotland when he succeeded Queen Elizabeth I on the English throne in 1603. In 1619 he granted Letters Patent to Edward Alleyn for the foundation of his College at Dulwich. He was an author (*Basilikon Doron*, 1599, and other works), but is better known as 'The wisest fool in Christendom'.

Canvas, 79 × 51in (200.5 × 129.5cm)

PROVENANCE Probably Holland House, passing to the Countess of Warwick, who married Joseph Addison in 1716. They lived at Bilton Hall, near Rugby; Bilton Sale, Christie's, 28.vi.1898 (12), bt H. Yates Thompson, who presented it to Alleyn's School

EXHIBITED RA, Kings and Queens, 1953 (113: as Attributed to Gheeraerts)

VERSIONS Other full-length versions include those in Cambridge University and the Prado, Madrid. There are three-quarter length versions in the National Maritime Museum, and the Scottish National Portrait Gallery. Versions of the head only are in the National Portrait Gallery, London, and 384 of this collection

LITERATURE L. Cust in *Walpole Society* (1914), III, 26; R. Strong, *Tudor and Jacobean Portraits* (NPG Catalogue, 1969), I, 179; *id, The English Icon* (1969), 259, 264

Aelbert **CUYP** (1620–91)

Cuyp was one of the greatest of Dutch landscape painters in the Italianate style derived from Claude and brought back to Holland by painters like Both (*cf* 12) and Berchem: Cuyp himself never went to Italy. The Dulwich pictures are among the finest examples of his work, ranging from the earliest, still under the influence of van Goyen (348), to the most mature examples of his Italianate style, with the wonderful golden light seen in 96 and 124. He married a rich widow in 1658 and was thus free to devote himself to his art, although he painted little in the last years of his life. British painters of the 18th and early 19th centuries were profoundly influenced by Cuyp, which probably explains the presence of most of his best works in this country. His imitator, Abraham Calraet, is also well represented at Dulwich.

4   *View on a Plain*

Signed: *A cuyp*

It has been suggested that between *A* and *cuyp* are the remains of a monogram of J. G. Cuyp (Aelbert's father). This is incorrect, and there seems to be no reason to doubt the authenticity of the signature. The painting is probably fairly early (*c* ?1645) and shows the influence of van Goyen. The view is thought to be near Rhenen.

Panel, $19\frac{3}{8} \times 28\frac{7}{8}$in (49.3 × 73.3cm)

PROVENANCE Bourgeois Bequest, 1811

EXHIBITED NG 1947 (4); RA, Dutch, 1952/3 (351); NG 1973 (6)

VERSIONS Two pictures in private collections (HdG nos 69a and 75)

DRAWING One in the Teyler Museum, Haarlem, seems to have been used for the distance, and also for a painting, dated 1641, in a private collection in Buenos Aires

ENGRAVING J. Cousen

LITERATURE HdG, II, no 694; S. Reiss in *Burl.Mag.* (1953), XCV, 42ff.; *id, A. Cuyp* (1975), 75, fig 42 (recanting his earlier attribution to J. G. Cuyp)

96   *An Evening Ride near a River*

Signed: *A. cuijp*

The signature seems perfectly authentic, but Reiss rejects the attribution.

Panel, $19\frac{1}{4} \times 25\frac{1}{4}$in (48.9 × 64.1cm)

PROVENANCE Possibly J. Barnard in 1769 and his Sale, 1798, bt Bourgeois; Bourgeois Bequest, 1811

EXHIBITED RA 1903 (99)

ENGRAVING T. Major, 1769 (if this picture)

LITERATURE Sm nos 261 and ?83; HdG, II, no 434 and probably no 467; S. Reiss, *A. Cuyp* (1975), 208 (identifying 96 with Sm no 261 and HdG no 434, but rejecting it)

124   *A Road near a River*

Probably a late work, *c* 1660. There is a similar picture in the Royal Collection. *See colour plate V.*

Canvas, $44\frac{1}{2} \times 66$in (113 × 167.6cm)

PROVENANCE Desenfans Sale, 1802 (142); Insurance List, 1804 (probably 60); Bourgeois Bequest, 1811

EXHIBITED Perhaps BI 1824 (64); RA 1903 (93); NG 1947 (5); RA, Dutch, 1952/3 (159); Dordrecht, 1977/8 (35)

LITERATURE Sm no 72; HdG, II, no 435; S. Reiss in *Burl.Mag.* (1953), XCV, 42 (as *c* 1660/65); D. Burnett in *Apollo* (1969), LXXXIX, 372–80; S. Reiss, *A. Cuyp* (1975), 181, pl 138 (as mid-1650s)

128   *Herdsmen with Cows*

Signed: *A. cuijp*

Probably a late work, *c* 1660.

Canvas, $39\frac{1}{2} \times 56\frac{3}{4}$in (99 × 144cm)

PROVENANCE Probably Bryan Sale, Coxe, Burrell & Co, 19.v.1798 (39); Bourgeois Bequest, 1811

EXHIBITED RA 1903 (97); Dutch, 1952/3 (185); The Hague, 1970, and London, Tate Gallery, 1971 (57)

VERSION Sm no 100 and HdG no 242 refer to a version sold in Paris in 1803, but this was very much smaller (13 × 19in)

LITERATURE Sm no 80 (wrongly identifying with a picture in Desenfans 1802 Catalogue); HdG, II no 330 (repeating Smith); S. Reiss in *Burl.Mag.* (1953), XCV, 42ff. (as early); *id*, *A. Cuyp* (1975), 77, fig 44

144   *Cattle near the Maas, with Dordrecht in the distance*

Signed: *A. cuyp*

Unlike most of Cuyp's landscapes this represents an actual place. The church is the Groote Kerk at Dordrecht, which may also be seen in the opposite direction in two pictures in the National Gallery (961 and 962)

Panel, 30 × 41in (76.2 × 106.4cm)

PROVENANCE Possibly in Desenfans Sale, Christie's, 11–14.v.1785 (68) and Private Sale, 8ff.iv.1786 (90); Bourgeois Bequest, 1811

EXHIBITED NG 1947 (6)

VERSIONS HdG nos 384 and 385 are in Rotterdam, Boymans-van Beuningen Museum and the Museum in San Diego, Calif.

DRAWING A drawing of the town and boat was sold at Sotheby's, London, on 21.x.1963. Another, related to the National Gallery pictures, is in the British Museum

LITERATURE HdG, II, no 201a; S. Reiss, *A. Cuyp* (1975), 117 and fig 80 (as late 1640s and also rep. the drawing)

348   *Landscape with Cattle and Figures*

Signed: *A. cuijp*

The marked influence of van Goyen makes it likely that it is a very early work, perhaps *c* 1640, since there are some identical details in a portrait group dated 1641 in the Israel Museum, Jerusalem, and Reiss (1975) points out that the two goats at the left must have been painted from Cuyp's father's drawings, used for engravings in *Diversa Animalia*, 1641.

Panel, $15\frac{7}{8} \times 23\frac{1}{2}$in ($40 \times 59$cm)

PROVENANCE Desenfans Sale, 1802 (144); probably Desenfans Insurance List, 1804 (31); Bourgeois Bequest, 1811

EXHIBITED NG 1947 (8); RA, Dutch, 1952/3 (358); NG, Cuyp, 1973 (1)

LITERATURE Sm no 77; HdG, II, nos 697 (and 239); S. Reiss in *Burl.Mag.* (1953), XCV, 42ff.; *id*, *A. Cuyp* (1975), 43, fig 15

Michael **DAHL** (1656/9–1743)

Dahl was a Swedish painter who came to London and developed into Kneller's only serious rival. He first visited London in 1682, after which he made a long Grand Tour, staying for some time in Rome, before settling in London in 1689. He outlived Kneller by 20 years, dying in extreme old age.

575
576
Unknown Man and *Unknown Woman*

The flowers may indicate that these were painted as marriage pictures. The attribution seems to be due to Fairfax Murray and is certainly correct, the date probably being in the 1690s.

Canvas, (575) $49\frac{5}{8} \times 40$in (126×101.6cm);
(576) $49\frac{1}{2} \times 40$in (125.7×101.6cm)

PROVENANCE Delme Sale (Different Properties), Christie's, 7.vii.1894 (68, 70) (as Anon. Painter), bt Fairfax Murray; his Gift, 1911

Dirck van **DELEN** (1604/5–71)

Van Delen painted only architectural fantasies, usually of a floridly Northern Renaissance style closer to the taste of Antwerp than to Holland; he was influenced by Steenwyck, the Antwerp architectural painter. Van Delen was born and died at Arnemuiden, near Middelburg in Zeeland, where he became Burgomaster.

470
The Entrance to a Palace

Signed and dated: *D. V. DELEN F 1654*

Delen's architectural fantasies bear dates between 1623 and 1668, and many of them are said to have the figures painted by other artists: the elaborate example in the National Gallery has figures ascribed to J. Olis, but no suggestion has been made that 470 is not entirely by Delen.

Panel, $19\frac{1}{2} \times 21\frac{1}{4}$in ($49.5 \times 54$cm)

PROVENANCE Bourgeois Bequest, 1811

LITERATURE H. Jantzen, *Das niederländische Architekturbild* (Leipzig, 1910), 65ff., Cat no 129

Stephen Poyntz **DENNING** (*c* 1787–1864)

Denning was principally a miniature painter, exhibiting at the Royal Academy from 1814 until 1852, but he was also the second Curator of the Dulwich Gallery, succeeding Cockburn in 1821 and serving until his death in 1864. With the help of his son, the Rev. Stephen Denning, he compiled a catalogue of the Gallery in 1858 and began a fair copy of it in 1859, but this was never completed: it was never published, perhaps because, as appears from the 1892 Catalogue 'it was removed from the College, and has not been recovered'. By 1905, however, the Ms (or perhaps both of them) had been recovered (*see* Introduction, p 22).

304 *Queen Victoria, aged Four*

The Princess Victoria (1819–1901) became Queen in 1837, succeeding her uncle, William IV. She is portrayed here at the age of four, in 1823. This charming little picture, for many years the most popular in the Gallery, was probably made, like most of Denning's works, for engraving. He also painted, much later, a portrait of her future husband, Prince Albert, which is now in Gotha.

Panel, $11 \times 8\frac{7}{8}$in (27.9 × 22.7cm)

PROVENANCE Bought by Dulwich College (£30), 1890

EXHIBITED Earl's Court, Royal Room, 1897 (651); London Museum, 1978

ENGRAVING Dowdeswell

William **DOBSON** *see* Gerard SOEST (592)

Carlo **DOLCI** (1616–86)

Dolci was the leading Florentine painter of the 17th century. Most of his works are highly detailed, small in scale, and devotional to the point of cloying. The *S. Catherine* is a characteristic example.

242 *S. Catherine of Siena*

S. Catherine (?1347–80) became a member of the Third Order of S. Dominic *c* 1367. In 1375 she received the Stigmata (but without visible lesions) and she is usually represented in art as a Dominican Tertiary (as here) and with the Stigmata. There was a controversy between the Franciscans and Dominicans over her in the 17th century. She is also remembered for her peremptory, but ineffectual, letters to the Popes at Avignon before and during the Great Schism (1378–1417).

Panel, $9\frac{5}{8} \times 7\frac{1}{8}$in (24.4 × 18.1cm)

PROVENANCE Bourgeois Bequest, 1811

VERSION The Royal Collection had a pair, *S. Catherine* and the *Magdalen*, in the time of George III, but nothing is now known of them

Gerrit (Gerard) **DOU** (1613–75)

Dou was a portrait and genre painter of Leyden, who was Rembrandt's pupil, though he shows little trace in his work of contact with that great genius. He was a meticulous painter (*fijnschilder*) in the tradition mainly founded by him: he is said to have claimed, when his painting of a broomstick was admired for its finish, that it still needed three days' work.

56 *A Lady playing a Clavichord*

Formerly called virginals, the instrument is a clavichord. The subject is rather unusual for Dou, and there is some confusion between the few known paintings by him of such scenes, although this one was clearly influential on Vermeer's *Lady at a Virginal* in the National Gallery. The Dou was probably painted about 1665 and the Vermeer some ten years later. It has been suggested that the birdcage, musical instruments, and wine are erotic symbols.

Panel, $14\frac{7}{8} \times 11\frac{3}{4}$ in (37.7×29.8cm)

PROVENANCE Possibly de Bye Collection, Leyden, 1665; Comte de Dubarry Sale, Paris, 21.xi.1774; Prince de Conti Sale, Paris, 8.iv.1777, bt Langlier (a note in the catalogue says it had previously been sold at Langford's, London, as by Schalken after Dou); Gildemeester Sale, 11.vi.1800 (34); certainly Desenfans by 1802 (127); Bourgeois Bequest, 1811

EXHIBITED NG 1947 (11: wrongly said to be signed); Art in 17th Century Holland, 1976 (32)

VERSIONS Confusion arises between this and a similar painting in New York (HdG no 133) and two others (HdG nos 133a, b), one of which—probably 133—was recorded as Sm no 45 and probably belonged to Desenfans in 1801

LITERATURE HdG, I, no 132 (partly confusing the provenance with no 133); A. Jameson, *Handbook to the Public Galleries* . . . (1842), 459, no 106 (as copy of the Wells picture—*ie* HdG no 133); W. Martin, *Dou* (KdK, 1913), 99 and p 184 (stating that the de Bye picture was either this or the New York version, his no 98); *Art in 17th Century Holland* (exhibition catalogue), NG, 1976, no 32 (with details of the symbolism)

Simon **DUBOIS** *see* Du BOIS

Gaspar **DUGHET** (1615–75)

Often called Gaspard Poussin, because his sister married Poussin in 1630, Gaspar was, with Poussin and Claude, the leading landscape painter in Rome in the 17th century, and, like them, he was of French origin although he spent his life in Rome. He was extremely popular among English collectors of the 18th and 19th centuries and had great influence on painters such as Richard Wilson.

70 *Landscape in the Roman Campagna*

Formerly catalogued as a School work, perhaps on account of the statement in the 1880 Catalogue that it is a replica of a picture in the Duke of Sutherland's collection. That landscape, though similar, is not identical in composition with 70, which, in fact, is closer to one in the Holt Collection in 1966.

Canvas, $28\frac{3}{4} \times 38\frac{3}{4}$ in (73×98.4cm)

PROVENANCE Possibly in Desenfans Private Sale, 8ff.vi.1786 (262); Bourgeois Bequest, 1811

Karel **DU JARDIN** (Dujardin) (?1621/2–78)
Du Jardin was born in Amsterdam and was a pupil of Berchem, whose Italianate landscapes he imitated (*cf* Berchem, 196), and he also occasionally imitated the style of Paulus Potter, his junior. He went to Rome before 1650 and was a member of the 'Bent', or Northern artists' club, and he was in Lyons in 1650, when he married. After working in Amsterdam and The Hague he returned to Italy in 1674/5 and died in Venice in 1678.

72   *Peasants and a White Horse*

Canvas, $17\frac{3}{8} \times 15\frac{5}{8}$in (44.1 × 39.7cm)

PROVENANCE Desenfans by 1802 (1802 Catalogue, 133); Bourgeois Bequest, 1811

EXHIBITED RA, Dutch, 1952/3 (475)

LITERATURE HdG, IX, no 70

82   *A Smith shoeing an Ox*

Signed: *K. DV. IARDIN fe*

A *bambocciata* subject, presumably painted in Italy.

Canvas, $15 \times 16\frac{7}{8}$in (38 × 42.8cm)

PROVENANCE Heemskirk, The Hague, 1770; P. van Spyck, Leyden, 1781; Geldermeester, 1800; possibly 'From Abroad' Sale, Christie's, 26.iv.1806 (1), bt North, and perhaps Crawford Collection, 1806; Bourgeois Bequest, 1811

EXHIBITED BI 1824 (116); RA, Dutch, 1952/3 (530)

VERSION A version or copy formerly in the National Gallery, Edinburgh (HdG no 336), and now in Edinburgh University, has been confused with this picture

LITERATURE Sm no 15; HdG, IX, no 336

Cornelis **DUSART** (1660–1704)
Dusart was a Haarlem painter, received into the Guild in 1679, who was a pupil and imitator of A. van Ostade (*cf* 45), some of whose works he finished.

39   *Figures in the Courtyard of an old Building*

This domestic scene may be a fairly late work, as it is less obviously influenced by Ostade than many of Dusart's works.

Panel, $19\frac{3}{8} \times 14\frac{3}{4}$in (49 × 37.2cm)

PROVENANCE Bourgeois Bequest, 1811

DUTCH SCHOOL *see* Roelof van VRIES (7)

Sir Anthony van **DYCK** (1599–1641)

Van Dyck was much influenced by Rubens, whose pupil he was, but he seems to have been an independent master by about the age of 16, although he may have acted as a sub-contractor for Rubens. In 1620 he visited England for the first time, returning to Antwerp the following year and then going to Italy, where he worked mainly in Genoa, although he went as far south as Sicily (*see* 173). In Italy he learned a more elegant style of portraiture which stood him in good stead in England later. He returned to the Netherlands in 1627/8 and to England in 1632, when he was knighted by Charles I. The rest of his short life was spent mainly in London, where he died in 1641.

90   *The Madonna and Child*

Several versions of this subject are known, the closest to 90 being those in the Fitzwilliam Museum, Cambridge (ex-Bridgewater Collection) and the Walters Art Gallery, Baltimore (ex-Blenheim Palace). Others are in Nancy, the Liechtenstein Collection, Vaduz, and Munich. Van Dyck's Italian sketch-book (British Museum) contains several drawings related to the composition, which is itself reminiscent of Italian Seicento painters like Reni. There are also similarities with *The Abbé Scaglia adoring the Virgin and Child*, of 1634, in the National Gallery. Our picture probably dates from just before van Dyck's return to England in 1632.

Canvas, $60\frac{1}{2} \times 45\frac{7}{8}$in (153.7 × 116.5 cm). The measurements are larger than those recorded in the 1880 (and later) Catalogues, and there is a strip about a foot deep at the top which may be an addition.

PROVENANCE The provenance in earlier catalogues is certainly wrong, and the history seems to be: Imported into France by Gersaint before 1750; Jullienne Collection before 1767; Desenfans Private Sales, 8ff.iv.1786 (187) and 8ff.vi.1786 (187) both as 53 × 44in (*ie* sight-size?); 13.vii.1786 (3rd day, 62), bt 'Debrun'; J. B. P. Lebrun Sale, Paris, 11ff.iv.1791 (90: as 56 × 39 *pouces*, ex-Gersaint and ex-Jullienne), withdrawn; Desenfans Sale, Skinner & Dyke, 26.ii.1795 (96); Desenfans Insurance List, 1804 (111); Bourgeois Bequest, 1811

EXHIBITED NG 1974 (with *Abbé Scaglia*)

ENGRAVING The composition was engraved by Pontius, Clouwet and Carmona, but it is not clear which version was the model. The Salvador Carmona engraving is from a picture in the Conte Vincii Collection, Paris, in 1757

LITERATURE Sm no 263 (for this and other versions); G. Glück, *Van Dyck* (KdK, 1931), 234, 541 (as autograph); L. van Puyvelde in *Journal of the Walters Art Gallery* (Baltimore, 1942), V, 114 (as copy of the Baltimore version); G. Hoogewerff in *Mitteilungen des Kunsthistorischen Institutes* (Florence, 1959), VIII, 179 (as autograph)

127   *Samson and Delilah*

The subject is from *Judges*, xvi, 4–19: 'And she made him sleep upon her knees; and she called for a man, and she caused him to shave off the seven locks of his head; and she began to afflict him, and his strength went from him'. The Vulgate version—'lay his head in her lap'—is closer to the scene depicted. The young van Dyck was greatly influenced by Rubens in this composition, since there exist a drawing, an oil-sketch (now in Cincinnati Art Museum), and a finished painting, all by Rubens, as well as an engraving by Matham. These are all in the opposite direction, but the likeness is clear. For this reason, our picture is probably to be dated around 1618/20, since there is also a strong resemblance to the *Continence of Scipio*, Christ Church, Oxford, in both the old woman and especially the younger one. The Oxford picture has been dated *c* 1620/21. In fact, 127 was attributed to Rubens by Desenfans and remained under that name until about 1906.

Canvas, $59\frac{3}{8} \times 90\frac{3}{4}$in ($151.4 \times 230.5$cm), including an added strip at the top about 5in deep

PROVENANCE David Amory, Amsterdam, in 1711; his Sale, 23.vi.1722; Sir Gregory Page before 1767; Anon. (Page) Sale, Bertels, 26ff.v.1783 (3rd day, 76), perhaps bt Desenfans, as van Dyck; Desenfans Private Sale, 8.iv.1786 (174: as ex-Page, and now as Rubens); not in 1802 Catalogue, but in the Insurance List, 1804 (99), still as Rubens; Bourgeois Bequest, 1811

EXHIBITED RA, 17th Century, 1938 (68); NG 1947 (13); RA, Flemish, 1953/4 (228)

VERSIONS Apart from the Rubens prototype and its variants there have been several copies of 127 in the sale-room, most recently Christie's, 25.x.1946 (129)

LITERATURE G. Hoet, *Catalogus . . . van Schilderyen* (1752), I, 25 (as in Amory Collection); T. Martyn, *The English Connoisseur* (Dublin, 1767), II, 59 (in Page Collection); W. Bode, *Great Masters of Dutch and Flemish Painting* (1909), 308 n (re-attributing to van Dyck); G. Glück, *Van Dyck* (KdK, 1931), 13, 518; H. Vey, *Van-Dyck-Studien* (Cologne Dissertation, 1958), Ch. III (comparing the Dulwich and Vienna versions); H. Gerson and E. ter Kuile, *Art and Architecture in Belgium, 1600–1800* (1960), 113–14; M. Jaffé in *Burl.Mag.* (1969), CXI, 436 n (drawing by van Dyck); M. Kahr in *Art Bulletin* (1972), LIV, 282 (on the Rubens versions)

132 *Sunset Landscape with a Shepherd and his Flock*

Previously regarded as by Rubens or a copy of his work, the balance of opinion now seems to favour an attribution to van Dyck. The subject is markedly Titianesque and is based on an engraving after Titian and a drawing, attributed to van Dyck, which is also Titianesque.

Canvas, $42\frac{3}{8} \times 62\frac{1}{4}$in ($107.6 \times 158.1$cm)

PROVENANCE Said to have come from the Cabinet of Prince Rupert (Desenfans, 1802, but probably wrongly); John Bertels Sale, Walsh, 8.iv.1775 (25: Rubens); Desenfans 1802 Catalogue (87) and Insurance List, 1804 (63); Bourgeois Bequest, 1811 (Rubens)

DRAWING At Chatsworth, attributed to van Dyck by Jaffé, 1966

LITERATURE Sm no 725 (as Rubens); J. Müller-Hofstede in *Pantheon* (1966), XXIV, 36ff. and rep. (as Rubens, *c* 1638/40); M. Jaffé in *Burl.Mag.* (1966), CVIII, 410ff.; *id*, *Burl.Mag.* (1969), CXI, 436 n (attributes to van Dyck, *c* 1621)

170 *A Young Man, perhaps the Earl of Bristol*

Three young noblemen have been proposed as the sitter for this portrait, which may be dated stylistically to the mid-1630s. They are William Russell, 5th Earl and 1st Duke of Bedford; George Digby, 2nd Earl of Bristol; and Philip Herbert, 5th Earl of Pembroke. Lord Pembroke is very unlikely—he was not born until early 1621, and, as van Dyck died in 1641, the date would have to be *c* 1640/41; nor is the sitter like any other portrait of him. Both Bedford and Bristol would fit the dates better—the Duke of Bedford was born in 1616 and the Earl of Bristol in 1612, so that either would be of the right age for a portrait painted *c* 1635. There is, fortunately, a portrait of them both by van Dyck at Althorp, Northants., in the collection of Earl Spencer, probably painted about 1633: neither is so like the sitter in 170 as to be overwhelmingly convincing, but the Duke of Bedford had markedly darker hair, and, therefore, the balance seems to be in favour of an identification with Lord Bristol. Against this, the early catalogues of Desenfans' collection mention van Dyck portraits of a Russell and/or an Earl of Pembroke, but not one of Lord Bristol.

Canvas, $40\frac{5}{8} \times 32\frac{3}{4}$in ($103.2 \times 83.2$cm)

PROVENANCE Probably the *Earl of Bedford* in Desenfans Private Sale, 8ff.iv.1786 (208) and *John Russell, 3rd Son to the Earl of Bedford*, 8ff.vi.1786 (151)—both given as 37 × 31in; Christie's,

14.vii.1786 (44), bt ?Wickstead; Bourgeois Bequest, 1811 (but as *Earl of Pembroke* in 1813 Inventory). If the earlier *Bedford* is a different picture from the Bourgeois *Pembroke* then the history of that picture may be: Sir J. Reynolds; Bryan Sale, P. Coxe, 17ff.v.1798 (3rd day, 2) and so on

EXHIBITED NG 1947 (14: as *Bedford*); RA, Flemish, 1953/4 (162: as *Bristol*)

LITERATURE Sm no 521, but probably wrongly, as *Pembroke*, ex-Reynolds; G. Glück, *Van Dyck* (KdK, 1931), 479; F. Grossmann in *Les arts plastiques* (1948), 47ff., quoting L. Burchard as identifying it with the 1786 Desenfans Sale *Bedford*

173 *Emmanuel Philibert of Savoy, Prince of Oneglia*

Painted in Palermo in the summer of 1624. According to the account given by Bellori (1672), 'Antonio [van Dyck] wished to go to Sicily, where Philibert of Savoy was then Viceroy, and he painted his portrait. At that time, however, there was an outbreak of plague, and the Prince died of it . . . Antonio having suffered some sort of disaster in Palermo left in haste, as if in flight, and returned to Genoa . . .'. Emmanuel Philibert (1588–1624) was the third son of Charles Emmanuel of Savoy and spent his life in the Spanish service. He was a Knight of Malta and was created Prince of Oneglia in 1620 and Viceroy of Sicily in 1621. Palermo was infected by plague in June 1624, and the Prince died of it on 3 August. Our portrait was identified with the one described in Bellori by A. van de Put in 1912, on the evidence of the armour with a Savoy motive of sprays in a coronet. A very similar suit of armour was sold at Christie's in June 1979. A bust in Turin seems to confirm the identification. *See* colour plate III.

Canvas, $49\frac{5}{8} \times 39\frac{1}{4}$in (126 × 99.6cm)

PROVENANCE Presumably in Palermo; V. Donjeux Sale, Paris, 29.iv.1793 (132), bt Desmarets; Bourgeois Bequest, 1811 (1813 Inventory as *Duke D'Alva*)

EXHIBITED BI 1828 (113: van Dyck, *Portrait in Armour*); NG 1947 (12); RA, Flemish, 1953/4 (153)

VERSIONS A contemporary copy was sold at Christie's, 6.iii.1936 (151), and a version of the head (according to Glück, the original sketch) was in a Swedish private collection in 1931

LITERATURE G. P. Bellori, *Vite dei Pittori* . . . (Rome, 1672), 257; Sm nos 682 and 831; A. van de Put in *Burl.Mag.* (1912), XXI, 311ff. and rep; (1914), XXV, 59; G. Glück, *Van Dyck* (KdK, 1931), 171 and p 538; C. Sterling in *Burl.Mag.* (1939), LXXIV, 53; F. Grossmann in *Les arts plastiques* (1948), 58

194 *Venetia Stanley, Lady Digby, on her Death-bed*

Venetia Stanley was born in 1600 and died very suddenly in 1633. She married Sir Kenelm Digby in 1625 or 1626, at about the time of the birth of their first child, and her life is best described by John Aubrey, writing about half-a-century after her death:

> She was a most beautiful desireable Creature. . . . The Earle of Dorset . . . was her greatest Gallant, who was extremely enamoured of her, and had one, if not more children by her. . . . Among other young Sparkes of that time, Sir Kenelm Digby grew acquainted with her, and fell so much in love with her that he maried her, much against the good will of his mother, but he would say that a wise man, and lusty, could make an honest woman out of a Brothell-house. . . . Sir Kenelme had several pictures of her by Vandyke, &c. He had her hands cast in playster, and her feet and Face. . . . She dyed in her bed, suddenly. Some suspected that she was poysoned. When her head was opened there was found but little braine, which her husband imputed to her drinking of viper-wine; but spitefull woemen would say 'twas a viper husband who was jealous of her that she would steale a leape.

In fact, Digby was distraught at his wife's death and asked van Dyck to paint her on her death-bed. His letter to his brother, dated 19 June 1633, describes the delivery of the picture to his house and continues:

> It is the Master peece of all the excellent ones that ever Sir Antony Vandike made, who drew her the second day after she was dead; and hath expressed with admirable art every little circumstance about her, as well for the exact manner of her lying, as for the likenesse of her face; and hath altered or added nothing about it, excepting onely a rose lying upon the hemme of the sheete, whose leaves being pulled from the stalke in the full beauty of it, and seeming to wither apace, even whiles you looke upon it, is a fitt Embleme to express the state her bodie then was in. . . . When we came in wee found her almost cold and stiffe; yet her blood was not so settled but that our rubbing of her face brought a litle seeming color into her pale cheekes, which continued there till she was folded up in her last sheete, and Sir Anthony Van Dike hath expressed excellently well in his picture.
>
> This is the onely constant companion I now have . . . it standeth all day over against my chaire and table . . . and att night when I goe into my chamber I sett it close by my beds side, and by the faint light of a candle, me thinkes I see her dead indeed; for that maketh painted colors looke more pale and ghastly than they doe by daylight . . .

Aubrey also records 'at Mr Rose's, a Jeweller in Henrietta-St in Convent Garden . . . an excellent piece . . . drawne after she was newly dead'.

Canvas, 29¼ × 32¼in (74.3 × 81.8cm)

PROVENANCE Presumably Sir Kenelm Digby; perhaps Mr Rose's picture; Bourgeois Bequest, 1811 (in 1813 Inventory as *Lady sleeping in bed*)

VERSION A version in the Spencer Collection, Althorp, was formerly believed to be the original, but is now catalogued as 'after Van Dyck'

LITERATURE Sm no 222 (noting that it was then wrongly called *Lady Penelope Digby*); J. Aubrey (ed. O. L. Dick), *Brief Lives* (before 1692), 3rd edn (1971), 100–101; V. Gabrieli, *Sir K. Digby* (Rome, 1957), 65, n 1 and 246ff.; K. Garlick, Althorp Catalogue in *Walpole Society* (1976), XLV, no 167

Studio of van **DYCK**

81   *Charity*

This is generally agreed to be one of the versions of the allegory of Charity produced in van Dyck's studio and under his supervision, perhaps with some touches from his own hand—at least, no other version has an obvious claim to be entirely by him. Smith's insinuation (1842) that 81 may be a copy by Bourgeois was probably inspired by malice.

Canvas, 55⅞ × 41½in (141.9 × 105.4cm)

PROVENANCE Bourgeois Bequest, 1811

ENGRAVING One of the versions was engraved by C. van Caukercken (*d* 1680); Ryland

LITERATURE Sm no 425, Supplement, no 125; G. Glück, *Van Dyck* (KdK, 1931), 259, 546 (endorsing Richter's attribution to van Dyck's studio, with possible participation by van Dyck)

Adam **ELSHEIMER** (1578–1610)

Elsheimer was a German landscape painter whose work in Rome in the last decade of his short life had a profound influence on Rembrandt and Claude, as well as his friend Rubens, especially in their treatment of light. His works are always small and on copper, but several of his contemporaries imitated him very closely, as is probably the case with our picture.

Circle of **ELSHEIMER**

22   *Susanna and the Elders*

The subject is from the Apocryphal *History of Susanna*, perhaps v, 24: 'Susanna cried with a loud voice: and the two elders cried out against her'. Although the painting has long been attributed to Elsheimer himself it now seems probable that it is by one of his circle in Rome. There are strong similarities with the *Bathsheba* (Ashmolean Museum, Oxford), which is a signed work by Johann Koenig (1586–1642); but the name of Thomann von Hagelstein, who joined Elsheimer's Roman circle about 1605, has also been suggested on the basis of analogies with a signed *Judith* of 1607. In the present state of knowledge an attribution to the Elsheimer circle seems the only prudent course.

Copper, $9\frac{1}{4} \times 11\frac{3}{4}$in (23.5 × 29.9cm)

PROVENANCE Perhaps the Elsheimer *Susanna* 'From Abroad' sold Christie's 23.iii.1781 (55); Bourgeois Bequest, 1811

EXHIBITED NG 1947 (15 : as Elsheimer)

LITERATURE W. Bode, *Elsheimer* (1920), 44; H. Weiszäcker in *Zeitschrift für bildende Kunst* (1928–9), LXII, 68; *id*, *Elsheimer* (1936), I, 133 and rep.; W. Drost, *Elsheimer* (1933), 75ff.; K. Bauch in *Kunstchronik* (1967), XX, 90 (as by Koenig); M. Waddingham in *Burl.Mag.* (1972), CXIV, 610–11 (as ?Hagelstein); K. Andrews, *Elsheimer* (1977), no A8 (as Circle of Elsheimer)

FLEMISH SCHOOL *see* ANTWERP MASTER (250)

FLEMISH SCHOOL(?)

14   *A Village on Fire*

Previously attributed to David Teniers II (before 1880) or David I (from 1880), but there seems no connection with the style of either, nor is the subject to be found in their work. The poor state of preservation and low quality make an attribution simply to the Flemish School advisable. The English painter Julius Caesar Ibbetson (*d* 1817) is known to have made forgeries of Teniers and the *Literary Gazette* describes how 'arriving at a picture which seemed to attract Ibbetson's particular regard, Mr Desenfans observed, "That, Mr Ibbetson, is a very beautiful example of the work of David Teniers". There was a pause. Mr Desenfans requested Ibbetson's opinion, whose answer, after another pause, was—"That picture, Sir?—that picture *I* painted . . .".'

Panel, $9\frac{1}{2} \times 13\frac{3}{4}$in (23.4 × 34.9cm)

PROVENANCE Bourgeois Bequest, 1811 (as Teniers)

LITERATURE W. T. Whitley, *Art in England, 1800–20* (Cambridge, 1928), 277–8 (for Ibbetson story)

Manner of Frans **FLORIS** *see* ANTWERP MASTER (250)

Francesco **FRACANZANO** (1612–*c* 1656)
Francesco was the son and younger brother of Neapolitan painters, and, in 1632, he married the sister of Salvator Rosa, whose first teacher he was (*see* Rosa, 216). He himself was much influenced by Ribera. He died young, either of plague or, according to some, under mysterious circumstances in prison.

558 *The Prodigal Son*

Luke, xv, 21: 'And the son said unto him, Father, I have sinned against heaven, and in thy sight, and am no more worthy to be called thy son . . .'. This is one of a series on the Prodigal Son theme, of which the closest parallels are in Capodimonte, Naples and Bristol Art Gallery. The present attribution is based on these pictures.

Canvas, $38\frac{3}{8} \times 48\frac{3}{4}$in (97.5 × 123.8cm)

PROVENANCE Perhaps the *Prodigal Son* attributed to 'Calabrese' (*ie* M. Preti) in Sir G. Page's collection by 1774; his Sale, 1783; John Willett Sale, Coxe, 2.vi.1813 (94); Fairfax Murray Gift (as Ribera), 1911

LITERATURE B. Nicolson in *Burl.Mag.* (1962), CIV, 317, suggests that the Bristol *Prodigal* may be by Passante

Jean-Honoré **FRAGONARD** *see* Jean-Alexis GRIMOU (74)

FRENCH SCHOOL *see* School of LEBRUN (188)

FRENCH SCHOOL *see* Aleksander KUCHARSKI (489)

Thomas **GAINSBOROUGH**, RA (1727–88)
Gainsborough was born in Suffolk and trained in London in the 1740s. At this time he studied (and may have forged) Dutch 17th-century landscapists such as Ruisdael, Hobbema and Wynants. His earliest works (*eg* 588) show this influence very clearly; nevertheless, he earned his living as a portraitist, first in Suffolk, then, from 1759, in Bath, where he painted all the fashionable people taking the waters. In 1774 he moved to London (having been made a Founder-Member of the RA in 1768), and soon became the only serious rival to Reynolds. He continued to paint landscapes as well as portraits in a style strongly influenced by van Dyck.

66 *Philipp Jakob de Loutherbourg*, RA

Loutherbourg (1740–1812) was a painter of picturesque landscapes (*cf* 297, 339) who was the teacher of Sir Francis Bourgeois, the co-founder of the Dulwich Gallery (*see* Beechey, 17). He was born in Strasbourg, the son of a painter, and trained in Paris from 1755 under C. van Loo and Casanova, the painter-brother of the celebrated amorist. Casanova was also the master of Vernet (*cf* 300, 319, 328), and Loutherbourg began by exhibiting landscapes of the Berchem/Vernet type. He first exhibited at the Salon in 1763 and was noticed favourably by Diderot, which made his name, so that he became a member of the Académie royale in 1766. He moved to London in 1771 and began to work as a stage-designer for David Garrick in 1772, revolutionising the art in the next few years. In 1778 he and Gainsborough painted each other (66 and the *Gainsborough* in the Paul Mellon Collection, U.S.A.). In 1780 he was elected ARA and in the following year RA; in 1781 he invented the *Eidophusikon* ('representation of nature'), a sort of peep-show with moving and fixed scenes, lights and sounds which has been called a precursor of the cinema, and which fascinated Gainsborough and other artists interested in picturesque effects. In 1786–8 he was involved with the quack Count Cagliostro and gave up painting for faith-healing and alchemy; in 1788 however, he challenged Cagliostro to a duel in Switzerland. This was averted and he returned to painting. In 1801 he published *Picturesque Scenery of Great Britain* and in 1805 *Romantic & Picturesque Scenery of England & Wales*, illustrated by coloured aquatints. He was a candidate for the Presidency of the Royal Academy in 1806; his fulsome epitaph in Chiswick churchyard reads:

Here, Loutherbourg, repose thy laurel'd head;
While art is cherished thou cans't ne'er be dead.
Salvator, Poussin, Claude, thy skill combines,
And beauteous nature lives in thy designs.

Our picture was painted *c* 1777/8 and exhibited at the Royal Academy in 1778.

Canvas, 30⅛ × 24⅞in (76.5 × 63.2cm)

PROVENANCE Bourgeois Bequest, 1811 (*ie* in the sitter's lifetime)

EXHIBITED RA 1778 (408); NG 1947 (21)

LITERATURE V. Manners and G. Williamson, *Zoffany* (1920), 12, reproduce a drawing, attributed to Zoffany and said to represent Garrick, after this picture; E. K. Waterhouse, *Gainsborough* (1958), no 456 and pl 197; J. Hayes, *Gainsborough* (1975), fig 11 and note 91

140 *Thomas Linley the Elder*

Thomas Linley (1732–95) was a singing master and composer and the father of a large musical family. He studied in Naples, but settled in Bath at least from the time of his marriage in 1752 and remained there until *c* 1777, when he moved to London. Gainsborough, who was in Bath at the same time, came to know the family well and painted several portraits of them (including 302, 320 and 331). In London the elder Linley was joint manager of the Drury Lane Oratorios and was associated with Drury Lane Theatre through his son-in-law, Richard Brinsley Sheridan. In addition to the Gainsborough portraits the Gallery also contains a portrait of his wife, by James Lonsdale (456), and three of his other children by Lawrence (178, 474, 475: *see also* Oliver, 476).

Canvas, 30⅛ × 25in (76.5 × 63.5cm)

PROVENANCE Linley family, bequeathed by William Linley, 1835

EXHIBITED NG 1947 (17); Kenwood, Gainsborough and his musical Friends, 1977 (4)

LITERATURE E. K. Waterhouse in *Walpole Society* (1953), XXXIII, 69; *id, Gainsborough* (1958), 78, no 446 and pl 107 (as probably later 1760s); C. Black, *The Linleys of Bath* (1971 edn), *passim*

302 *Samuel Linley*, RN

Samuel (1760–78) was the son of Thomas Linley (*see* 140) and, like his brothers and sisters, was trained as a musician but became a midshipman in the Navy. He died of fever at the age of 18, so the portrait must date from 1777/8 and was perhaps painted when he went to sea. A Ms catalogue in the Gallery by S. P. Denning (*see* 304) in 1858 records: 'This picture was commenced and finished as it now exists in one sitting, and that sitting less than an hour. The authority for this is the testimony of his own brother'.

Canvas, 29⅞ × 25 in (75.8 × 63.5 cm)

PROVENANCE Linley family, bequeathed by William Linley, 1835

EXHIBITED NG 1947 (19)

LITERATURE E. K. Waterhouse in *Walpole Society* (1953), XXXIII, 69; *id, Gainsborough* (1958), 78, no 445; C. Black, *The Linleys of Bath* (1971 edn), 119 and rep. p 120

316 *Mrs Moody and two of her Children*

Mrs Moody (*c* 1756–82) was the first wife of Samuel Moody (or Moodey), whose portrait by Russell (601) belongs to the Gallery. She died at the age of 26: this portrait was probably painted before the birth of her two sons Samuel and Thomas. Thomas, the donor of this picture, seems to have been about eight months old when his mother died, so he was born in 1781/2. The two children in the painting are clearly girls, which puts the date of the portrait back to about 1775/6, which accords with the style of the picture. Her husband Samuel (1733–1808) married again and had children by his second wife, but very little is known about the family, nor is it clear why Captain Thomas Moody should have given the portrait to Dulwich, with which he had no connection; however, he is known to have disliked his step-mother and may have wanted to see that her family did not have the picture.

Canvas, 92⅛ × 60¾ in (234 × 154.2 cm)

PROVENANCE Presented by Captain Thomas Moody, 1831

EXHIBITED NG 1947 (22); RA, 18th Century, 1954/5 (63)

LITERATURE E. K. Waterhouse in *Walpole Society* (1953), XXXIII, 77 (mid-1770s); *id, Gainsborough* (1958), 82, no 498 (later 1770s)

320 *The Linley Sisters (Mrs Sheridan and Mrs Tickell)*

Elizabeth (1754–92), the standing figure, and Mary (1758–87) were the elder daughters of Thomas Linley (*see* 140), and were trained by him as concert singers. Gainsborough, who was passionately fond of music, lived in Bath 1759–74 and knew the family there. Elizabeth eloped with Richard Brinsley Sheridan the playwright in 1772, and Mary married Richard Tickell in 1780. The music held by Mary is said to be *A Song of Spring* by Tickell, set to music by Linley. Probably painted in 1772.

Canvas, 78⅜ × 60¼ in (199 × 153.1 cm)

PROVENANCE Linley family; R. B. Sheridan in 1814; returned to William Linley in part-payment of a debt, deposited by him in the Gallery in 1822 and presented in 1831

EXHIBITED Probably RA 1772 (95); BI 1814 (97), lent by Sheridan; International Exhibition 1862 (74); NG 1947 (20); RA, 18th Century, 1954/5 (64); NPG 1972 (25); Kenwood, 1977 (6)

VERSIONS Other portraits of Elizabeth by Gainsborough are in Philadelphia and the National Gallery, Washington, and one of Gainsborough's Fancy Pictures, called *Miss Linley & her Brother*, is in the Clark Art Institute, Williamstown, Mass.

LITERATURE W. T. Whitley, *Artists and their Friends . . .* (1928), II, 378; id, *Art in England, 1800–20* (Cambridge, 1928), 230; E. K. Waterhouse in *Walpole Society* (1953), XXXIII, 70; id, *Gainsborough* (1958), 79, no 450 and pl 145; C. Black, *The Linleys of Bath* (1971 edn), *passim*; J. Hayes, *Gainsborough* (1975), pl 102 and note 77; *Gainsborough and his Musical Friends* (exhibition catalogue), Kenwood, 1977, no 6 and rep. (for details of the sitters)

331 *Thomas Linley the Younger*

Thomas (1756–78) was the son of Thomas the Elder (*see* 140) and was a prodigy both as a violinist and composer. Mozart, who met him in Florence, thought that, had he lived, he might have become 'one of the greatest ornaments of the musical world'. This portrait was probably painted *c* 1773/4; one in the Prince of Liechtenstein's collection at Vaduz is somewhat later.

Canvas, $29\frac{7}{8} \times 25$ in (75.9×63.5 cm)

PROVENANCE Linley family, bequeathed by William Linley, 1835

EXHIBITED NG 1947 (18)

LITERATURE E. K. Waterhouse in *Walpole Society* (1953), XXXIII, 69; id, *Gainsborough* (1958), 79, no 447 and pl 155; C. Black, *The Linleys of Bath* (1971 edn), 46, 117–18, rep. p 118

588 *An Unknown Couple in a Landscape*

This is one of the finest of Gainsborough's small portraits of a husband and wife in a landscape, most of which were painted in the 1750s in Ipswich. The *Mr and Mrs Andrews* in the National Gallery is a well-known example, and the *Girl in a Park* (Trustees of the Cook Collection) seems to have been a pendant to 588, although the history of both is obscure. *See* colour plate VII.

Canvas, $30 \times 26\frac{3}{8}$ in (76.2×67 cm)

PROVENANCE John Doherty, Birmingham, 1858; Doherty, Foxlydiate House, Redditch, 1880; with Lesser; Fairfax Murray Gift, 1911

EXHIBITED NG 1947 (16)

LITERATURE E. K. Waterhouse in *Walpole Society* (1953), XXXIII, 117; id, *Gainsborough* (1958), 99, no 753 (as mid-1750s)

Aert de **GELDER** (1645–1727)
De Gelder was a Dordrecht painter who became a pupil of Rembrandt in Amsterdam in the 1660s, when Rembrandt's art was totally neglected. He remained faithful to his master's late style until well into the 18th century.

126 *Jacob's Dream*

Signed: probably *ADe* in monogram and *Gelder*

The signature was discovered during cleaning in 1946 and is incised with the brush handle, a method often used by de Gelder (as in the foliage in this picture), but it is extremely difficult to read. The subject is from *Genesis*, xviii, 12: 'And he dreamed, and behold a ladder set up on the earth, and the top of it reached to heaven: and behold the angels of God ascending and descending on it . . .'. This picture was ascribed to Rembrandt until 1914, and was one of the most popular in the gallery throughout the 19th century: the attribution to de Gelder was first proposed by Hofstede de Groot about 1914, and was confirmed 32 years later by the discovery of the signature. Lilienfeld regards it as a late work, comparing it with paintings in Aschaffenburg and the former Cook Collection.

Canvas, $26\frac{1}{4} \times 22\frac{3}{8}$in (66.7 × 56.9cm)

PROVENANCE Le Brun of Paris Sale, Christie's, 18–19.iii.1785 (81: as Rembrandt), bt Dillen (?Desenfans); Desenfans by 1802 (as Rembrandt); Bourgeois Bequest, 1811

EXHIBITED NG 1947 (23); RA, Dutch, 1952/3 (107); NG, Dutch, 1976 (43)

LITERATURE Sm no 12; K. Lilienfeld, *A. de Gelder* (The Hague, 1914), 130, 157 and Cat no 10 (acknowledging de Groot's attribution); HdG, VI, no 456, n 8 (as Gelder); W. Bernt, *Netherlandish Painters of the 17th Century* (1970), I, 42 (for monogram)

Marcus **GHEERAERTS** *see* BRITISH SCHOOL (443) and John De CRITZ(?) (548)

John **GREENHILLS** (*c* 1640/45–76)
For biography *see* 418 (*Self-portrait*).

374 *Unknown Man, perhaps an Actor*

Signed: *J.G.*

Described in the 1686 Inventory as 'A man with a bald head . . . by grinhill'. It has been plausibly suggested that, beards being almost unknown in the Restoration period, it represents an actor in a character part. In view of the known interests of both the artist and the donor (*see* 393) this seems quite probable; but the alternative suggestion advanced by Collins-Baker, that it is a copy of an Italian portrait, also has much to be said for it.

Canvas, $29\frac{3}{4} \times 24\frac{3}{4}$in (75.5 × 62.8cm)

PROVENANCE Cartwright Bequest, 1686 (117)

LITERATURE D. Lysons, *Environs of London* (1796), I, 108ff.; C. Collins-Baker, *Lely and the Stuart Portrait Painters* (1912), II, 157; E. K. Waterhouse, *Painting in Britain . . .* (1953), 74

387 *Jane Cartwright*

William Cartwright (*see* 393) was married three times. This picture must be the one recorded in the Cartwright Inventory as 'my Last wifes pictur, with a black vaile on her head', so it must represent Jane Hodgson, whom he married on 19 November 1654. She apparently predeceased him, but the picture must date from before 1676 when Greenhill died. An earlier Mrs Cartwright, also painted by Greenhill, is 399.

Canvas, $29\frac{3}{8} \times 23\frac{5}{8}$in (74.5 × 60cm)

PROVENANCE Cartwright Bequest, 1686 (116)

LITERATURE C. H. Collins-Baker, *Lely and the Stuart Portrait Painters* (1912), II, 8; E. Boswell in *Modern Language Review* (1929), XXIV, 125ff. (for Cartwright family)

393 *William Cartwright*

William Cartwright (1606/7–86) was an actor before and after the Civil War and a bookseller during the Commonwealth, when the theatres were closed. On the Restoration in 1660 he immediately went back to the stage, and it was probably Cartwright who was meant when Pepys saw the *Merry Wives of Windsor* on 5 December 1660, and complained 'Sir J. Falstaffe as bad as any'. He was less censorious in 1667. The Cartwright Inventory, now in the Gallery archives, is an ill-written Ms, probably in Cartwright's own hand, listing some 239 pictures in his collection. The Inventory cannot be later than December 1686 and may be earlier (*see* Introduction, p 17). Many of the pictures bequeathed by him to Alleyn's College have been lost or never arrived: only about 18 are actually on exhibition. Nevertheless, it was the most important bequest before the Desenfans–Bourgeois gift. This portrait is recorded as 'My pictur in a black dress with a great doge', the pose with the sitter's hand on the head of a large dog being a clear reference to van Dyck's portrait types. The initials on the dog's collar presumably refer to Cartwright and no painter's name is given in the Inventory, but the portrait is accepted as by Greenhill, which means that it cannot be later than 1676. Cartwright was married three times (*see* 387, 399).

Canvas, $40\frac{1}{2} \times 33\frac{1}{2}$in (102.8 × 84.9cm)

PROVENANCE Cartwright Bequest, 1686 (234)

EXHIBITED National Portrait Exhibition, 1866 (667); NPG, Samuel Pepys Esq, 1970 (67)

VERSION Another portrait of Cartwright, by Riley, belonged to Lord Sackville in 1949; *see also* British School, 411

LITERATURE Vertue, *Notebooks . . .*, II, 13 ('W. Cartwright after Lilly his hand on a great dog'); D. Lysons, *Environs of London* (1796), I, 108ff. (as by Greenhill); C. H. Collins-Baker, *Lely and the Stuart Portrait Painters* (1912), II, 8; E. Boswell in *Modern Language Review* (1929), XXIV, 125ff. (on Cartwright); Highfill, Burnim and Langhans (eds), *A Biographical Dictionary of Actors . . .* (Carbondale, Ill., 1975), III (*s.v.* Cartwright)

399 *Elisabeth Cartwright*

Signed: *J.G.*

William Cartwright (*see* 393) was married three times, first to Elisabeth Cooke on 1 May 1633, when he was about 27. She must have died soon afterwards, since he married Andria Robins on 28 April 1636. She died in 1652 and he married his third wife (*see* 387) in 1654. He does not seem to have owned a portrait of Andria, but this picture is recorded in the Cartwright Inventory as 'my first wifes pictur Like a Sheppardess'. As this is signed by Greenhill, who was not born until after Elisabeth's death, it must be based on an earlier likeness, but the pose and the pastoral setting derive from Lely and the dress and hair-style are those of the 1660s. The lamb is usually an attribute of S. Agnes, but Lely painted great ladies dressed up as shepherdesses.

Canvas, $37\frac{1}{8} \times 28\frac{3}{4}$in (94.3 × 73cm)

PROVENANCE Cartwright Bequest, 1686 (78)

LITERATURE C. H. Collins-Baker, *Lely and the Stuart Portrait Painters* (1912), II, 8 and rep.; E. Boswell in *Modern Language Review* (1929), XXIV, 125ff. (for details of Cartwright's wives); M. D. Whinney and O. Millar, *English Art, 1625–1714* (Oxford, 1957), 179 and pl 51b (as the second Mrs Cartwright)

416   *James, Duke of York, later James II*

James Stuart (1633–1701), Duke of York and later King James II. This portrait shows him as Duke of York and Lord High Admiral, at the period when Pepys knew him best: the picture is datable from Pepys's diary entry of 15 February 1664—'Duke . . . first put on a periwigg today . . . his hair cut short thereto . . .'. As he is wearing his own hair the portrait must date from shortly before then. It is recorded in the Cartwright Inventory as the 'Duke of Yorke' (although he became King James II on 6 February 1685) and as by 'grinhill'.

Canvas, 29½ × 24½in (74.9 × 62.2cm)

PROVENANCE Cartwright Bequest, 1686 (68)

LITERATURE C. H. Collins-Baker, *Lely and the Stuart Portrait Painters* (1912), II, 8; E. K. Waterhouse, *Painting in Britain* . . . (1953), 74; D. T. Piper, *Catalogue of 17th Century Portraits* (NPG Catalogue, 1963), 178

418   *Self-portrait*

John Greenhill (*c* 1640/45–76) was a pupil and assistant of Lely, setting up on his own about 1665—approximately the date of this self-portrait and of the *First Mrs Cartwright* (399). He was acquainted with Soest, and his early works are closer to Soest (*cf* 573) than to Lely, although after about 1670 he seems to have moved back towards a Lely style. He was interested in the stage and in literature, which probably explains his connection with William Cartwright (*cf* 393), but he fell into a 'loose and unguarded Manner of Living' and died young as a result of a drunken fall. The paper in his hand has a profile sketched on it which may be the portrait of Greenhill by Lely now in the British Museum. Another self-portrait, by R. Walker, of *c* 1645, now in the Royal Collection, is almost identical in pose, so probably both derive from a prototype by van Dyck. Our picture is recorded in the Cartwright Inventory of 1686 as 'grenhills pictur . . . dun by himselfe'. The Inventory records four other pictures as by Greenhill (374, 387, 393 and 399) and this group is the basis for all attributions to him.

Canvas, 41⅞ × 32⅝in (106.3 × 82.9cm)

PROVENANCE Cartwright Bequest, 1686 (95)

EXHIBITED National Portrait Exhibition, 1866 (1005)

DRAWINGS There are two in the British Museum; one, a profile of Greenhill by Lely, may be the original of the drawing shown in this painting. The other, said to be a self-portrait, may represent the same man

LITERATURE D. Lysons, *Environs of London* (1796), I, 108ff.; C. H. Collins-Baker, *Lely and the Stuart Portrait Painters* (1912), II, 8 and rep.; E. K. Waterhouse, *Painting in Britain* . . . (1953), 74; M. D. Whinney and O. Millar, *English Art, 1625–1714* (Oxford, 1957), 179 (as *c* 1665); E. Croft-Murray and P. Hulton, *Catalogue of British Drawings . . . in the British Museum* (1960), I, 338–40 and pl 141 (for Greenhill drawing), 417–18 and pl 213 (Lely drawing)

John **GREENHILL** *see* After John Michael WRIGHT (424)

Jean-Alexis **GRIMOU** (1678–1733)
Grimou, formerly confused with a Swiss painter of a similar name, was born at Argenteuil, near Paris, and was probably a pupil of De Troy. He was received into the Académie royale in 1705, but was subsequently struck off for failing to present a diploma work. He was sometimes called 'le Rembrandt français', which was a gross exaggeration, but his style is much influenced by Rembrandt and by the general Netherlandish tendency of the early 18th century on French painting, so evident in Watteau. According to 18th-century gossip, Grimou was a prodigious drinker who was finished off by a pint of brandy on top of half-a-dozen bottles of burgundy.

74 *Young Woman*

Signed: *Grimou*

One of several fancy portraits of this type, some of which are closer to Rembrandt. This is a premonition of Fragonard, to whom it has recently been attributed, in spite of the apparently authentic signature.

Canvas, $24\frac{3}{4} \times 20\frac{3}{4}$in (62.9 × 52.7cm)

PROVENANCE Bourgeois Bequest, 1811

LITERATURE L. Dimier, *Les peintres français du XVIIIᵉ siècle* (Paris, 1930), II, 185ff. and Cat no 40; P. Rosenberg in *Revue du Louvre* (1974), no iii, 191 and rep. (as by Fragonard)

GUERCINO (1591–1666)
Francesco Barbieri, called Guercino ('Squint-eyed'), was born at Cento, near Bologna, and worked there from 1613. He was deeply influenced by Lodovico Carracci and also by the strong chiaroscuro of Caravaggio in his early works. He arrived in Rome in 1621, but returned to Cento in 1623 and worked there and in Bologna for the rest of his life, taking over from his rival Guido Reni.

282 *The Woman taken in Adultery*

The subject is from *John*, viii, 3–5: 'This woman was taken in adultery . . . Now Moses in the law commanded us, that such should be stoned: but what sayest thou?'. Probably painted *c* 1621, just before or just after Guercino's arrival in Rome.

Canvas, $38\frac{5}{8} \times 48\frac{3}{8}$in (98.2 × 122.7cm)

PROVENANCE Mari family, Genoa, until *c* 1806; probably bought from them by J. Irvine; Anon. (Champernowne) Sale, Christie's, 24.v.1806 (52; 'received within a few days from Italy, and has long been admired . . . in the palace of the Mari family at Genoa'), bt Sir F. B. (*ie* Bourgeois); Bourgeois Bequest, 1811

LITERATURE C. G. Ratti, *Description des Beautés de Gênes* . . . (Genoa, 1781), 112; W. T. Whitley, *Art in England, 1800–20* (Cambridge, 1928), 61–2 (on Champernowne)

Jakob T. von **HAGELSTEIN** *see* Circle of ELSHEIMER (22)

Adriaen **HANNEMAN** (*c* 1601–71)
Hanneman was born, and probably trained, in The Hague. He came to London in 1626 and was influenced by van Dyck, whose style he introduced into The Hague on his return there in 1637.

572 *Unknown Man*

Signed and dated: *An° 1655/Adr Hanneman F.*

Canvas, $32\frac{3}{8} \times 25\frac{3}{4}$in (82.2 × 65.4cm)

PROVENANCE Collection of William Dyce, RA (*d* 1864); Fairfax Murray Gift, 1911

LITERATURE C. H. Collins-Baker, *Lely and the Stuart Painters* (1912), I, 88 (rep.); *id* in *Onze Kunst* (1915), 101ff. and rep. (wrongly dated 1654 in text); O. Ter Kuile, *Hanneman* (Alphen am Ryn, 1976), 85 and pl 9 (as perhaps pendant to *Unknown Woman*, *c* 1653)

Guilliam van **HERP I** (*c* 1614–77)
Van Herp was an Antwerp painter who was influenced by Rubens (whom he copied) and also by Teniers.

332 *Figures and Sheep at a Well*

The attribution to van Herp depends upon the evident likenesses to both Rubens and Teniers, although the subject is not typical of Herp. A signed *Interior* in the London trade in 1973 showed remarkably similar facial characteristics. Our picture was attributed, not unreasonably, to Le Nain in the 1816 Catalogue of the Gallery.

Panel, $22\frac{1}{2} \times 29\frac{5}{8}$in (57.2 × 75.2cm)

PROVENANCE Bourgeois Bequest, 1811

VERSION A very similar composition, but closer to the Le Nain style, is in Glasgow University Gallery, attributed to the 'Maître aux béguins'

Jan van der **HEYDEN** (1637–1712)
Van der Heyden specialised in townscapes, often imaginary, with figures by other painters, including A. van de Velde (who died in 1672). Most of his pictures date from the 1660s and a little later, since about 1670 he began to be interested in fire-engines and street lighting, both of which made his fortune: his *Fire-Engine Book* was published in 1690.

155 *Two Churches and a Town Wall*

Signed: *V Heyden*

The figures are attributed to Adriaen van de Velde.

Panel, $11\frac{1}{8} \times 13\frac{1}{4}$in (28.2 × 33.6cm)

PROVENANCE Probably Desenfans Sale, 8ff.vi.1786 (217: 'Vander Heyde and A. Van de Velde'

... panel, 23 × 27in, including frame); possibly one of pair in Desenfans Sale, Skinner & Dyke, 28.ii.1795 (90); Bourgeois Bequest, 1811

LITERATURE HdG, VIII, no 126; H. Wagner, *Jan van der Heyden* (Amsterdam, 1971), no 188 (noting some similarity between the church and Sta Francesca Romana, Rome)

Meindert **HOBBEMA** (1638–1709)

Hobbema was the friend and pupil of the other great Dutch landscape painter, Jacob van Ruisdael (*see* 105, 168), but he is less Romantic in his approach than Ruisdael. In 1668 he obtained a minor post in the Amsterdam Excise and it used to be thought that he gave up painting, but it is now clear that he continued, though less actively. Most of his best works— such as 87—were bought by English 18th-century collectors and are still here.

87   *Wooded Landscape with Water-mill*

Signed (damaged): *Hobbema*

See colour plate IV.

Panel, $24\frac{3}{8} \times 33\frac{5}{8}$in (61.9 × 85.4cm)

PROVENANCE Probably in Desenfans Sale, Skinner & Dyke, 28.ii.1795 (23); perhaps 1802 Catalogue (111); Desenfans Insurance List, 1804 (95); Bourgeois Bequest, 1811

EXHIBITED NG 1947 (24); RA, Dutch, 1952/3 (330)

VERSION A similar composition was sold in Brussels, Giroux, 12.iii.1927 (36: as signed)

LITERATURE Sm no 123; HdG, IV, no 82; G. Broulhiet, *Hobbema* (Paris, 1938), no 218 and rep. p 211

Gerard **HOET** (1648–1733)

Hoet was a Dutch landscape painter who, like Lairesse, was influenced by contemporary French ideas, especially in his Arcadian landscapes with nude figures. He also painted quite different tavern scenes. His son, Gerard II, was also a painter and was one of the first people to realise the importance of collecting sale catalogues of pictures as a historical record.

176   *Apollo and Daphne* and *Pan and Syrinx*

179   Both signed: *G. Hoet*

Until they were cleaned in the 1940s the signatures were invisible and the pictures were attributed to Gerard de Lairesse. The subjects are from Ovid's *Metamorphoses* (I, v) and both deal with nymphs pursued by gods. Daphne was pursued by Apollo and transformed into laurel, hence the laurel-wreath as a symbol of Apollo and the poet's crown. Syrinx was turned into a reed, and Pan made his pipes from the reed-bed. Robert Browning, who was familiar with the Gallery, had them in mind in his poem on Lairesse.

Canvas, (176), $15\frac{1}{8} \times 18\frac{5}{8}$in (38.4 × 47.3cm);
       (179) $15\frac{1}{8} \times 18\frac{3}{4}$in (38.3 × 47.5cm)

PROVENANCE Bourgeois Bequest, 1811 (as Lairesse)

William **HOGARTH** (1697–1764)

Hogarth was apprenticed to a goldsmith, but married Sir James Thornhill's daughter and, according to his autobiographical notes: 'I then [*ie* 1729] married, and commenced painter of small conversation pieces . . .' (*cf* 562). His reputation was made with his modern moral subjects, engraved and painted, but he continued to paint portraits such as 580. He was early influenced by French Rococo art, and especially by Watteau and his followers, though he remained a lifelong xenophobe.

562   *A Fishing Party ('The Fair Angler')*

There are the remains of a signature at the lower left centre. This, which probably dates from *c* 1730, is one of the early conversation pieces in which Hogarth comes very close to contemporary French painters such as Watteau and Lancret.

Canvas, $21\frac{5}{8} \times 18\frac{7}{8}$in ($54.9 \times 48.1$cm)

PROVENANCE J. H. Manners-Sutton; Anon. Sale, Robinson & Fisher, London, 29.v.1902 (87), bt Agnew; Fairfax Murray by 1908; his Gift, 1911

EXHIBITED Perhaps BI, 1817 (56 or 113, *A Fishing Party*, lent by T. Mathias); RA 1908 (113); Tate Gallery, Hogarth, 1971/2 (34); Arts Council, London and elsewhere, British Sporting Pictures, 1974 (22)

LITERATURE R. Beckett, *Hogarth* (1949), 42 and fig 29; F. Antal, *Hogarth* . . . (1962), 35, 111 and pl 31b; R. Paulson, *Hogarth; His Life, Art and Times* (1971), I, 218, 230 and pl 77

580   *Unknown Man*

Signed and dated: *Wm Hogarth Anglus Pinxit 1741*

It has been suggested that the sitter may be a member of the Coxe family, but there seems no good reason for this. Waterhouse suggests that the suffix *Anglus* was directed against the French portrait painter J. B. Vanloo, who was much patronised by the nobility and gentry 1737–42.

Canvas, $30 \times 25\frac{1}{8}$in (76.2×63.8cm)

PROVENANCE Fairfax Murray by 1908; his Gift, 1911

EXHIBITED RA 1908 (88); NG 1947 (25); Tate Gallery, Hogarth, 1971/2 (111)

LITERATURE A. Dobson and W. Armstrong, *Hogarth* (1902), 130, 172; R. Beckett, *Hogarth* (1949), 51 and pl 132; E. K. Waterhouse, *Painting in Britain* (1953), 132; R. Paulson, *Hogarth, His Life, Art and Times* (1971), I, 428, 456 and pl 173

Gerard van **HONTHORST** (1590–1656)

Honthorst was one of the leading Dutch Caravaggists at the beginning of his career, as may be seen from his *Christ before the High Priest* in the National Gallery; however, he changed his style completely after visiting England in 1628, when he began to paint elegant portraits in the van Dyck manner. He became Court Painter at The Hague in 1637.

571   *A Lady aged 40*

Signed and dated: *GHonthorst 1639* and inscribed: *AE 40*

This is a good example of his later style.

Panel, $29\frac{1}{8} \times 23\frac{5}{8}$in (74 × 60cm)

PROVENANCE Said to have come from the Mniszech Collection, Paris; Fairfax Murray Gift, 1911

LITERATURE C. H. Collins-Baker, *Lely and the Stuart Portrait Painters* (1912), I, 60; *id* in *Onze Kunst* (1915), 101ff. and rep.

Attributed to John **HOPPNER**, RA (1758–1810)

589 *Unknown Man*

Formerly attributed to Hoppner and called *A Divine*, but there seems no reason to believe either statement. The style is probably closer to that of Raeburn than that of Hoppner, and there is no reason to suppose that the sitter was a cleric. It probably dates from the turn of the century or the first years of the 19th century.

Canvas, 30 × 25in (76.2 × 63.5cm)

PROVENANCE Fairfax Murray Gift, 1911

Gerrit Willemsz. **HORST** (*c* 1612–52)
Horst was very much influenced by Rembrandt—as this picture shows—between about 1635 and 1640. He also painted a few still-lifes.

214 *Isaac blessing Jacob*

Signed and dated: *Horst 1638*

There is a false Rembrandt signature at the right. The subject is from *Genesis*, xxvii—'And Jacob went near unto Isaac his father; and he felt him, and said, The voice is Jacob's voice, but the hands are the hands of Esau'. The picture passed as a Rembrandt until the 1880s, when Dr Richter attributed it to Jan Victors, another follower of Rembrandt active at the same time. Traces of a false Victors signature were said to be discernible over the Horst one when it was cleaned in the 1950s.

Canvas, $64\frac{1}{4} \times 79\frac{1}{4}$in (163.2 × 201.3cm)

PROVENANCE Desenfans Sale, Christie's, 13.v.1785 (74: as Rembrandt); his Private Sales, 8ff.iv and 8ff.vi.1786 (191); his Sale, Christie's, 14.vii.1786 (69); his Sale, Skinner & Dyke, 27.ii.1795 (98); Bourgeois Bequest, 1811

VERSION A very similar picture, in reverse, was formerly in the Berlin Museum, attributed to Horst

LITERATURE W. Bernt, *Netherlandish Painters of the 17th Century* (1970), II, pl 555 (the Berlin picture)

Thomas **HUDSON** (1701–79)
Hudson was the son-in-law of Jonathan Richardson and the master of Reynolds. Most of his best portraits were painted as man-and-wife pairs between 1745 and 1760, although after Reynolds set up in London in 1753 Hudson's business declined and he virtually retired *c* 1760.

578
579

Unknown Lady and *Unknown Gentleman*

Both signed and dated: *T Hudson Pinxit 1750* (*TH* in monogram)

The man is wearing Court dress. They may be members of the Hollond family, perhaps painted on the occasion of their betrothal. These are good examples of the rather stiff portraits usual before the rise of Reynolds.

Canvas, both $50\frac{1}{8} \times 40\frac{1}{8}$ in (127.3 × 102cm)

PROVENANCE Robert Hollond of Stanmore Hall; his Sale, Christie's, 27.iv.1889 (32, 34), bt Murray; Fairfax Murray Gift, 1911

EXHIBITED Kenwood, 1979 (46, 47)

Ozias **HUMPHREY** *see* James LONSDALE (456)

Jan van **HUYSUM** (1682–1749)
Jan van Huysum—more correctly, Huijsum—was the most famous of a family of Amsterdam flower painters. He was the son of Justus (1659–1716) and the brother of Jacobus (*c* 1687/9–?1740), his imitator, who worked in England and died in London. Jan was the first to introduce light backgrounds to set off his flowers, which are usually of different seasons. Several of his pictures have double dates, indicating that he worked on them as the flowers became available.

42
A Delft Bowl with Fruit

Signed: *Jan Van Huysum*

Pendant to 61.

Panel, $15\frac{3}{4} \times 12\frac{3}{4}$ in (40 × 32.4cm)

PROVENANCE Braamcamp Collection in 1752; his Sale, Amsterdam, 31.vii.1771 (95/96), bt Fouquet; Desenfans 1802 Catalogue (137); Bourgeois Bequest, 1811

LITERATURE Sm no 24; HdG, X, no 114

61
A Delft Vase with Flowers

Signed (damaged): *f Jan Van Huijsum*

Pendant to 42.

Panel, $15\frac{3}{4} \times 12\frac{3}{4}$ in (40 × 32.4cm)

PROVENANCE As 42

LITERATURE Sm no 23; HdG, X, no 205

120   *Vase with Flowers*

Signed: *Jan van Huysum fecit*

The flowers include tulips, roses, French marigolds, poppies, auriculas, salvias, orange-blossom, forget-me-not, London pride, iris, larkspur, veronica, flax, and convolvulus minor.

Panel, $31\frac{1}{8} \times 23\frac{7}{8}$in (79.1 × 60.6cm)

PROVENANCE Bourgeois Bequest, 1811

EXHIBITED RA, Dutch, 1952/3 (310)

LITERATURE Sm no 107; HdG, X, no 125 (confusing Sm no 107 with 139 of this Gallery)

139   *Vase with Flowers*

Signed: *Jan Van Huysum*

The flowers are a tulip, tuberoses, double stocks, roses, auriculas and a hollyhock. Not a pendant to 120, to which it is inferior, and, because of its lighter background and broader handling, probably considerably later.

Canvas, $33\frac{1}{8} \times 24\frac{1}{2}$in (84.1 × 62.2cm)

PROVENANCE Bourgeois Bequest, 1811

LITERATURE Not in Sm; HdG, X, no 126 (confused with Sm no 107 and wrongly said to have belonged to Desenfans)

Charles **JERVAS** (?1675–1739)
Jervas was Kneller's assistant and lived in his shadow. He is best remembered as the friend of Pope.

567   *Dorothy, Lady Townshend*

Inscribed: *Dorothy, Sister of Sir Robert Walpole &/Second Wife of Charles Lord Viscount/Townsend*

Dorothy Walpole was the sister of the Prime Minister, Sir Robert Walpole, and married Charles, 2nd Viscount Townshend, as his second wife in 1713. Her reputation was such that a contemporary recorded the 'yet greater folly of Lord Townshend . . . had occasioned his being drawn in to marry her'. Her ghost, the Little Brown Lady of Raynham, is said, rather unusually, to haunt both Raynham and Houghton. The attribution to Jervas, though unsupported, seems probable. The tents in the background are unexplained, but the coat of arms is Townshend impaling Walpole and the Garter was conferred on Townshend in 1724, though the portrait may well be earlier. Dorothy died in 1726.

Canvas, $50 \times 40\frac{7}{8}$in (127 × 103.8cm)

PROVENANCE Walpole family, Raynham, in 1802; Townshend family, Raynham, but not in the Townshend Heirlooms Sale, 1904 (an unidentified sale mark on the back of the canvas does not refer to the Christie Sale of 1904); Fairfax Murray Gift, 1911

ENGRAVING E. Harding, 1802

VERSIONS Other portraits of her, by Kneller, were in the 1904 Sale, and another is at Holkham; *see also* NPG 2506

LITERATURE E. Sherson, *The Lively Lady Townshend* (1926), rep. p 170 (from the engraving)

Cornelius **JOHNSON** (1593–1661)

Jonson or Johnson, often wrongly called Janssens, was born in London of Netherlandish parents and was one of the leading portrait painters in England before van Dyck's arrival. In 1643 he went to Holland on account of the Civil War and remained there for the rest of his life. His son, also Cornelius, worked in his manner. He was born in London, after 1622 and died in Holland after 1698, but he seems to have returned to England about 1675 for a time. Little is known about his work, but he was fond of the blue-grey background which his father used in his later works, and the few known signatures by him seem to copy his father's (*see also* British School, 411).

564   *A Dutch Gentleman*

Signed and dated: *Cornelius Jonson van Ceulen Fecit 16.7*

The signature and date are very damaged, and the 1926 Catalogue said that they had been destroyed by cleaning, but they were recorded in 1915 and are still sufficiently legible to confirm the accuracy of that reading. The date is not clear, but must be 1657, both for stylistic reasons and because the form of the signature is that used by Johnson during the latter part of his life: however, it is also the form used by his son, and the weakness of the picture makes it likely that it is by Cornelius the Younger.

Canvas, $36\frac{1}{4} \times 28\frac{1}{2}$in (92 × 72.4cm)

PROVENANCE Perhaps Colonel W. Pinney Sale, Arber, Rutter and Waghorn, 21.vii.1898 (33, 34: *Dutch Lady, Dutch Gentleman*), bt Colnaghi; Fairfax Murray Gift, 1911

LITERATURE C. H. Collins-Baker in *Onze Kunst* (1915), 101ff. and rep. (as signed and dated); A. J. Finberg in *Walpole Society* (1922), X, 37, no 114 (as damaged in cleaning and dated conjecturally 1657); H. Schneider in Thieme-Becker, *Allgemeines Lexikon der bildenden Künstler* (1926), XIX, 144 (as by Cornelius II)

George **KNAPTON** (1698–1778)

Knapton was a pupil of Richardson and went to Italy in 1725 for seven years. He is best known for his series of 23 portraits of the members of the Dilettanti Society. There is a very large group-portrait by him in Marlborough House, London.

606   *Lucy Ebberton*

This portrait was engraved by J. McArdell between 1746 and 1765, as by G. Knapton. An impression of this mezzotint was annotated by Horace Walpole: 'Afterwards wife of Capt Greig, of the Marines . . . resided at Blandford and . . . Exeter. Banton, who kept the London Tavern in Poole, was her uncle . . .'. According to the Royal Marines Historian, no Capt. Greig served at the relevant time, but there was a Capt. Thomas Cregg who entered as 2nd Lieutenant in 1757 and was promoted Captain in June 1765. He served until 1782, when he presumably died. The style of this portrait is different from that of the Marlborough House group of Frederick, Prince of Wales, and his family, of 1751, and is markedly more French. Our picture may, therefore, date from somewhat later, perhaps 1760/65.

Canvas, $30\frac{1}{8} \times 25\frac{1}{4}$in (76.5 × 64.1cm)

PROVENANCE Fairfax Murray by 1908; his Gift, 1917

EXHIBITED RA 1908 (107); Paris, Cent Portraits de Femmes, 1909 (21)

LITERATURE G. Goodwin, *J. McArdell* (1903), no 130; A. Staring in *Nederlands Kunsthistorisch Jaarboek* (1968), XIX, 200ff. (with unfounded attribution to van der Mijn); letter from Royal Marines Historian in Gallery archives (14 January 1971)

Sir Godfrey **KNELLER** (1646/9–1723)

Gottfried Kneller was born in Germany and trained in Amsterdam under Rembrandt's pupil F. Bol, and he may even have met Rembrandt himself. He finished his education in Italy and arrived in England *c* 1676, where he rapidly became the leading portrait painter, taking over from Lely. His fame lasted at least until Reynolds returned from Italy in 1753, 30 years after Kneller's death. Nevertheless, much of his large output is stiff and mechanical, because of his reliance upon assistants. His best works are the Kit-Cat series of 42 portraits (now in the National Portrait Gallery).

570   *Two Children, perhaps of the Howard Family*

Signed and dated: *G. Kneller f/1694*

The last figure of the date was once a *3* (or *?5*), but the inscription has been altered by Kneller himself. Formerly called *Lord Carlisle and his Sister*. There is a label on the back, of the second half of the 19th century: *Honble Mary Howard*, which presumably refers to the owner rather than the sitter, and there was an Hon. Mary, born in 1865, who was a Norfolk Howard, not a Carlisle one. In fact, no Lord Carlisle was the right age in 1694, being either grown up or not yet born, and no children of the Carlisle branch of the Howard family can be made to fit. The Norfolk branch is not much better, though Edward Henry, Duke of Norfolk, was born in 1686. It is unlikely to represent him, however, since the boy seems less than eight, and, in two other similar paintings (Althorp, Northants., 1688, and Knole, Kent, *c* 1695) the children wear adult dress from about the age of seven, and the loose wrap is reserved for children of about four or five. The Knole picture, *Lord Buckhurst and Lady Mary Sackville*, is very similar to 570 and there the boy wears adult dress.

Canvas, 50⅛ × 40½in (127.3 × 102.9cm)

PROVENANCE Hon. Mary Howard; Fairfax Murray Gift, 1911

LITERATURE J. D. Stewart, *Kneller* (exhibition catalogue), NPG, 1970, reproduces two drawings for the boy's hands and feet, and the girl's hands, both in the British Museum

Godfrey **KNELLER** *see* Attributed to John Baptist CLOSTERMAN (611)

Johann **KOENIG** *see* Circle of ELSHEIMER (22)

Aleksander **KUCHARSKI** (1741–1819)

Born in Warsaw, Kucharski spent most of his life in Paris and his style is completely French. He was sent to study in Paris by Stanislas Poniatowski before 1760—*ie* before Stanislas was elected King.

489   *Michael Poniatowski, Prince Primate of Poland* and *Stanislas Augustus Poniatowski,*
490   *King of Poland*

Michael Poniatowski (1736–94), younger brother of the King, was a friend of Noel
Desenfans and suggested to his brother the idea of employing Desenfans to collect pictures
for a future National Gallery of Poland. For this purpose Desenfans was made Polish
Consul-General in London. Stanislas (1732–98) had been one of Catherine of Russia's
lovers, and she procured his election as King of Poland in 1764. Stanislas was an educated
and travelled man, a typical product of the Age of Enlightenment, but no match for the power-
politics of Russia and Prussia. During his reign Poland was partitioned three times and in
1792 a Russian army was sent by Catherine to 'restore freedom to Poland'. In 1795 Stanislas
abdicated and retired to St Petersburg as a pensioner of Catherine. He had commissioned
Desenfans to buy paintings in 1790—a very favourable moment, since many French
collections were being dispersed by the Revolution—and in 1798, when Stanislas died,
Desenfans realised he had the pictures on his hands. Some are now in Dulwich (*see*
Introduction, p 19).

The attribution to Kucharski is based on the markedly French style which can be seen in
the few certain pastels by him, and on the known connection between him and Stanislas. In
the Bourgeois Inventory of 1813 no artist's name is given.

Pastel on paper, mounted on canvas, (489) 24 × 20in (60.9 × 50.6cm);
(490) 24 × 20in (60.9 × 50.8cm)

PROVENANCE Bourgeois Bequest, 1811

Gerard de **LAIRESSE** *see* Gerard HOET (176, 179)

Nicolas **LANCRET** *see* Circle of WATTEAU (167)

Samuel **LANE** (1780–1859)
Lane was an East Anglian and a friend of Constable. He was Lawrence's principal assistant
and a portrait painter in his own right, exhibiting at the Royal Academy, 1804–57.

449   *George Bartley*

Bartley (1782–1858) was a comic actor who made his first stage appearance in 1802 and
retired some 50 years later.

Canvas, 30 × 25in (76.2 × 63.5cm)

PROVENANCE Presented by the sitter, 1854

Jan **LAPP** (active 1625–70)
Jan Lapp is recorded in the Guild at The Hague in 1625, where he seems to have been active as late as 1670. He produced Italianate landscapes in the style of Berchem or Du Jardin, to whom this picture was once attributed (*see* Du Jardin, 72). He is thought to have worked in Italy, where he was known as Giovanni Lap.

330   *An Italian Landscape with Figures and Cattle*

The fragments of antiquity, the convent and the cypresses are all characteristic of the Dutch vision of Italy in the 17th century, but the attribution of this picture has always presented problems. It probably belonged to Desenfans as early as 1785, when he attributed it to A. van de Velde: he certainly owned it by 1802, when he described it minutely and attributed it then to K. Du Jardin. It seems, therefore, not to have been clearly signed at that time. In 1816 it was catalogued by the Gallery as by Du Jardin, but the 1876 Catalogue re-attributed it to J. van der Does (1623–73) on the grounds that it was signed with his initials; in 1880, however, Richter rejected this attribution (and presumably the initials) and re-attributed it to Dirk van Bergen (1645–after 1690), under whose name it was last catalogued. By 1928, however, the 'remains of the signature' of Jan Lapp had been read, and close examination (1974) confirms that something very like *J* . . . *L.p* exists below and to the left of the elbow of the boy seated on the sarcophagus. The actual sarcophagus is in the Villa Torlonia, Rome.

Canvas, $22\frac{3}{8} \times 25\frac{3}{8}$in ($56.8 \times 64.3$cm)

PROVENANCE   Probably in Desenfans Sale, Christie's, 11ff.v.1785 (28) and 8ff.iv.1786 (267) in both as A. van de Velde; not in later Desenfans sales, but certainly in 1802 Catalogue (130: as Du Jardin); Bourgeois Bequest, 1811

LITERATURE   N. Desenfans, *Descriptive Catalogue . . . of . . . Pictures . . . purchased for His Majesty the late King of Poland* (1802), II, no 130; Thieme-Becker, *Allgemeines Lexikon der bildenden Künstler* (1928), XXII, unsigned article (?by H. de Groot) on Lapp, as bearing remains of Lapp's signature; C. Vermeule in *Transactions American Philosophical Society* (1966), N.S. 56, pt. 2, no 8748 and fig 219a (Villa Torlonia sarcophagus); W. Bernt, *Netherlandish Painters of the 17th Century* (1970), II, fig 663 (as signed by Lapp)

Filippo **LAURI** (1623–94)
Filippo, the son of a Flemish painter, Lauwers, was born in Rome and lived there all his life. He worked mainly on a small scale and occasionally painted the figures in Claude's landscapes.

164   *Apollo and Marsyas*

The gruesome story, told by Ovid, recounts how Marsyas the flute player challenged the god Apollo to a musical contest. The Muses judged the competition, awarded the victory to Apollo, and the god then flayed the mortal alive for his presumption.

Canvas, $19\frac{1}{4} \times 14\frac{1}{2}$in ($48.9 \times 36.8$cm)

PROVENANCE   Desenfans Private Sale, 8.iv.1786 (365: Albano, *Apollo and Martius*, 29×23in framed); Bourgeois Bequest, 1811 (1813 Inventory: 186 Laura)

LITERATURE   G. J. Hoogewerff in Thieme-Becker, *Allgemeines Lexikon der bildenden Künstler* (1928), XXII (*s.v.* Lauri)

Sir Thomas **LAWRENCE**, PRA (1769–1830)

Sir Thomas Lawrence began as a boy prodigy, drawing heads in pastel in the West Country and Oxford (*see* 474, 475), but in 1787 he was a student at the Royal Academy and an exhibitor in the same year. He was a particular favourite of the Prince Regent, for whom many of his best works were painted. He became President of the Royal Academy in 1820, having been knighted five years earlier. His collection of Old Master drawings was one of the greatest ever formed.

178   *William Linley*

William (1771–1835) was the youngest of the 12 children of Thomas Linley (*see* Gainsborough, 140 for details of the family). He spent many years in India, wrote plays and was—like the other Linleys—a fine singer and musician. He bequeathed the family pictures to the Gallery.

Canvas, 30 × 25 in (76.2 × 63.5 cm)

PROVENANCE Bequeathed by the sitter, 1835 (but on loan to the Gallery from *c* 1822)

EXHIBITED RA 1789 (171); BI 1833 (32: as lent by Dulwich College); RA 1904 (61) and 1951/2 (421)

LITERATURE W. T. Whitley, *Artists and Their Friends* . . . (1928), II, 385; K. Garlick, *Lawrence* (1954), 46; *id* in *Walpole Society* (1964), XXXIX, 126

474   *The Rev. Ozias Thurstan Linley, as a Boy* and his sister *Maria Linley*
475
Two of the children of Thomas Linley (*see* Gainsborough, 140 for details of the family), and brother and sister of William (178), the donor of the portraits. Ozias, like the rest of the family, was a skilled musician and after holding three livings he resigned in order to become Junior Fellow and Organist at Dulwich College. He was born in 1765, died in 1831 and is buried in the Chapel (*see* Oliver, 476). He was responsible for lending the family portraits to the Gallery (*c* 1822) and his brother William finally bequeathed them in 1835. His elder sister Maria (1763–84) had a fine voice. She died at 21.

Since Lawrence himself was born only in 1769 the portraits can hardly be earlier than 1779, when Lawrence was certainly making drawings of this kind, and from *c* 1782 he was producing oval pastel portraits for a guinea each in Bath. The difference in quality between the two portraits may be explained by the youth of the artist.

Pastel on paper on canvas (oval), both 12 × 10 in (30.5 × 25.4 cm)

PROVENANCE As 178

LITERATURE C. Black, *The Linleys of Bath*, 3rd edn (1971), rep. 124, 132; K. Garlick in *Walpole Society* (1964), XXXIX, 263 (confusing two portraits of each sitter)

Charles **LEBRUN** (1619–90)

Lebrun was the virtual artistic dictator of France in the late 17th century, acting as Colbert's aide in the glorification of Louis XIV's rule. He was a pupil of Vouet and in 1642 went to Rome, probably with Poussin, who was a major influence on him. There he studied the works of the great Baroque decorators, returning to France in 1646 as he had become bored with Rome. He was one of the leaders of the Académie from its foundation in 1648, and became Director of it, as well as First Painter to the King and Director of the Gobelins

Tapestry Factory. His most important works are in the Galerie des Glaces and the Salons de la Guerre and de la Paix, all at Versailles, where he was in charge of the decoration.

202   *The Massacre of the Innocents*

In spite of *Matthew* ii, 16–18, Lebrun has set his scene in Rome, since the pyramid is clearly that of Cestius, and the strange temple with trees growing out of it is based on the Mausoleum of Augustus. The picture was begun in 1647—the background and small figures—and finished, in a different style, many years later.

Canvas, $52\frac{3}{8} \times 73\frac{3}{4}$in ($133 \times 187.4$cm)

PROVENANCE M. Metz, Garde du Trésor Royale; Duc d' Orléans Collection, before 1734; to England with the Orléans Collection, and bt by Desenfans, probably 1802/4; Insurance List, 1804 (80); Bourgeois Bequest, 1811

ENGRAVING Le Noir, *c* ?1716 and Bertaux, both while in the Orléans Collection

LITERATURE E. Johnston (ed.), *Highmore's Paris Journal, 1734*, in *Walpole Society* (1970), XLII, 81 and n 96 (describes it in Orléans Collection); C. Stryienski, *La galerie du . . . Duc d'Orléans* (Paris, 1913), no 365; A. F. Blunt in *Burl.Mag.* (1944), LXXXV, 168

244   *Horatius Cocles defending the Bridge*

Horatius Cocles ('one-eyed') was a Roman hero of the 6th century BC who traditionally held the wooden Sublician bridge against the Etruscans who were attempting to invade Rome. The bridge was cut down behind him and he then swam the Tiber to safety: in the words of Macaulay's *Lays of Ancient Rome*: 'Even the ranks of Tuscany/Could scarce forbear to cheer'. Probably painted in Rome 1642/6, when Lebrun was influenced by his surroundings and by Poussin in particular.

Canvas, $48 \times 67\frac{5}{8}$in (121.9×171.8cm). A strip about $2\frac{1}{2}$in deep has been added at the bottom

PROVENANCE Probably Vaudreuil, before *c* 1784; Desenfans Insurance List, 1804 (110); Bourgeois Bequest, 1811

EXHIBITED NG 1947 (26)

LITERATURE A. F. Blunt in *Burl.Mag.* (1944), LXXXV, 165ff. and rep.

School of **LEBRUN**

188   *A Man, called Molière*

When this portrait was presented to the Gallery by the actor George Bartley (*see* Lane, 449) in 1854 it was as Molière by Maratta. The Maratta attribution was soon abandoned, and the 1880 Catalogue noted the connection with a portrait of Molière, attributed to the School of Lebrun, in 'the Musée Royale'. The picture in question cannot now be traced, but the engraving by J. Posselwhite (*c* 1833) certainly shows a marked likeness to 188. However, it has long been suggested that the sitter is not Molière, and a positive identification with Michel Baron (*b* 1653), an actor in Molière's company, has been made by Mlle S. Chevalley, the author of an authoritative biography of Molière. Her re-identification rests mainly on a portrait of Baron by Largillierre at Tours. While the case against Molière is strong, that for

Baron is much less so. It is significant that a *Molière* by Mignard, dated 1671, belonged to the Duke of Sutherland and was exhibited in London in 1846 and 1854, the year in which our picture was presented, so the identification as Molière may well have sprung from comparison with the Mignard, which shows an older man. H. Y. Thompson, according to the 1926 Catalogue, compared 188 with a version of the Mignard in the Musée Condé at Chantilly and was convinced that they represent the same man.

Canvas, 29 × 23¾in (73.7 × 60.4cm)

PROVENANCE Given by George Bartley, 1854

ENGRAVING J. Posselwhite in *Gallery of Portraits with Memoirs* (1833), I

LITERATURE S. Chevalley, *Molière et son temps* (Paris and Geneva, 1973), 234 and figs 523, 698

Sir Peter **LELY** (1618–80)

Peter van der Faes, better known as Lely, was the leading painter in England during the reign of Charles II. He was of Dutch origin and studied in Haarlem, where he became a Master in 1637. He was in London by 1647, when he had already painted Charles I. During the Interregnum he painted mythological and even religious subjects, but he soon became established as a portrait painter and began his huge output of likenesses of the leading figures of the Restoration, including the beauties of Charles II's Court. Pepys described him in 1667 as a 'mighty proud man and full of state'. He was knighted in 1680.

555 *Nymphs by a Fountain*

This picture was, apparently, once signed and dated 1670, but there is no trace of this now. The date must be wrong, since the style is that of about 1650/55, when Lely is known to have painted similar subjects (*eg Cimon and Iphigenia* at Knole, Kent). A *Sleeping Girl* at Hatfield House, Herts., is a variant in reverse of the nymph at the right with her head propped on her hand. Surprisingly, Lely seems to have painted these subjects during the Commonwealth period. He also painted them earlier, which makes the suggestion that our picture was painted before he came to England in the 1640s more plausible.

Canvas, 50¾ × 57in (128.9 × 144.8cm)

PROVENANCE Bt in Paris by Fairfax Murray; presented by him, 1911

EXHIBITED RA 1960/61 (17); NPG, Lely, 1978 (25)

DRAWING A drawing attributed to Rubens, but from Lely's collection and probably by him, was in the C. R. Rudolf Collection, London, sold in Amsterdam, 1977. It represents a reclining nude, reversed from the one on the right, and with a different pose of the arm: it is even closer to another Lely, *Shepherd and Nymphs* (private collection)

LITERATURE C. H. Collins-Baker, *Lely and the Stuart Portrait Painters* (1912), I, 139 n (as 'said to be signed and dated earlier than his arrival in England'—*ie* pre-1647); R. Beckett, *Lely* (1951), 67–8 and pl 52 (as signed, but date 'not discoverable'); E. K. Waterhouse, *Painting in Britain* ... (1953), 64 (as mid-1650s); M. D. Whinney and O. Millar, *English Art, 1625–1714* (Oxford, 1957), 172; J. Sunderland, *Painting in Britain, 1525–1975* (1976), 233 and pl 38; Sir O. Millar, *Lely* (exhibition catalogue), NPG, 1978, no 25, rep. colour pl II and p 49

559 *Lady in Blue* and *Lady in Blue holding a Flower*
560
Signed: (559) *PL* in monogram

The two ladies are strikingly alike, and, as they have probably always been a pair, the portraits may represent two sisters, perhaps of the Townshend family. The spray of white jasmine held by one may symbolise her betrothal. Although sold in 1904 as by Lely they were attributed to Daniel Mytens by Fairfax Murray, who gave them to the Gallery in 1911. They were correctly re-attributed to Lely in 1915 by Collins-Baker, and this was confirmed by the discovery of the *PL* monogram on 559. He dated them *c* 1660.

Canvas, both $49\frac{7}{8} \times 40\frac{3}{8}$in (126.7 × 102.5cm)

PROVENANCE Marquess of Townshend, Raynham Hall; Townshend Heirlooms Sale, Christie's, 5.iii.1904 (78, 80), bt Fairfax Murray; his Gift, 1911

LITERATURE C. H. Collins-Baker in *Onze Kunst* (1915), 101ff. (as by Lely *c* 1660)

563   *Young Man as a Shepherd*

Signed: *PL* in monogram

Although this was regarded as a portrait of the poet Abraham Cowley at least as far back as the late 18th century, it cannot represent him. Cowley was born in 1618 and can hardly be more than 20 if he is represented here, but Lely did not come to London until well after 1638. In any case, this Romantic image does not correspond with the genuine portraits by Lely himself (*eg* in the National Portrait Gallery) (*see* Beale, 574).

Canvas, $36 \times 29\frac{3}{4}$in (91.4 × 75.6cm)

PROVENANCE E. Lovibond, Hampton; Lovibond Sale, 1776, bt Horace Walpole; (his) Strawberry Hill Sale (11th day) 6.v.1842 (21: as Cowley), bt Sir Robert Peel; Peel Heirlooms Sale, Robinson & Fisher, 10.v.1900 (203); Fairfax Murray Gift, 1911

EXHIBITED RA 1908 (157); NG 1947 (27); NPG, Lely, 1978 (28)

ENGRAVING An 18th-century engraving by Sherlock and Simon, as Cowley

VERSION/COPIES An enamel copy by Zincke, mentioned in the Walpole Sale Catalogue, is now in the Fitzwilliam Museum, signed and dated 1716. According to the 1926 Dulwich Catalogue there was then a copy or version with a blue mantle

LITERATURE C. H. Collins-Baker, *Lely and the Stuart Portrait Painters* (1912), II, 122; *id* in *Onze Kunst* (1915), 101ff. as Cowley, but *c* 1645; R. Beckett, *Lely* (1951), 42, no 129 and pl 38, not Cowley and *c* 1657; Sir O. Millar, *Lely* (exhibition catalogue), NPG, 1978, no 28 and rep. colour pl III and p 51

Johannes **LINGELBACH** (1622–74)

Lingelbach was born in Germany and worked in France before going to Rome *c* 1644–50. He spent the rest of his life in Amsterdam. His works are mainly in imitation of Wouwermans (an example is in the National Gallery) or in imitation of the exotic Italian seaports of J. B. Weenix (as 326): there is a fine Weenix of a similar scene at Kenwood.

326   *An Italian Seaport*

Signed and dated: *I LINGELBACH/FECIT/1670*

Canvas, $27\frac{3}{8} \times 34\frac{3}{8}$in (69.5 × 87.3cm)

PROVENANCE Said to have been bought by Desenfans at Moses Vanhausen Sale, 1783; Bourgeois Bequest, 1811

James **LONSDALE** (1777–1839)

Lonsdale was a pupil of Romney who became Portrait Painter to Queen Caroline. Although a successful portrait painter who exhibited 138 pictures at the Royal Academy, he never became a member.

456   *Mrs Thomas Linley*

Mary Johnson (1729–1820) married Thomas Linley (*see* Gainsborough, 140) in 1752 and bore him 12 children, almost all of the survivors being distinguished musicians. This portrait was wrongly attributed to Ozias Humphrey (a friend of the family) in the 1892 Catalogue, but there is no resemblance to Humphrey's style, and, in any case, it is known that her son William, who left the family pictures to Dulwich in 1835, had two portraits of her—one by Lonsdale and the other by Oliver (*see* 476). The Oliver portrait has not been traced, but this is stylistically identical with Lonsdale's work. Mrs Linley used to play whist with Mrs Lonsdale, presumably the painter's mother. Mrs Linley died, at the age of 91, in January 1820, and her portrait by Lonsdale was exhibited at the Royal Academy that year, presumably as a memorial, since she appears less than 90 in it.

Canvas, $30\frac{1}{8} \times 25$in (76.5 × 63.5cm)

PROVENANCE Bequeathed by William Linley, 1835

EXHIBITED RA 1820 (33)

LITERATURE C. Black, *The Linleys of Bath*, 3rd edn (1971), *passim*

Claude **LORRAINE** *see* CLAUDE

Philipp Jakob de **LOUTHERBOURG**, RA (1740–1812)

For biography *see* Gainsborough, 66.

297   *Landscape with Cattle*

Signed and dated: *P J de Loutherbourg 176(?7)*

If the date has been correctly read—and there seems no doubt about the *6*—the picture was painted in Paris (*cf* 339) and must have been brought to London, where Loutherbourg's pupil Bourgeois acquired it.

Canvas, $22\frac{3}{8} \times 27\frac{3}{4}$in (57 × 70.5cm)

PROVENANCE Bourgeois Bequest, 1811

LITERATURE L. Herrmann, *British Landscape Painting of the 18th Century* (1973), 113–16

339   *Landscape with Cattle and Figures*

Signed: *P J de Loutherbourg*

It has been suggested that this was one of a group of landscapes exhibited by Loutherbourg at the Salon in Paris in 1765: if so, it is slightly earlier than 297. It must, however, have come to England, where Loutherbourg's pupil Bourgeois acquired it. The importance of

Loutherbourg as a link between the landscapes of Dutch artists like Wynants and those of Gainsborough in the 1770s and later, can be seen in the composition generally as well as in the trees at the right.

Canvas, $27\frac{7}{8} \times 38\frac{1}{4}$in (70.8 × 97.2cm)

PROVENANCE Bourgeois Bequest, 1811

EXHIBITED Possibly Paris, Salon, 1765 (140); RA, France in 18th Century, 1968 (457)

LITERATURE D. Diderot, *Salon de 1765*, in J. Adhémar and J. Seznec (eds), *Diderot's Salons* (1957–63), (1765) 39 and fig 65; L. Herrmann, *British Landscape Painting of the 18th Century* (1973), 113–16

MABUSE (active 1503–32)

Jan Gossaert, called Mabuse, was one of the principal Romanists active in Flanders in the early 16th century. He was greatly influenced by Dürer, and even more by the experience of High Renaissance Italy, where he went in 1508.

Circle of MABUSE

505 *The Fall of Man*

The scene is from *Genesis*, iii, 6: 'she took of the fruit thereof . . . and gave also unto her husband . . . and he did eat'. The left background shows the sequel—24: 'and at the east of the Garden of Eden Cherubims, and a flaming sword . . .'. The composition is closely based on the famous engraving by Dürer of 1504 but there are about half-a-dozen versions by Mabuse or from his circle which are variations on the theme. The closest to the Dürer engraving is the painting of *c* 1509 now in the Thyssen-Bornemisza Collection at Castagnola in Switzerland. Next probably comes the Dulwich picture, followed by the original work by Mabuse in the Royal Collection and at least two derivatives from it, and, finally, a much more elaborate version, incorporating motives from Leonardo da Vinci, now in the Bode-Museum in East Berlin. Although our picture cannot be regarded as by Mabuse himself it must be a product of his studio about 1520/30.

Panel, $42 \times 25\frac{1}{2}$in (106.7 × 64.8cm)

PROVENANCE Unknown, but possibly from the Alleyn Bequest, 1626, or the Cartwright Bequest, 1686 (one page of the Inventory is missing); it appears in old inventories as 76 and has, therefore, probably been in the College for a long time

LITERATURE M. J. Friedländer, *Early Netherlandish Painting* (1972), VIII, nos 8–11 (not mentioning our painting)

Alessandro MAGNASCO (1677–1749)

Magnasco was a Genoese painter of extremely melodramatic landscapes, usually with storms raging and theatrical monks in attendance. He was a late follower of Salvator Rosa (*cf* Rosa, 216).

279   *The Entombment of Christ*

This small *bozzetto* for an unknown altarpiece exists in several versions. Formerly attributed to a variety of painters including Agostino Carracci, A. M. Fabrizzi, Sacchi, and Salvator Rosa, it is a version of the composition known from examples in a private collection in Cardiff; one in Genoa formerly with the Newhouse Galleries, New York, and another with a dealer in Vienna, related to a *Crucifixion* in the Akademie, Vienna. Strangely, although so many versions of the *modello* are known, there is no trace of the large altarpiece for which they were presumably preparatory studies.

Canvas, $21\frac{3}{8} \times 13\frac{3}{8}$in ($54.3 \times 33.9$cm)

PROVENANCE Bourgeois Bequest, 1811 (as Agostino Carracci, later changed to A. Sacchi)

LITERATURE *Pittori Genovesi* . . . (exhibition catalogue), Palazzo Bianco, Genoa, 1969, no 137 (the New York/Genoa version, 53×34cm, said to show the influence of S. Ricci)

Carlo **MARATTA** (1625–1713)
Maratta was the leader of the Classical school in late Baroque painting. He was very precocious and was an independent master before 1650. He worked for many years under Sacchi and by the end of the century he had become virtually dictator of the arts in Rome.

Attributed to **MARATTA**

274   *The Holy Family with S. Anne, the Baptist and Zacharias*

This picture has been attributed to Carlo Maratta since 1785 and, indeed, looks extremely Marattesque. It is, however, identical in composition with the only known signed work by Giovanni Battista Mola, dated 1657, now in the Seattle Art Museum, U.S.A. Mola was the father of the better-known Pier Francesco Mola, and was active as an architect in Rome 1616–65. The Seattle painting is slightly larger than 274—$25\frac{3}{4} \times 18\frac{1}{2}$in—and there are various differences between them—*eg* in the Seattle picture the head of the Madonna is tilted slightly to the right, S. Joseph's head is at a different angle, Zacharias has his head covered. The Seattle picture also seems rather timid in handling, which suggests the possibility that 274 is a *modello* by Maratta—whose style was well established by 1657—which, for some reason, he never executed and which was copied by Mola.

Canvas, $19\frac{3}{8} \times 15\frac{3}{8}$in ($49.2 \times 39$cm)

PROVENANCE Possibly the *Madonna* in the Crozat Inventory of 1740 (20×15in, which is nearer 274 than the Seattle painting); Desenfans Sale, Christie's, 11.v.1785 (2nd day: 23); his Sale, 8ff.iv.1786 (296); Bourgeois Bequest, 1811

LITERATURE R. Cocke, *Mola* (Oxford, 1972), 70, no R48 and pl 145 (the Seattle picture)

Juan Bautista del **MAZO** (*c* 1612–67)
Mazo was apprenticed to Velazquez (*see* 249), whose daughter Francisca he married in 1634. In 1657 he went to Italy for some months, and, after Velazquez's death in 1661, he was appointed Painter to the King.

277 *One of the Painter's Sons*

A study for the head of one of the children in *The Painter's Family* (Kunsthistorisches Museum, Vienna). Mazo's first wife, Velazquez's daughter, died before 1654, so this group represents his second wife and children. The Vienna picture is datable *c* 1660/61 on the ages of the children: our study must therefore date from *c* 1660. It was previously attributed to Juan de Pareja, another of Velazquez's followers and assistants.

Canvas, $14\frac{7}{8} \times 10\frac{3}{4}$in (37.8 × 27.1cm)

PROVENANCE Bourgeois Bequest, 1811

EXHIBITED Madrid, 1960–1 (133: as Mazo)

LITERATURE C. Justi, *Velazquez and his Times* (1889), 422–5 (first recognising the connection with the Vienna picture, then attributed to Velazquez); Allende Salazar, *Velazquez* (KdK, 1925), 241; J. Lopez-Rey, *Velazquez' Work and World* (1968), 131–2 and pl 165

Jan **MIEL** (1599–1663)

Miel was born in Antwerp, and was in Rome by 1636. In Italy he became a member of the 'Bamboccianti', a group of Northern artists who painted scenes of Italian low life. Miel is said to have painted the figures in some of Claude's landscapes. In 1658 he went as Court Painter to Turin, where he died.

Attributed to Jan **MIEL**

20 *Landscape with Figures*

There are traces of what may have been Miel's complicated *JM* monogram, but they may be accidental. The subject is not quite typical of Miel's *bambocciate*—the figures are too well-dressed—and the quality is not as good as in his best works, so the attribution is made with some reservations.

Copper, $8 \times 11\frac{7}{8}$in (20.4 × 30cm)

PROVENANCE Perhaps Desenfans Sale, 8ff.iv.1786 (346); Bourgeois Bequest, 1811

Giovanni Battista **MOLA** *see* Carlo MARATTA (274)

Circle of Pier Francesco **MOLA** (1612–66)

75 *Pluto and Proserpine*

According to the Greek myth Pluto, King of Hades, carried off Proserpine, the daughter of Zeus and Demeter, while she was picking flowers in a Sicilian meadow. She was later allowed to return to earth for part of the year, the myth being a symbol of the burying of seed in the earth and the subsequent corn crop, Demeter being the goddess of harvests. Titian is known to have painted the subject for the Duke of Mantua, but the picture is lost. It may be reflected in this composition, but the authorship of 75 is difficult to determine. It was attributed to Mola until 1880, when Richter demoted it to Venetian School, but there are links with Mola, and perhaps also with Pietro della Vecchia and Baldi, so it seems worthwhile to return tentatively to the earlier attribution.

Canvas, 25¾ × 19¼in (65.4 × 48.9cm)

PROVENANCE Desenfans Insurance List, 1804 (74); Bourgeois Bequest, 1811 (both as Mola)

LITERATURE G. F. Waagen, *Treasures of Art in Gt Britain* (1854), II, 347 (as by Mola)

Jakob van **MOSCHER** (active 1635–55)
Van Moscher was a Haarlem painter who worked in the styles of Jan van Goyen and Salomon van Ruysdael (to whom 16 was long attributed). The moss-like pattern of the foliage is characteristic of his pictures and can be seen in a very similar landscape in Munich which is signed.

16 *A Road near Cottages*

Signed: *J van . . . o . . .*

In the 1816 Catalogue this picture was attributed to I. van Ostade, but in 1880 the attribution was changed to School of S. van Ruysdael and it was noted that the remains of a signature could be read as (?)*P van olo*. In 1974 it seems clearly to be *J van . . . o . . .*, but the *olo* could well have been *ofc*, since Moscher did use the long *s*. The stylistic evidence seems conclusive.

Panel, 19¾ × 25¾in (50.2 × 65.3cm)

PROVENANCE Perhaps Desenfans Sale, 8ff.iv.1786(7) and 8ff.vi.1786 (31), both as S. Ruysdael; Bourgeois Bequest, 1811

LITERATURE I. Q. van Regteren Altena in Thieme-Becker, *Allgemeines Lexikon der bildenden Künstler* (1931), XXV (*s.v.* Moscher, first attributing 16 to him); W. Bernt, *Netherlandish Painters of the 17th Century* (1970) II, 82 (rep. of a signature), figs 805, 806 (signed pictures)

Robert **MULLER** (active 1789–1800)
Muller was a portrait painter in London, but nothing seems to be known about him now, except the two portraits mentioned below.

587 *Mrs George Morland*

Anne Ward, the sister of James Ward RA, and of William Ward the engraver, married Morland the painter in 1786. Muller seems to have painted a pair of portraits of the couple before 1796, when he exhibited *George Morland* at the Royal Academy. It was engraved by William Ward in 1806, but 587 was not in the Royal Academy exhibition of 1796, nor was it engraved. The *George Morland* is now in the Lady Lever Art Gallery, Port Sunlight, Merseyside, but it seems to have become separated from *Mrs Morland* before 1905, when it was sold by itself. It was probably at that time that our picture was bought by Fairfax Murray, since there is no other reason for the attribution and identification than that he presented it in 1911 as *Mrs Morland* by Muller: it is also said that H. B. Chalon the animal painter was responsible for the dog, which seems plausible.

Canvas, 30 × 25in (76.3 × 63.5cm)

PROVENANCE Fairfax Murray Gift, 1911

LITERATURE J. T. Smith, *Nollekens and his Times* (1829), II, 339–340 (for Mrs Morland's unhappy married life)

Bartolomé Estéban **MURILLO** (1617/18–82)

Murillo was the leading painter in Seville in the 17th century. In his youth he was influenced by Ribera and Zurbarán, though he came to influence Zurbarán's own later works. He made his name with a series of paintings for the Franciscans of Seville in 1645, but a later visit to Madrid, where he saw the work of Rubens and van Dyck in the Royal Collections, changed his style into a much softer one, with golden light effects. All the Dulwich pictures are in this later style, and the beggar-boy pictures here, with those in Munich and Paris, form a important part of his work, much prized in the 18th and 19th centuries.

199 *The Flower Girl*

Similar genre subjects, dating from Murillo's later years, are in Munich and Leningrad (*The Fruit-Seller*, *The Orange Girl*). Our picture probably dates from 1665/70.

Canvas, $47\frac{3}{4} \times 38\frac{7}{8}$in (121.3 × 98.7cm), enlarged from $41\frac{1}{2} \times 33\frac{1}{2}$in (105.4 × 85.1cm), probably in the 18th century

PROVENANCE Comtesse de Verrue before 1737; passed to Comte de Lassay, *d* 1750; passed to Comte de la Guiche; Blondel de Gagny; his Sale, Paris, 10.xii.1776 (3), bt Basan (as ex-Verrue and Lassay); probably wrongly said to have been in the Randon de Boisset Collection; Le Brun of Paris Sale, Christie's, 18–19.iii.1785 (2nd day, 29); C. A. de Calonne; his Sale, Skinner & Dyke, 23ff.iii.1795 (4th day, 99: as ex-Randon de Boisset), bt Desenfans; Bourgeois Bequest, 1811

EXHIBITED BI 1816 (21); NG 1947 (28)

VERSION There is an old copy in the Akademie, Vienna

LITERATURE W. Buchanan, *Memoirs . . .*, I, 255 (as ex-R. de Boisset, Calonne Collections); C. B. Curtis, *Velazquez and Murillo* (London and New York, 1883), no 426; A. L. Mayer, *Murillo* (KdK, 2nd edn, 1923), 216; G. Kubler and M. Soria, *Art and Architecture in Spain and Portugal* (1959), 276 and pl 147; J. A. Gaya Nuño, *L'opera completa di Murillo* (Milan, 1978), no 169 and pl 39

222
224 *Two Peasant Boys and a Negro Boy* and *Two Peasant Boys*

These are, with the comparable pictures in Munich and Paris, among the most celebrated of Murillo's later genre scenes. The three examples in Munich (487, 597, 605) are similar in several respects, but do not repeat any of the motives exactly. The whole group probably dates from the late 1660s.

Canvas, (222) $66\frac{1}{4} \times 43\frac{1}{4}$in (168.3 × 109.8cm);
(224) $64\frac{3}{4} \times 43\frac{1}{2}$in (164.9 × 110.5cm)

PROVENANCE Possibly Desenfans Sale, 8ff.iv.1786 (177, 178: the size differing); Insurance List, 1804 (8, 9); Bourgeois Bequest, 1811

EXHIBITED BI 1828 (66, 69)

LITERATURE C. B. Curtis, *Velazquez and Murillo* (London and New York, 1883), nos 435, 452; A. L. Mayer, *Murillo* (KdK, 2nd edn, 1923), 212, 213; H. Soehner, *Spanische Meister* (Munich Gallery Catalogue, 1963); J. A. Gaya Nuño, *L'opera completa di Murillo* (Milan, 1978), nos 167, 168 and pl 38

281 *The Madonna of the Rosary*

Probably a late work, *c* 1679/80.

Canvas, 79 × 50⅝in (200.8 × 128.2cm)

PROVENANCE Apparently bought by Alleyne Fitz Herbert, Lord St Helens (1753–1839), in Spain while he was Ambassador there (1791–94); Desenfans after 1802 and before 1804 (Insurance List, 3); Bourgeois Bequest, 1811

EXHIBITED BI 1816 (75)

VERSIONS There is a copy at Corsham Court, Wilts., and another was in trade in Vienna in 1936. A similar picture belonged to J. B. Lebrun, Desenfans' partner, bought in Spain *c* 1807.

LITERATURE C. B. Curtis, *Velazquez and Murillo* (1883), no 78 (giving provenance, for which there is no other evidence); A. Calvert, *Murillo* (1907), 114, no 21 (as in Curtis); A. L. Mayer, *Murillo* (KdK, 2nd edn, 1923), 176 (as 1665/82); J. A. Gaya Nuño, *L'opera completa di Murillo* (Milan, 1978), no 286

Pieter **NASON** (*c* 1612–*c* 1689)
Little is known about Nason, who worked mainly as a portrait painter in The Hague. He painted Oliver St John in 1651, either there or in London, and was certainly in England in 1663 (the date of the Dulwich picture) and in Berlin in 1666.

556 *Unknown Man*

Signed and dated: *P Nason F 1663* (PN in monogram)

It has been suggested that the sitter was a doctor, but the skull may be no more than a *memento mori*. There is a portrait of Lord Shaftesbury by Nason, also dated 1663, so it is likely that our picture was painted in England. There are only two other examples of Nason's work in public collections in Britain: the *Oliver St John* of 1651 now in the National Portrait Gallery, and the *Man and Wife* in the National Gallery, Edinburgh.

Canvas, 35¼ × 26⅝in (89.5 × 67.7cm)

PROVENANCE Bt in Paris by Agnew's, 20.v.1904; Fairfax Murray Gift, 1911

EXHIBITED NG 1947 (29); RA, Dutch, 1952/3 (623)

LITERATURE C. H. Collins-Baker, *Lely and the Stuart Portrait Painters* (1912), II, 2; *id* in *Onze Kunst* (1915), 101ff. and rep.

NEAPOLITAN School *see* Francesco FRACANZANO (558)

Peeter **NEEFFS I** (active 1605–*d* in or after 1656)
Neeffs worked in Antwerp, more or less in the style of Steenwyck. He painted exclusively church interiors, usually Gothic, and mostly versions of Antwerp Cathedral. It is said that the figures in his pictures were usually painted by others. His son Peeter was an assistant and imitator.

141 *Interior of a Gothic Church*

Signed: *PEETER NEEFFS*

The figures have been attributed to Frans Francken II (1581–1642). The building is probably an imaginary one, but it resembles many other pictures by Neeffs, especially those of *Antwerp Cathedral* in the Victoria and Albert Museum (244 and 247) and the Wallace Collection: probably they are all loosely based on the actual building. The subjects of the altarpieces on the nave piers are, on the right, an *Ecce Homo*, a *Madonna*, a *Descent from the Cross*, a *Gethsemane*(?), a *Bishop*, a *Way to Calvary*; on the left, a *Holy Family*.

Panel, $21\frac{1}{2} \times 33\frac{3}{4}$in ($54.4 \times 85.7$cm)

PROVENANCE Possibly the Steenwyck in Desenfans Sale, 8ff.iv.1786 (304), but not the Neeffs *Church by candlelight* in his Sale, Skinner & Dyke, 24ff.ii.1795; Bourgeois Bequest, 1811

LITERATURE H. Jantzen, *Das niederländische Architekturbild* (Leipzig, 1910), 165–7 (for variations on Antwerp theme) and Cat no 268; W. Bernt, *Netherlandish Painters of the 17th Century* (1970), II, pl 833

James **NORTHCOTE**, RA (1746–1831)
Northcote was a pupil and assistant of Reynolds 1771–5, before going to Rome 1778–80. He painted history pieces and portraits (in the manner of Reynolds), but is perhaps best remembered as the author of a *Life of Reynolds* (1813) and for his conversations with Hazlitt (published in 1830).

28 *Noel Joseph Desenfans*

Desenfans (1745–1807) was, with Bourgeois, the major benefactor of the Gallery. For details of his life and collection, *see* Introduction p 19. According to Northcote's own list this portrait was painted in 1796, when Desenfans was just over 50. A Northcote portrait of Bourgeois is 172.

Canvas (elliptical), $28\frac{7}{8} \times 24$in (73.3×60.9cm)

PROVENANCE Bourgeois Bequest, 1811

ENGRAVING S. Freeman, *c* 1809 as frontispiece to the *Monthly Mirror*, December 1809, and for *Memoir of . . . Desenfans*, 1810

LITERATURE S. Gwynn, *Memorials of an Eighteenth Century Painter* (1898), 275, no 305 (Northcote's own list, as 1796); F. Herrmann, *The English as Collectors* (1972), 173 (rep. the Freeman engraving)

172 *Sir Peter Francis Bourgeois*, RA

For information on the sitter, whose Bequest was the foundation of this Gallery, *see* Beechey, 17. According to Northcote's own list of his works this portrait was painted in 1795, but it is much more likely to have been the *Portrait of an artist* exhibited by Northcote at the Royal Academy in the previous year, as recorded in an annotated edition of the Catalogue. Northcote seems also to have been mistaken about the engraver.

Canvas, 30×25in (76.2×63.5cm)

PROVENANCE Bourgeois Bequest, 1811

ENGRAVING W. Leney, 1795

LITERATURE S. Gwynn, *Memorials of an Eighteenth Century Painter* (1898), 275, no 301 (based on Northcote's own list of his works, but wrongly dating the picture 1795 and giving the engraver as Reynolds)

Archer James **OLIVER** (1774–1842)
Oliver was a prolific portrait painter, who became an ARA in 1807 and was later appointed Keeper of the Academy's Painting School, but never became a full member, although he exhibited at the Royal Academy over half a century.

476   *A Man of the Linley Family, probably the Rev. Ozias*

This pciture, since 1876, has been called a portrait of Desenfans by William Owen, RA. It has nothing to do with Owen (who worked in the Reynolds tradition), and it is clearly a much younger man than Desenfans, whose authentic portrait by Northcote (28) shows him in 1796 at the age of about 50 (he was born in 1745). This picture was obviously painted about 1810 and represents a man of very much less than 65, which Desenfans would then have been, had he lived (he died in 1807). The error began in 1873, when a picture was discovered 'lying in or near the Mausoleum' and was, therefore, assumed to represent Desenfans. The Governors' Minutes for December 1873, record this and attribute the portrait to an unknown painter. By the time of the 1876 Catalogue this had become *Desenfans* by Owen. In fact, the three portraits of Desenfans which came to the Gallery with the Bourgeois Bequest in 1811 are all accounted for, and do not resemble 476 in the least degree. On the other hand, the Linley family portraits bequeathed to the College in 1835 by William (*see* Lawrence, 178) had obviously been muddled up (*see* Lonsdale, 456), and the will records two portraits by Oliver—one of Mrs Linley and the other of either William himself or his brother, the Rev Ozias Linley, Organist of Dulwich College (1765–1831) (*see* Lawrence, 474). This picture is clearly by Oliver and must date, on grounds of costume and hair-style, from about 1810. In fact, Oliver exhibited a portrait of William Linley at the Royal Academy in that year, when Linley would have been about 39; on the other hand, the sitter is wearing black, the usual clerical dress of the day, and the will seems to specify Ozias, then about 45, as the sitter. Oliver exhibited many 'Portraits of Gentlemen' at the Royal Academy before and after 1810, but there is no firm reason to identify any of them with Ozias, and the 1810 exhibit of *William Linley* would then remain unaccounted for. The attribution to Owen, otherwise inexplicable, may be a misreading of Oliver.

Canvas, $30\frac{1}{2} \times 25\frac{1}{4}$in (76.8 × 64.2cm)

PROVENANCE Presumably the Linley Bequest, 1835

EXHIBITED ?RA, 1810 (179: *W. Linley Esq*)

LITERATURE C. Black, *The Linleys of Bath*, 3rd edn (1971), *passim* for both brothers

Adriaen van **OSTADE** (1610–85)
Ostade was a Haarlem painter of peasant genre scenes who was principally influenced by Brouwer (*see* 108), although he was also influenced by Rembrandt in the 1640s. He is known to have worked on occasion with his own pupil Dusart (*see* 39).

45 *Interior of a Cottage*

A work of the painter's later period. On the back of the panel are three unidentified seals and the remains of a fourth.

Panel, $13\frac{1}{2} \times 10\frac{7}{8}$in ($34.1 \times 27.5$cm)

PROVENANCE Perhaps J. P. Wierman Sale, Amsterdam, 18.viii.1762 (37: if identifiable with HdG no 294); Desenfans Sale, 1802 (75); Insurance List, 1804 (122); Bourgeois Bequest, 1811

LITERATURE Sm no 124; HdG, III, no 290 and almost certainly no 294

98 *A Woman with a Beer-jug*

Signed: *Av Ostade* (*Av* joined)

S. P. Denning, in his manuscript catalogue of 1858/9, noted that he thought the picture was by Dusart and the signature forged, but later writers accept it as genuine.

Panel, $6\frac{3}{8} \times 5\frac{5}{8}$in ($16.2 \times 14.2$cm)

PROVENANCE Bourgeois Bequest, 1811

LITERATURE HdG, III, no 221

113 *A Man Smoking*

Signed: *Av Ostade* (*Av* joined)

Although probably intended as a pendant to 98, Denning does not seem to have doubted the authenticity of this signature. Both seem to be late works.

Panel, $6\frac{3}{4} \times 5\frac{1}{2}$in ($17.1 \times 14.1$cm)

PROVENANCE Bourgeois Bequest, 1811

LITERATURE HdG, III, no 174

115 *Boors making Merry*

Signed and dated: *Av ostade 1647* (*Av* joined)

Panel, $10\frac{3}{4} \times 8\frac{1}{2}$in ($27.1 \times 21.6$cm)

PROVENANCE Probably the *Boors Singing* in Desenfans Sale, Skinner & Dyke, 28.ii.1795 (54); Insurance List, 1804 (44); Bourgeois Bequest, 1811

EXHIBITED RA, Dutch, 1952/3 (497)

ENGRAVING J. Suyderhoef before 1686, as *Jan de Moff*

LITERATURE Sm no 125; HdG, III, no 327; W. Bernt, *Netherlandish Painters of the 17th Century* (1970), II, pl 890

William **OWEN** *see* Archer James **OLIVER** (476)

Juan de **PAREJA** *see* Juan Bautista del **MAZO** (277)

Pierre **PATEL** *see* School of CLAUDE (53)

Jean-Baptiste **PATER** *see* Circle of WATTEAU (167)

Imitator of Jean-Baptiste **PATER** (1695–1736)

620 *Encampment of Soldiers*

Like Circle of Watteau, 167, this was formerly attributed to Lancret. Both pictures derive from the work of Watteau, but this seems a rather poor pastiche of a military scene by Pater. Lancret never painted such scenes, although they were common in Watteau's earlier period (*eg* pictures in Glasgow and London, Soane Museum). This may well be an English imitation.

Canvas, $19\frac{5}{8} \times 24\frac{1}{2}$in ($49.8 \times 62.2$cm)

PROVENANCE Bequest of Miss Gibbs, 1951

PIERO DI COSIMO (*c* 1462–?1521)

Piero di Cosimo's eccentricities—such as living on hard-boiled eggs—are described by Vasari. He worked with the pedestrian Florentine painter Cosimo Rosselli in the 1480s, but his own highly personal style seems to have developed after 1500, although there are no securely dated works to act as a guide to his development. He was influenced by Leonardo da Vinci.

258 *A Young Man*

This is probably a work of about 1500 or a little later, although it is not of the same high quality as the two Sangallo portraits of *c* 1505 now in Amsterdam. It is also somewhat damaged and has been cut, apparently on all four sides, although it now has an added strip at the bottom: if it was always intended as a portrait (and is not a donor-portrait cut out of a damaged altarpiece), on the analogy of the Sangallo pair it would have been about 4in wider and would have a strip about 1in at the top as well as a deeper strip with a painted parapet at the bottom—*ie* the whole would have been about $27\frac{3}{4} \times 20$in. An X-ray has shown that the hair was originally shorter and less full. *Pentimenti* are also visible in the shoulders.

It was first recorded in Desenfans' collection as by Leonardo da Vinci and it bore this attribution until 1854, when Waagen attributed it more reasonably to Boltraffio. The attribution to Piero di Cosimo was first made by Frizzoni in 1879, and followed by Richter in his 1880 Catalogue. It has been generally accepted ever since, although Mina Bacci tentatively suggested (1966) Ridolfo Ghirlandaio, mainly on the grounds of admitted similarity to a portrait belonging to the Earl of Plymouth, which she (and others) have denied to Piero.

Panel, $15\frac{3}{8} \times 16$in (38.7×40.5cm). A strip $3\frac{7}{8}$in (9.8cm) wide has been added at the bottom

PROVENANCE Desenfans Insurance List, 1804 (69); Bourgeois Bequest, 1811

EXHIBITED NG 1947 (30); Florence, Lorenzo de' Medici, 1949 (XII, 3)

LITERATURE G. F. Waagen, *Treasures of Art in Gt Britain* (1854), II, 346; G. Frizzoni in *Archivio Storico Italiano* (1879), ser. IV, 258; L. Douglas, *Piero di Cosimo* (1946), 76, 110 (with bibliography); B. Berenson, *Italian Pictures . . . Florentine School* (1963), I, 175; M. Bacci, *Piero di Cosimo* (1966), 109, 125 (tentatively ascribed to R. Ghirlandaio); *id*, *L'opera completa di Piero di Cosimo* (Milan, 1976), no 66 (as ?Piero)

PIETRO DA CORTONA (1596–1669)

Pietro Berrettini was born in Cortona but worked mainly in Rome, where, with Bernini and Borromini, he was one of the leading exponents of Roman High Baroque, both in painting and in architecture. His principal work in painting was the huge ceiling in the Barberini Palace (1633–9), but he also painted a very important series of frescoes in the Pitti Palace, Florence (*see* 121), and rebuilt the church of SS. Martina e Luca in Rome (*see* 226), where he is buried.

121 *The Age of Bronze*

This is the only known *modello* for the Age of Bronze fresco in the Pitti Palace, Florence. In 1637 Pietro was commissioned by the Grand Duke to paint the Camera della Stufa in the palace with a series of the Four Ages of Mankind—Gold, Silver, Bronze and Iron—from Ovid's *Metamorphoses* (I), and for the next ten years he worked in the Palace on this and other schemes. There are at least seven drawings known—one in Dulwich—for this fresco. The Dulwich drawing differs mainly in the group of figures in the foreground. Campbell suggests a date after 1641 for the fresco, so the *modello* must be datable 1637/41, probably *c* 1640.

Canvas, $32\frac{1}{4} \times 25\frac{7}{8}$in ($81.9 \times 65.4$cm)

PROVENANCE Desenfans Sale, Skinner & Dyke, 27.ii.1795 (76: *Vespasian rewarding his Soldiers*); Bourgeois Bequest, 1811. (The drawing was lent to the Gallery by H. Yates Thompson in 1913 and subsequently given by him.)

DRAWINGS Apart from the one in the Gallery, others are in the Uffizi, Florence; Munich; Prague; Metropolitan Museum, New York (2); and a private collection

LITERATURE M. Campbell, *Pietro da Cortona at the Pitti Palace* (Princeton, N.J., 1977), 46–58 and pls 10, 13–18 (not including the Dulwich painting or drawing)

After PIETRO DA CORTONA

226 *Sta Martina calling down Lightning on the Idols*

Sta Martina was a Roman girl martyred at Ostia in 228 for refusing to sacrifice in the Temple of Apollo. In 1634 what were thought to be her remains were found in Rome in a chapel belonging to the Painters' Guild. It was rebuilt (and partly paid for) by Pietro da Cortona himself, and is now in the church of SS. Luca e Martina. The original picture of *c* 1656, slightly smaller, is in the Pitti Palace, Florence, and a replica, still smaller and on copper, is in the Louvre, Paris. Our painting seems to be a copy rather than an autograph replica.

Canvas, $45\frac{3}{8} \times 34\frac{1}{4}$in ($115.3 \times 87$cm)

PROVENANCE The *Triumph of Religion* described in Desenfans 1802 Catalogue does not correspond at all closely, but 226 is certainly the *Triumph of Religion* in the 1813 Inventory (147); Bourgeois Bequest, 1811

VERSIONS Apart from those mentioned above, there is one reproduced by Briganti as in a Florentine private collection; his version in an English private collection is perhaps 226

LITERATURE G. Briganti, *Pietro da Cortona* (Florence, 1962), 258–9, nos 128–30, 275 (as replica), pls 271, 272 (the Pitti original and the Florentine private collection)

Cornelis van **POELENBURGH** (*c* 1586–1667)

Poelenburgh was an Utrecht painter who was in Rome by 1617, where he was influenced by the works of Elsheimer and his followers. He returned to Holland before 1627, and visited London in 1637 to work for Charles I.

25   *Nymphs and Satyr*

Signed: *C.P*

A characteristic example of Poelenburgh's small Italianate landscapes with mythological—or sometimes religious—subject-matter. Compare the works of Breenbergh (23, 26, 338) and Hoet (176, 179) in this Gallery.

Panel, $15\frac{1}{8} \times 20\frac{1}{4}$in ($38.4 \times 51.2$cm)

PROVENANCE Desenfans Sales, Christie's, 12.v.1785 (29) and 8ff.iv.1786 (61); perhaps 14.vii.1786 (13, bt Podd—*ie* bt in?); probably Desenfans Sale, Skinner & Dyke, 28.ii.1795 (27); Bourgeois Bequest, 1811

Gaspard **POUSSIN** *see* Gaspar DUGHET

Nicolas **POUSSIN** (1594–1665)

Poussin was born in Normandy, but went to Paris *c* 1612 and worked there until he went to Rome in 1624, where he spent almost all the rest of his life. He was persuaded to return to Paris in 1640 to work for the King and Cardinal Richelieu, but, after some 18 months, he returned to Rome in 1642 and remained there. Much of his work was for French patrons and he never felt at home in the world of Baroque patronage, since, like his early master, Domenichino, he represents the pure Classical tradition. His work had enormous influence in France, but many of his best works are (or were) in England: the Dulwich group is one of the finest collections.

203   *A Roman Road*

Very probably painted in 1648 as a pendant to the *Landscape: a man washing his feet at a fountain* (National Gallery). Both these paintings have been denied to Poussin, and the fact that X-rays show the beginnings of another composition by Poussin underneath the Dulwich picture has been regarded as evidence that it is a copy. Anthony Blunt, however, regards both our picture and the National Gallery landscape as originals, in spite of the figures in the X-ray which correspond closely with three in *Moses trampling on Pharaoh's Crown* (Louvre, Paris). Turner, in a lecture in 1811, praised it as 'a powerful specimen of Historic landscape'.

Canvas, $31\frac{1}{4} \times 39\frac{3}{8}$in (79.3 × 100cm)

PROVENANCE Referred to by Félibien as belonging to the Chevalier de Lorraine in 1685; Desenfans 1802 Catalogue (55); Bourgeois Bequest, 1811

EXHIBITED Paris, Louvre, Poussin, 1960 (84)

ENGRAVING E. Baudet, in or before 1684

VERSIONS At least three recorded by Blunt

LITERATURE A. Félibien, *Entretiens sur les vies . . . des plus excellens peintres . . .* (1688) (1725 edn) IV, 59; Sm no 310 (as *c* 1650 for M. Passart—but his picture is now identified with one in Ottawa); A. F. Blunt, *Poussin* (1967), 253, 257, 291f., 296 and pl 184; *id, Poussin Catalogue* (1966), no 210; J. Thuillier, *Tout l'oeuvre peint de Poussin* (Paris, 1974), no 157* (as a copy of lost original)

234   The Nurture of Jupiter

According to Greek myth, the young Jupiter was brought up on the island of Crete by two nymphs, Adrastea and Ida, and fed on honey and the milk of the goat Amalthea. The most likely literary source is Callimachus's *Hymn to Jupiter*—'Adrastea lulled thee in a golden cradle; thou suckedst the full teat of the goat Amalthea, and moreover atest sweet honey'. It is not unlikely that Poussin was conscious of the parallel with *Isaiah*, vii, 14–15: 'Butter and honey shall he eat'. The actual composition is partly derived from one by Giulio Romano, engraved by Bonasone, and perhaps also from a woodcut in the 1546 French edition of the *Hypnerotomachia Poliphili*. The painting is generally dated in the mid-1630s—Blunt puts it at 1636/7—but Thuillier, uniquely, is doubtful of its autograph quality and dates it *c* 1639, the generally accepted date for the version of the subject in Berlin.

Canvas, $37\frac{7}{8} \times 47\frac{1}{8}$in (96.2 × 119.6cm)

PROVENANCE Blondel de Gagny Collection, Paris, by 1757; his Sale, Remy, Paris, 10.xii.1776 (94); Ogilvie Sale, Christie's, 7.iii.1778 (85: as ex-Gagny), bt Campbell; Desenfans by 1804 (Insurance List, no 55); Bourgeois Bequest, 1811

EXHIBITED BI 1816 (117); RA, French Art, 1932 (173: Commemorative Catalogue no 120); NG 1947 (35); RA, Landscape, 1949/50 (24); Paris, Louvre, Poussin, 1960 (48)

LITERATURE A. Dézallier d'Argenville, *Voyage pittoresque de Paris*, 3rd edn (Paris, 1757), 279; Sm no 208 (wrongly as *Bacchus*); W. Friedländer, *Poussin* (1966), 152 and pl 111; A. F. Blunt, *Poussin* (1967), 148, 150 and pls 106, 108, 109; *id, Poussin Catalogue* (1966), no 161; J. Thuillier, *Tout l'oeuvre peint de Poussin* (Paris, 1974), no 120

236   The Triumph of David

The subject represents David with the head of Goliath (I *Samuel*, xvii, 54; xviii, 6–9): 'And David took the head of the Philistine, and brought it to Jerusalem . . . the women came out of all cities of Israel, singing and dancing, to meet King Saul, with tabrets, with joy, and with instruments of musick. And the women answered one another as they played, and said, Saul hath slain his thousands, and David his ten thousands. And Saul was very wroth . . . And Saul eyed David from that day and forward'. Saul may be the figure on the extreme right. X-rays show that there have been many changes, particularly in the architecture, and it is thought that the picture was painted in two stages, beginning before 1628 and completed after 1631, the group of women on the left showing stylistic differences from the central group of a woman with two children. Another version of the same subject (Prado, Madrid) is quite different. *See* colour plate VIII.

Canvas, $46\frac{5}{8} \times 58\frac{3}{8}$in ($118.4 \times 148.3$cm)

PROVENANCE Pierre Lebrun, Paris, sold to B. Vandergucht, London, before 1771; 2nd Lord Carysfort by 1776; C. A. de Calonne, *c* 1787; his Sale, Skinner & Dyke, London, 26.iii.1795 (92), bt Desenfans; Bourgeois Bequest, 1811

EXHIBITED BI 1816 (19); NG 1947 (33); Paris, Louvre, Poussin, 1960 (9)

ENGRAVING/DRAWINGS Two drawings are in the Royal Library, Windsor, and Chantilly. Engraved by S. Ravenet, 1776, with arms of Lord Carysfort

LITERATURE Letter to Desenfans from J. B. Lebrun, 25 February 1789, printed in G. F. Warner, *Catalogue of the Manuscripts . . . at Dulwich* (1881), 212–14; W. Buchanan, *Memoirs . . .*, I, 252; Sm no 38; W. Friedländer, *Poussin* (1966), 31 and fig 18 (as early 1630s); A. F. Blunt, *Poussin* (1967), 59, 70ff., 73, 127 and fig 67 and pls 15–17; *id, Poussin Catalogue* (1966), no 33; J. Thuillier, *Tout l'oeuvre peint de Poussin* (Paris, 1974), no B.76 (as possibly 1632/3 or maybe by Mellin imitating Poussin)

238   *Rinaldo and Armida*

The subject is from Torquato Tasso's heroic poem *Gerusalemme Liberata*, completed in 1575, which deals with the liberation of Jerusalem from the heathen by the First Crusade. Rinaldo, the imaginary Christian hero, has been enchanted by the magic powers of Armida, the Saracen heroine, but, as she is about to kill him, she is overwhelmed by love—'E di nemica ella divenne amante' (Canto XIV, lxvii). X-rays show that Poussin seems to have begun another picture, perhaps of a related subject, beneath this one: he also painted several others on themes from Tasso's poem, which he interpreted allegorically, in this case perhaps as Reason conquering Concupiscence. It was formerly believed that this was the picture of *Rinaldo and Armida* painted for Jacques Stella about 1637/8, but that one, now lost, is known from copies and it is generally agreed that our picture must be much earlier: Thuillier dates it *c* 1625, Blunt 'before 1630' and Friedländer 1635.

Canvas, $32\frac{3}{8} \times 43$in (82.2×109.2cm)

PROVENANCE Possibly Anon. Sale, Christie's, 29.iv.1788 (88); Desenfans by 1804 (Insurance List, 55); Bourgeois Bequest, 1811

EXHIBITED NG 1947 (32); Paris, Louvre, Poussin, 1960 (14)

ENGRAVING G. Audran (with additions at top); P. Dupin, 1722

LITERATURE Sm no 286; W. Friedländer, *Poussin* (1966), 49–50 and fig 39; A. F. Blunt, *Poussin* (1967), 83, 90, 148–50 and pls 58–9; *id, Poussin Catalogue* (1966), no 202; J. Thuillier, *Tout l'oeuvre peint de Poussin* (Paris, 1974), no 24

240   *The Return of the Holy Family from Egypt*

This painting has often been called a *Flight into Egypt*, but must, in fact, represent the much rarer subject of the Return to Israel (*Matthew*, ii), since the Child is at least two years old and the vision of the cross is meaningful only on His return: 'Out of Egypt have I called my son'. There is another version of the subject, formerly in the Liechtenstein Collection, Vienna, and now in the Cleveland Museum, Ohio, but it is now thought that the Cleveland version is not an original work by Poussin (contrary to the general view earlier this century): the problem is complicated by a full description of this unusual subject in a poem by Hilaire

Pader, published in 1653. Pader describes the boatman bringing his boat to the bank where Mary and Joseph are with the Child, who contemplates a vision of the Cross, raising His hands and opening His mouth ('Sa belle bouche semble estre preste à parler/Pour chérir une Croix qu'il apperçoit par l'air,/Que des enfants aislés de l'empirée apportent . . . Il élève les mains et monstre par son geste/Que son coeur reconnoist la machine céleste'). Both the Dulwich and Cleveland pictures have winged cherubs, but only in the Cleveland version does the Child raise both hands; on the contrary, the Dulwich version seems better to express the open-mouthed recognition of the Cross, so it may well be that Pader's description applies to our picture, though Blunt doubts this. Further, as Mitchell points out, the symbolism in 240, with the boatman as Charon and the implication of the river of Death, is more subtle than in the Cleveland version. Friedländer, however, thinks that the boatman is not Charon but 'Christophoros' (presumably S. Christopher).

Desenfans recorded the picture in his 1802 Catalogue—the only one of all the Poussins now in the Gallery to be so listed—and identified it with a *Flight into Egypt* known to have been painted for Mme de Montmort, but that picture is now identified with one in Leningrad, and ours is dated much earlier: 1628/9 by Blunt, 1629/30 by Thuillier, and 1637/8 by Friedländer.

Canvas, $46\frac{3}{8} \times 39\frac{1}{8}$in (117.8 × 99.4cm)

PROVENANCE J. Purling in 1792; his Sale, White, London, 16f.ii. 1801 (47), bt Burch (?Bourgeois); Desenfans by 1802 (1802 Catalogue, 53); Bourgeois Bequest, 1811

EXHIBITED NG 1947 (34)

ENGRAVING J. Fittler, 1792

LITERATURE Sm no 86; C. Mitchell in *Journal of the Warburg Institute* (1937–8), I, 340, with rep. and rep. of Cleveland picture; W. Friedländer, *Poussin* (1966), 43 and fig 31; A. F. Blunt, *Poussin* (1967), 128, 184 and pl 36; id, *Poussin Catalogue* (1966), no 68; J. Thuillier, *Tout l'oeuvre peint de Poussin* (Paris, 1974), no 60

263 *Sta Rita of Cascia*

The identification of the subject of this picture presents considerable difficulty. X-rays show that Poussin originally painted a nymph in a landscape on this panel, but, as the nymph is now unusually large in scale for Poussin's work, it is probable that he turned the panel upside down and trimmed it before re-using it for a new subject. The panel has certainly been cut at the top and both sides, and probably also at the base; so that it may be suggested that the present subject is a traditional Assumption with the empty tomb and the group of apostles missing at the bottom. The panel, however, is only about $\frac{1}{4}$in thick, and was, therefore, originally not much more than $2\frac{1}{2}$ to 3ft high and perhaps 2ft wide, which would hardly allow so great an addition to the composition. A second difficulty is that the city in the background is obviously an important feature, and it has been convincingly identified by Blunt as Spoleto: the Cathedral of Spoleto is dedicated to Maria Assumpta (not to the Assumption) and it would therefore be reasonable to assume that the work was commissioned by, or for, a Spoletan. In 1813 the picture was recorded as *Ascension of the Virgin*; ten years later as *Apotheosis of the Virgin*; and in 1880 as *Translation of a Female Saint*. It is proposed here that Sta Rita of Cascia (*d* 1457) meets all the requirements, because of her connection with Spoleto, and especially with the Barberini family. Rita was born near Spoleto and wished to be a nun, but submitted to her parents' wishes and married. For some 20 years she endured a thoroughly bad husband, and, after his violent end, she applied to join an Augustinian convent at Cascia, near Spoleto. She was rejected at first, but was carried through the air into the convent, after which she was accepted by the community. After her death her cult became popular in the district and continued to spread, so that Urban VIII

Barberini authorised the cult in 1626 and beatified her in 1627. Her usual attributes are a white veil (present here) and, more importantly, a thorn in the forehead, but it is not possible to say whether this was ever represented in our picture. Nothing is now visible, but, since the picture is recorded as having 'paint rubbed off' in 1813, it may have disappeared. The Barberini-Spoleto connection is much strengthened by the fact that Urban himself had been Bishop of Spoleto and was succeeded there by his nephew Cardinal Francesco Barberini (Cardinal from 1623), and it is known that the Papal architect was working on the Cathedral from about 1626.

Poussin is not known to have visited Spoleto; was first recorded as a landscape painter in 1630; and almost never painted recognisable topographical views—certainly no other picture of his can be compared with this. The attribution has, therefore, been frequently questioned, but the X-rays seem to have settled that objection. The most likely date is in the 1630s, so that it is one of Poussin's earliest landscapes: Blunt dates it *c* 1635, Mahon at 1636/8, Thuillier 1630/40.

Panel, $19\frac{1}{4} \times 14\frac{7}{8}$in ($48.8 \times 37.8$cm)

PROVENANCE Blunt suggested that it may have been painted for Poussin's regular patron, Cassiano del Pozzo, who was connected with Cardinal Barberini, but there is an Inventory of Taddeo Barberini of 1648–9 which records 'un quadretto della B. Rita in taffetta giallo con Cornice . . .', without naming the painter; Bourgeois Bequest, 1811

EXHIBITED BI 1823 (135); NG 1947 (31); RA, Landscape, 1949/50 (26); Paris, Louvre, Poussin, 1960 (43)

LITERATURE *Acta Sanctorum*, May, V, (22 May) for the early *Life* of Sta Rita; A. F. Blunt in *Burl.Mag.* (1948), XC, 8; *id*, *Poussin* (1967), 269f., 272, pl 95; *id*, *Poussin Catalogue* (1966), no 94; D. Mahon, *Poussiniana* (1962), xiii; W. Friedländer, *Poussin* (1966), 76 (as attributed to Poussin); *Bibliotheca Sanctorum* (1968), XI, 212ff.; J. Thuillier, *Tout l'oeuvre peint de Poussin* (1974), no 96; M. Lavin, *Seventeenth Century Barberini Documents . . .* (New York University, 1975), 202, no 316

481 *Venus and Mercury*

This is part of a larger composition which once included several more children to the left. A fragment with a group of five children is now in the Louvre, Paris, and was once attached to the lower left-hand part of 481. Above the Louvre fragment there was once a strip about 8in high and at least 20in wide. It is not known when the picture was cut up, but it was probably about 1764. The composition as a whole is known from a drawing by Poussin and an engraving by F. Chiari dated 1636. Venus and Mercury were the parents of Cupid, but the struggle between the winged Eros and the goat-legged Anteros is probably intended as an allegory of the triumph of poetical love over sensuality, the two aspects of Venus.

The painting was formerly regarded as a copy, but, since the Paris exhibition of 1960, it has become accepted as an original, now dated by Blunt *c* 1627/9.

Canvas, $31\frac{1}{2} \times 34\frac{1}{2}$in ($80 \times 87.6$cm)

PROVENANCE Almost certainly in the Lankrinck Sale, Smith & Bassett, London, 11.i.1693 (309); J. Meijers Sale, Willis, Rotterdam, 9.ix.1722 (2); Elector of Cologne Sale, Paris, 1764 (52), bt Basan; Anon. Sale, Christie's, 11.ii.1778 (22), bt Lebrun (who was often in partnership with Desenfans); ?Desenfans; Bourgeois Bequest, 1811

EXHIBITED Paris, Louvre, Poussin, 1960 (35)

VERSIONS Blunt lists one in the museum at Lille and three others, all showing the whole composition

LITERATURE Sm no 196; A. F. Blunt, *Poussin* (1967), 108f., 112, 114, 134, figs 104, 105 and pls 33*a* and *b*; *id*, *Poussin Catalogue* (1966), no 184; J. Thuillier, *Tout l'oeuvre peint de Poussin* (Paris, 1974) no 32A

Copy after **POUSSIN**

227 *The Adoration of the Magi*

An old copy of the painting of 1633 in Dresden.

Canvas, $50\frac{7}{8} \times 55\frac{1}{2}$in ($129.2 \times 141$cm)

PROVENANCE Sir Edward Walpole (*d* 1784); Sir J. Reynolds Sale, Christie's, 17.iii.1795 (98), bt Lawrence (?bt in); Reynolds Sale, Phillips, 9.v.1798 (47), bt Bourgeois; Desenfans Insurance List, 1804 (49); Bourgeois Bequest, 1811

EXHIBITION Ralph's Exhibition (*ie* Reynolds Collection), 1791 (77)

LITERATURE Sm no 56 (with wrong provenance); A. F. Blunt, *Poussin Catalogue* (1966), no 44 (as copy of Dresden picture); J. Thuillier, *Tout l'oeuvre peint de Poussin* (Paris, 1974), no 75* (copy of Dresden picture)

Cornelis **PRONK** (1691–1759)
Pronk (or Pronck) was an Amsterdam painter who began as a portraitist, but who later specialised in topographical drawings and designs for porcelain made (from 1734) for the Dutch East India Company, sent for manufacture in China. His paintings are extremely rare and this is probably the only one in this country.

615 *Unknown Man*

Signed and dated: *am 1714/C. Pronk*

The letters *am* presumably are the final letters of Amsterdam, the rest being concealed by the fold in the paper. It is known that Pronk's portraits were painted in his early period.

Canvas, $35\frac{3}{8} \times 27\frac{5}{8}$in ($90.5 \times 70.2$cm)

PROVENANCE Gift of Professor C. D. Broad, 1946

Adam **PYNACKER** (1622–73)
Pynacker was born in Delft and spent three years in Italy. He settled in Amsterdam and, like Berchem and Both, became one of the leading Italianate landscape painters in Holland.

86 *Landscape with Sportsmen and Game*

Signed: *A Pynacker* (*AP* in monogram)

This is a characteristic Italianate landscape by Pynacker (compare with the similar one in the Wallace Collection), but the blue leaves in the foreground are rather unusual. Their shape is quite common in Pynacker's works (a landscape in Bonn has identical leaves), but the blue colour is probably due to the fading out of a yellow (gamboge?) which was mixed with the blue to make green.

Canvas, $54\frac{1}{4} \times 78\frac{1}{4}$in ($137.8 \times 198.7$cm)

PROVENANCE Possibly in C. Backer (1633–81) Collection; C. Backer Sale, Leyden, 16.viii.1775 (4), bt Delfos; van Leyden Sale, Paris, 10.ix.1804 (75), bt Paillet; Desenfans; Bourgeois Bequest, 1811

EXHIBITED Almost certainly BI 1824 (81: as Pynacker and Berchem); RA, Dutch, 1952/3 (445); NG 1976 (83)

VERSIONS Possibly HdG no 72

LITERATURE Sm no 28; HdG, IX, no 9 (and also perhaps no 72—decoration in the house of C. Backer, Amsterdam); H. Gerson in *Burl.Mag.* (1953), XCV, 34, 51 and fig 26

183 *Bridge in an Italian Landscape*

Recorded as signed in the 1880 Catalogue, but this was a confusion with 86.

Panel, $17\frac{1}{4} \times 20\frac{3}{4}$in ($43.8 \times 52.7$cm)

PROVENANCE C. A. de Calonne; his Sale, Skinner & Dyke, 24.iii.1795 (46); Desenfans; Bourgeois Bequest, 1811

EXHIBITED BI 1824 (81); RA, Dutch, 1952/3 (285)

LITERATURE Sm no 17; HdG, IX, no 74; S. Reiss, *A. Cuyp*, 1975, 176 (rep., emphasising its similarity to a Cuyp in the Royal Collection)

Allan **RAMSAY** (1713–84)
Ramsay was born in Edinburgh, the son of the author of *The Gentle Shepherd*. He was trained in Italy and settled in London, where his cosmopolitan style was not approved by the local face painters. He was appointed Painter to George III, but he spent much time in travel and social life so that his fame has been eclipsed by Reynolds.

Attributed to **RAMSAY**

596 *Unknown Man*

The strong French influence is comparable with that in several signed portraits by Ramsay of the later 1740s, but both Hudson and Cotes seem possible alternative attributions.

Canvas, 30×25in (76.2×63.5cm)

PROVENANCE Unknown; Fairfax Murray Gift, 1915

LITERATURE A. Smart (letter in the Gallery archives) rejects the attribution to Ramsay and suggests Hudson, in the mid- or late 1740s

RAPHAEL (1483–1520)
Raffaello Sanzio, better known as Raphael, was the son of a minor painter in Urbino. After his father's death he studied in Perugia with Perugino, about 1500, and his work at this date was almost indistinguishable from his master's. By about 1504, however, he was in Florence, and the altarpiece from which our panels come is one of the first works in which he begins to absorb the new Renaissance ideas, which, in less than a decade, he was himself to advance to such a high degree. He went to Rome about 1508, and from then until his premature death at 37 he was fully occupied with the Vatican frescoes, the cartoons (now in the V & A Museum) for the Sistine Chapel tapestries, and other great undertakings.

241
243
S. Francis of Assisi and *S. Anthony of Padua*, from the *Colonna Altarpiece*

About 1504/5 Raphael was commissioned by the Franciscan nuns of Perugia to paint an altarpiece for the Church of S. Antonio da Padova. This was described by Vasari as consisting of two main panels—a *Madonna and Child Enthroned with Saints*, and a lunette of *God the Father with Angels*—and a predella with three scenes from the Passion. In addition, there were two small figures of SS. Francis and Anthony, perhaps on the base of the frame. The two main panels and one predella are now in the Metropolitan Museum, New York; another predella is in the Gardner Museum, Boston; and the third, the *Carrying of the Cross*, is in the National Gallery, London. That panel is generally thought to be entirely Raphael's own work, but the Dulwich pair have been damaged and may be only partly by his own hand, although Oskar Fischel, the greatest modern authority on Raphael, said in 1935 that both were his work.

S. Francis of Assisi (c 1181–1226), one of the most famous of medieval saints, was the founder of the Order, and S. Anthony of Padua (1195–1231) was the patron of the church for which the altarpiece was painted. S. Francis is recognisable by the Stigmata which he received in 1224. Unfortunately, damage and restoration (pre-1880) to 241 have removed the marks from hands and feet, but the wound in the side, together with the facial type, make the identification certain. S. Anthony was a Portuguese, who was one of the first Franciscans and is identified by the lily.

Panel, (241) 10⅛ × 6⅝in (25.8 × 16.8cm);
(243) 10⅛ × 6½in (25.6 × 16.4cm)
Both panels have a strip added at the side, but these are very old and probably original

PROVENANCE Painted for S. Antonio, Perugia; sold with the three predelle ('cinque quadretti di divotione') to Queen Christina of Sweden in Rome, 1663; passed with other pictures of hers to Livio Odescalchi, Duca di Bracciano, c 1689; passed to Prince Baldassare Odescalchi-Erba, Rome; sold to the Regent Orléans, Paris, 1721, and recorded in Orléans Catalogue, 1786; brought to England with the Orléans Collection, and probably exhibited 26 December 1798 at the Bryan Gallery and acquired by Desenfans before 1804; Bourgeois Bequest, 1811

EXHIBITED RA 1902 (12, 17)

LITERATURE Vasari, *Vite* (1568), ed. Milanesi (1879), IV, 324f.; G. F. Waagen, *Treasures of Art in Gt Britain* (1854), II, 346—'neither by Raphael . . . nor Perugino'; O. Fischel in Thieme-Becker, *Allgemeines Lexikon der bildenden Künstler* (1935), XXIX, 434; id, *Raphael* (1948), I, 46; C. Gould, *Italian 16th Century* (NG Catalogue, 1962), no 2919; L. Dussler, *Raffael, Krit. Verzeichnis* . . . (1966), no 25 (and cf 90) and English edn (1971); B. Berenson, *Italian Pictures . . . Central and North Italian Schools* (1968), I, 351, as partly autograph

Copy after **RAPHAEL**

507   *The Transfiguration*

Raphael was originally commissioned to paint an altarpiece for the Cathedral at Narbonne by Cardinal Giulio de' Medici, *c* 1517. The picture, which represents both the Transfiguration of Christ on Mount Tabor (*Mark*, ix, 2–13; *Matthew*, xvii, 1–13) and the unrelated miracle of the healing of the possessed boy (*Mark*, ix, 14ff. and *Matthew*, xvii, 14ff.), was still unfinished when Raphael died in 1520 and was finally placed in S. Pietro in Montorio in Rome, 1523, where it remained until stolen by Napoleon and exhibited in Paris 1797–1815. It is now in the Vatican Museum. Vasari records that after Raphael's premature death his assistants Giulio Romano and Gianfrancesco Penni completed some of his unfinished works and began a copy of the *Transfiguration* which, after they fell out, was completed by Penni and went to Naples. This is certainly the picture now in the Prado, Madrid. It was probably on account of the description given in Vasari that the Sale Catalogue of 1796 described our version as 'visibly by Julio Romano'. In fact, all three versions are approximately the same size and ours may well be Italian and 16th century. It was formerly ascribed to Pierino del Vaga, but there does not seem enough evidence for so precise an attribution. (*This picture is in the College Chapel.*)

Canvas, 148¼ × 104¼in (376.6 × 264.8cm)
(The original is on panel, 405 × 278cm)

PROVENANCE   B. Vandergucht (*d* 1794); his Sale, Christie's, 11.iii.1796 (92), bt Thomas Mills, of Saxham Hall, Sussex, and presented by him, 1796

LITERATURE   Vasari, *Vite* (1568), ed. Milanesi (1879), IV, 646 (for Penni's copy); L. Dussler, *Raphael, a Critical Catalogue* (1971), 52–4 (for details of the original and the Madrid copy)

REMBRANDT van Ryn (1606–69)

Rembrandt, the greatest of Dutch painters, was the son of a miller at Leyden. His early works were influenced by Caravaggio and Elsheimer, whom he probably learned about from his master, Pieter Lastman. By 1628 Rembrandt was sufficiently established to have a pupil of his own, Dou (*see* 56). He moved to Amsterdam in 1631 or 1632 (*see* 99) and became a successful portrait painter there for about ten years. His wife died in 1642, and then his fortunes declined until 1656, when he was declared bankrupt. During these years of adversity his art became deeper and his insight into human nature ever more profound.

99   *Jacob III de Gheyn*

Signed and dated: *RHL van Ryn/1632* (RHL in monogram) and inscribed on the back:
JACOBUS GEINIUS IUNᴿ/ H . . . NI IPSIUS/EFFIGIE/EXTREMUM MUNUS MORIENTIS/R/. . . MO.I E.STE. UN. HABET ISTA SECUNDUM HEV:

The inscription refers to the bequest of the sitter's portrait, and identifies him. Jacob de Gheyn (*c* 1596–1641) was the son and grandson of artists and practised as an engraver, and probably also as a painter, but later became a canon of Utrecht. He was a friend of the Huygens family, and visited London in 1618 with Constantijn Huygens, brother of the Maurits Huygens who inherited this portrait. The companion portrait by Rembrandt of Maurits is in the Kunsthalle, Hamburg.

Panel, 11⅞ × 9¾in (29.9 × 24.9cm)

PROVENANCE J. de Gheyn, bequeathed by him to M. Huygens (*d* 1642); Huygens family; A. R. van Waay Sale, Utrecht, 27.ii.1764 (123); possibly Desenfans Private Sale, 8ff.vi.1786 (264: 'Rembrandt, A head, 1ft. by 11in. on pannel'), not in later Desenfans Catalogues; perhaps van Leyden Sale, Paris, 10.ix.1804 (152); Bourgeois Bequest, 1811

EXHIBITED RA 1899 (16); NG 1947 (36); Edinburgh 1950 (5); Amsterdam, Drie Eeuwen . . ., 1952 (136); RA, Dutch, 1952/3 (126); V & A, Orange and the Rose, 1964 (59, 60) together with the Hamburg picture

LITERATURE HdG, VI, no 745; H. E. van Gelder in *Oud Holland* (1943), LX, 33 (first identifying Gheyn) and (1953), LXVIII, 107; A. Bredius, rev. by H. Gerson, *Rembrandt* (1969), no 162; B. Haak, *Rembrandt* (1969), 81–3, with colour pls of 99 and the Hamburg picture

163   *Girl leaning on a Window-sill*
Signed and dated: *Rembrandt/ft. 1645*

The girl seems to be about 14, which makes the identification with Hendrickje Stoffels, first documented in Rembrandt's household in 1649, unlikely, as she was probably about 20 in 1645. There are several variations by Rembrandt on this theme (*eg* in the Royal Collection). X-rays have shown that the top was originally different, and the restoration of the late 1940s removed a green curtain in the background.

Canvas, $32\frac{1}{8} \times 26$in (81.6×66cm)

PROVENANCE In England (Lord Polwarth Collection?) by 1774, when a drawing by A. G. Scott was made, and a copy by Reynolds, *c* 1780, now in the Hermitage, Leningrad; before then perhaps in France (copy by Santerre, early 18th century); Desenfans Private Sale, 8ff.iv.1786 (390: as *Dutch Woman*, 33 × 29in framed); Insurance List, 1804 (88); Bourgeois Bequest, 1811

EXHIBITION BI 1815 (14) and 1843 (107); RA 1899 (32); NG 1947 (37); Edinburgh 1950 (21); Amsterdam, Drie Eeuwen . . ., 1952 (142); RA, Dutch, 1952/3 (122)

DRAWING Executors of Count Seilern

LITERATURE Sm no 178; HdG, VI, no 327; O. Benesch, *Rembrandt Drawings* (1955), IV, no 700 and fig 841 (for Seilern drawing); A. Bredius, rev. by H. Gerson, *Rembrandt* (1969), no 368; B. Haak, *Rembrandt* (1969), 190 and colour pl and rep. of Reynolds copy

221   *A Young Man, perhaps the Artist's Son Titus*
Signed and dated: *Re . . . f . . . 63*

Formerly regarded as the work of a pupil or imitator, this portrait was attributed to Rembrandt himself and identified as his son Titus (1641–68) by Valentiner in 1921; subsequent cleaning revealed the traces of a signature and date (Valentiner had suggested 1658 on stylistic grounds). The attribution to Rembrandt is now universally accepted, but there is less agreement over the identity of the sitter. The earliest gallery records call him Wouwerman, but that would be very unlikely, since Philips Wouwerman was 44 in 1664. *See* colour plate II.

Canvas, $31 \times 25\frac{1}{4}$in (78.6×64.2cm)

PROVENANCE Possibly Calonne Sale, Skinner & Dyke, 23ff.iii.1795 (3rd day, 78); Bourgeois Bequest, 1811

EXHIBITED RA, Dutch, 1952/3 (179); Rotterdam 1956 (93: *Young Man*, not Titus)

LITERATURE Sm no 443(?); HdG, VI, no 705; W. R. Valentiner, *Rembrandt, Wiedergefundene Gemaelde* (KdK, 1921), XXIII and pl 86; A. Bredius, rev. by H. Gerson, *Rembrandt* (1969), no 289 (as ?Titus)

Guido **RENI** (1575–1642)

Reni was the great exponent of Bolognese Classicism in the generation after the Carracci, by whom he was much influenced. He worked in Rome for a few years at the beginning of the 17th century and was temporarily influenced by Caravaggio (who is said to have threatened to kill him), but returned to a more idealised Raphaelesque style.

262   *S. John the Baptist in the Wilderness*

'I am the voice of one crying in the wilderness' (*John*, i, 23). The composition is closely based on the *Baptist* by Raphael (Accademia, Florence) and is now generally dated in the last years of Reni's life, *c* 1640/2. The picture belonged to the Balbi family of Genoa for generations, but during the Napoleonic upheavals several British dealers attempted to buy it and other pictures. James Irvine, who acted for William Buchanan (*cf* Rubens, 148), saw the Balbi pictures in Piedmont and wrote to Buchanan on 12 May 1804, that he was disappointed by them as they had suffered from over-cleaning—'the St John and St Jerome of Guido are almost the only pictures that are untouched, and worth about 700 guineas each'. His offer must have been too low, for another Scottish dealer, Andrew Wilson, secured the *S. John* and also the *S. Jerome* (now in the Detroit Institute of Arts) and others in January 1805, subsequently selling the *S. John* to Desenfans for 1,000 guineas. *See* colour plate I.

Canvas, $88\frac{3}{4} \times 63\frac{7}{8}$in (225.4 × 162.2cm)

PROVENANCE Probably in Genoa by 1678; Balbi di Piovera family, Genoa; bt by A. Wilson, 1805; Desenfans before March, 1807; Bourgeois Bequest, 1811

EXHIBITED BI 1816 (50); RA 1950/51 (298); Bologna, Reni Exhibition, 1954 (18)

VERSIONS Of the three versions of this subject recorded by Malvasia before 1678 ours is now known to be the one in Genoa: the others may be the equally large, and very similar, picture in Temple Newsam House, near Leeds, which was in England by 1808, and the rather different version now in a private collection in Rome (Garboli and Baccheschi, no 106)

DRAWING A drawing in Dresden is closer to the Roman version than to 262

LITERATURE C. Malvasia, *Felsina Pittrice* (1678), II, 65 (recording three versions, one in Genoa); W. Buchanan, *Memoirs* . . ., II, 151, 166 (for Irvine's letters); T. Constable, *Life . . . of Archibald Constable* (1873), I, 107 (letter describing the picture and recording Desenfans' purchase of it from Wilson); O. Kurz in *Jahrbuch der k.k. Sammlungen in Wien* (1937), NF XI, 189ff.; (D. Mahon) Reni Exhibition Catalogue (Bologna, 1954), no 18 (with history); C. Gnudi and G. Cavalli, *Reni* (Florence, 1955), 96, no 102, and pls 176–8; C. Garboli and E. Baccheschi, *L'opera completa di Guido Reni* (Milan, 1971), no 204 and pl LVI

Attributed to **RENI**

204   *Lucretia*

Lucretia was the wife of Tarquinius Collatinus and was raped by her cousin Sextus, son of Tarquinius Superbus, King of Rome. She told her husband and then stabbed herself. He, with his friends, overthrew the Tarquin dynasty in 510 BC and established a Republic. Lucretia became an example of female virtue which lasted for more than 2000 years and was often treated by poets, painters, and composers—Britten's *Rape of Lucrece* being the latest of a long line. There are several versions of this composition by Guido Reni, but none seems to be the original, which may have been the one in the Sanford Collection in 1839. The original may have dated from *c* 1620.

Canvas, 39 × 29⅜in (99 × 54.6cm)

PROVENANCE Perhaps Christie's, 8.iv.1788 (78); Bourgeois Bequest, 1811

VERSION One was in a Swiss private collection in 1973

LITERATURE B. Nicolson in *Burl.Mag.* (1955), XCVII, 207 (on the Sanford pictures); C. Garboli and E. Baccheschi, *L'opera completa di Guido Reni* (Milan, 1971), no 124

Sir Joshua **REYNOLDS**, PRA (1723–92)

Reynolds was the son of a clergyman and became the most important figure in British art of the 18th century. He went to Italy in 1749, returning in 1752 and setting up in London in the following year, determined to introduce the principles of Italian Renaissance and Baroque art into what was a routine procedure of face-painting. With Gainsborough he became the leading portrait painter in London. He was also a friend of Johnson and Goldsmith and his intellectual interests and powers made him the leading figure in the arts. His appointment as President of the new Royal Academy (1768) and his knighthood were tributes to his work in raising the standard of British painting as much as to his own work as a painter.

17a *A Girl with a Baby*

One of a series of sketches of children, some with titles like *Robinetta, Puck, The Infant Academy*, mostly dating from the 1780s. Many, like this one, were technical experiments which have deteriorated badly.

Panel, 29½ × 24½in (74.9 × 62.2cm)

PROVENANCE Beechey before 1811 (*see* 17), and perhaps bought by him at one of the Reynolds Sales which contained sketches and unfinished works; presented by Beechey, 1836

LITERATURE Graves and Cronin, *Works of Sir J. Reynolds* (1899–1901), 4 vols, contains many similar subjects, but none can be identified with 17a with certainty

102 *Recovery from Sickness, an Allegory*

A sketch for an unexecuted history painting, showing the child's guardian angel warding off Death. The title is that given in the Reynolds Sale of 1796, but the Inventory of 1813 calls it *Mother and Sick Child*. Probably painted 1768/9.

Canvas, 27⅞ × 23⅞in (70.8 × 91.1cm)

PROVENANCE Reynolds Sale, Greenwood's, 16ff.iv.1796 (3rd day, 16), bt Bourgeois; Desenfans Insurance List, 1804 (96); Bourgeois Bequest, 1811

LITERATURE Graves and Cronin, *Works of Sir J. Reynolds* (1899–1901), III, 1191; E. K. Waterhouse, *Reynolds* (1941), 60 (as 1768/9); R. Paulson, *Emblem and Expression* (1975), 92 and pl 48

104 *Self-portrait*

Reynolds painted a self-portrait in spectacles in 1788; what is presumably the original, presented by his niece, Lady Thomond, to George IV, is now in the Royal Collection, but there are several replicas, more or less by his own hand, made for friends. Two similar versions in London are those in the Wellington Museum, Apsley House, and the Iveagh Bequest, Kenwood. Ours is probably a studio repetition.

Canvas, 30 × 25⅛in (76.2 × 63.8cm)

PROVENANCE Bourgeois Bequest, 1811

LITERATURE Graves and Cronin, *Works of Sir J. Reynolds* (1899–1901), II, 806

223 *The Infant Samuel*

The subject is from I *Samuel*, iii, 10: 'The Lord . . . called . . . Samuel, Samuel. Then Samuel answered, Speak; for thy servant heareth'. Reynolds painted several versions of the story. Hannah More described a visit to his studio in 1776: 'I wish you could see a picture Sir Joshua has just finished of the prophet Samuel on his being called . . . Sir Joshua tells me that he is exceedingly mortified when he shows this picture to some of the great; they ask him who Samuel was'.

Canvas, 30⅛ × 27⅛in (76.3 × 68.9cm)

PROVENANCE Reynolds Sale, Greenwood's, 16ff.iv.1796 (3rd day, 12), bt Bourgeois; Desenfans Insurance List, 1804 (6); Bourgeois Bequest, 1811

LITERATURE Graves and Cronin, *Works of Sir J. Reynolds* (1899–1901), III, 1202; IV, 1467

318 *Mrs Siddons as the Tragic Muse*
Inscribed: *REYNOLDS PINXIT 1789*

This is a version, painted for Desenfans, of the original of 1784, now in the Henry Huntington Art Gallery, San Marino, Calif. In keeping with the grandeur of the subject, Reynolds has adapted Michelangelo's *Isaiah inspired by Genii* in the Sistine Chapel of the Vatican. Sarah Siddons was the sister of J. P. Kemble and perhaps the greatest tragic actress of the 18th and 19th centuries (she retired in 1812, just before her brother—*see* Beechey, 111). Her account of the genesis of the picture is probably no more untruthful than is usual in the memoirs of actresses: 'About this time he produced what is reported to be the finest female Picture in the world, his glorious Tragedy. In tribute to his triumphant Genius, I cannot but remark his instantaneous decision on the attitude and expression. In short, it was in the twinkling of an eye.

'When I attended him for the first sitting, after many more gratifying encomiums than I dare repeat, he took me by the hand, saying, "Ascend your undisputed throne, and graciously bestow upon me some grand Idea of the Tragick Muse". I walked up the steps and seated myself instantly in the attitude in which She now appears. This idea satisfied him so well that he without one moments hesitation determined not to alter it. . . . He . . . most flatteringly added, "And to confirm my opinion, here is my name, for I have resolved to go down to posterity upon the hem of your garment" '.

Reynolds's ledger shows that our picture was a replica; but, since the price was so high, it may well be largely by Reynolds himself—'Feb. 1790. Mrs Siddons—sold to Mr Desenfans £735'.

Canvas, 94⅜ × 58⅛in (239.7 × 147.6cm)

PROVENANCE Bought from Reynolds by Desenfans, 1790; Bourgeois Bequest, 1811

EXHIBITED International Exhibition, 1862 (110); Port Sunlight, Lady Lever Gallery, 1949 (171); Hayward Gallery, Georgian Playhouse, 1975 (98)

ENGRAVING J. Bromley, 1832

LITERATURE Graves and Cronin, *Works of Sir J. Reynolds* (1899–1901), III, 892ff.; IV, 1411; W. T. Whitley, *Artists and their Friends* . . . (1928), II, 10–13; M. Cormack in *Walpole Society* (1970), XLII, 164 (Reynolds's ledger)

333   *A General on Horseback*

'This portrait is asserted by some to be that of Lord Albemarle, by others of Lord Ligonier: we leave the decision to those who have known them': thus the Desenfans 1802 Catalogue, but it seems certain that the General is not Albemarle, and the *Ligonier*, now in the Tate Gallery, is not very close in pose. Our sketch was probably made as an experiment for a possible portrait of a victorious general, based on Bernini's equestrian statue of Louis XIV. Two such sketches were in the sale of Reynolds's portraits, studies and sketches, held in 1796, and, as Sir Francis Bourgeois bought them both, it is impossible to be sure which this one is. It was previously catalogued as 'English School', but is clearly the picture recorded in the 1813 Bourgeois Inventory (127: Reynolds, *An Officer (Military) on Horseback*). The *Ligonier*, though not directly connected, is probably of about the same date—*ie* early 1760s.

Canvas, $30\frac{3}{8} \times 25\frac{1}{4}$in (77.2 × 64.1cm)

PROVENANCE Reynolds Sale, Greenwood's, 14ff.iv.1796 (49: *General on horseback, a sketch* or 52: *A sketch, of a general on horseback*), both bt Bourgeois; Desenfans 1802 Catalogue (187); Bourgeois Bequest, 1811

LITERATURE Graves and Cronin, *Works of Sir J. Reynolds* (1899–1901), III, 1090 (identifying 333 with no 52 in the 1796 Sale)

598   *Robert Dodsley*

Inscribed: *To/Mr Dodsley/in Bruton [Street] London* on the envelope

Robert Dodsley (1703–64) was a celebrated publisher who started life as a footman. His authors included Pope, Johnson, Goldsmith and Gray and he also published *A Select Collection of Old Plays* (1744), as well as founding, with Edmund Burke, the *Annual Register*, which still appears. This portrait was begun in 1760/61 and was given to his friend the poet Shenstone in exchange for one of him.

Canvas, $29\frac{7}{8} \times 25$in (75.8 × 63.5cm)

PROVENANCE W. Shenstone (*d* 1763); returned to Dodsley family and passed by descent to James Dodsley Tawney; passed to Miss Cuff; Miss Charles, Bristol; bequeathed to Miss Wigmore; Christie's (Different Properties), 10.xii.1898 (62), bt Lesser; H. Y. Thompson; presented by him in memory of George Smith, founder of the *Dictionary of National Biography*, 1917

LITERATURE Graves and Cronin, *Works of Sir J. Reynolds* (1899–1901), I, 255–6; IV, 1299; E. K. Waterhouse, *Reynolds* (1941), 48; M. Cormack in *Walpole Society* (1970), XLII, 116 (Reynolds's Ledger, 1760–61); J. Kerslake, *Early Georgian Portraits* (NPG Catalogue, 1977) (*s.v.* Dodsley)

Copy after **REYNOLDS**

627   *Margaret Desenfans*

Margaret Morris was one of three sisters, all of whom were painted by Reynolds. Their brother John (later Sir) owned Clasemont, Glamorgan, and Margaret is said to have brought Desenfans a dowry of £5000, with which he began to collect pictures (*see* Introduction, p 18). This is a copy by M. Ayoub of the original Reynolds, which belonged to Agnew's in 1930. The original was engraved in 1757, as Miss Margaret Morris.

Canvas, $29\frac{7}{8} \times 25$ in (75.9×63.5 cm)

PROVENANCE Commissioned by the Governors, 1930

Jusepe **RIBERA** *see* Francesco FRACANZANO (558)

Neapolitan Follower of Jusepe **RIBERA** (?1591–1652)

233 *The Locksmith*

The saying 'Love laughs at locksmiths' has an equivalent in most languages, but this painting probably illustrates a proverb, certainly known in Naples before 1634: 'Chiave incinto, Martino dinto'—which may be rendered 'You can lock up your wife/daughter and keep the key on your belt, but her lover will get in'. For a reason not immediately obvious Martino is a Neapolitan term for a cuckold, and on S. Martin's day popular processions made allusion to deceived husbands. In 1801 the picture was attributed to Caravaggio and called 'the Famous Bolognese Locksmith, of singular character'; by 1813 (Bourgeois Inventory) he had become 'of Antwerp', neither being easily explicable. The attribution to Caravaggio lasted until 1854, when Waagen suggested Pietro della Vecchia, which was rightly rejected by Richter (1880 Catalogue) in favour of Ribera. The style, however, does not seem his, although the subject is close to many of his works: Francesco Fracanzano (*see* 558) and his brother Cesare (*c* 1605–53) both have points in common with the style of the *Locksmith*, but not sufficient to warrant a positive attribution. Another possibility is Bartolomeo Passante (1618–48).

Canvas, $52\frac{1}{8} \times 39\frac{1}{4}$ in (132.3×99.5 cm). The strip at the top may be an addition

PROVENANCE Earl of Bessborough Sale, Christie's, 6–7.ii.1801 (77); Bourgeois by 1810; Bourgeois Bequest, 1811

LITERATURE G. Basile, *Pentamerone*, 2a Giornata, 1634 or earlier; G. F. Waagen, *Treasures of Art in Gt Britain* (1854), II, 347; C. Speroni, *Proverbs . . . in Basile's Pentameron* (University of California Publications in Modern Philology, 1941), XXIV, 2, 181ff.; N. Zingarelli, *Vocabolario della Lingua Italiana* (*s.v.* Martino)

Sebastiano **RICCI** (1659–1734)

Ricci was the first of the itinerant Venetian painters of the 18th century, working all over Italy, in Vienna, and in London from *c* 1712 until 1716. He failed to get the commission for the decoration of the dome of St Paul's, as well as Hampton Court Palace, but he was given the commission for Chelsea Hospital Chapel (*see* 195), as well as Burlington House and other private houses. Many of his works are in the Royal Collection, including several which show how closely he could imitate Veronese, his great Venetian predecessor; indeed, he may have produced several pastiches of Veronese.

134   *The Fall of the Rebel Angels*

Michael the Archangel is shown thrusting down the rebel angels: *Epistle of Jude*, 6; 'And the angels which kept not their first estate, but left their own habitation, he hath reserved in everlasting chains under darkness unto the judgment of the great day'. Perhaps part of a S. Michael series, dating from *c* 1720.

Canvas, $32\frac{1}{4} \times 26\frac{5}{8}$in (81.9 × 67.6cm), excluding added strip at bottom

PROVENANCE Probably Marshal Schulenburg by 1738; his Sale, London, 12–13.iv.1775; Bourgeois Bequest, 1811

DRAWINGS Five drawings at Windsor Castle and one in the Accademia, Venice, are related. These came from Consul Smith's collection and he may have owned 134 as well. The drawings date from *c* 1720

LITERATURE A. F. Blunt and E. Croft-Murray, *Venetian Drawings at Windsor* (1957), 62, nos 355–9 and rep.; A. Binion in *Burl.Mag.* (1970), CXII, 297; J. Daniels, *S. Ricci* (Hove, 1976), no 176; *id, L'opera completa di S. Ricci* (Milan, 1976), no 372 and colour pl 48 (as *c* 1720)

195   *The Resurrection*

One of two *modelli* for the painting in the chapel of the Royal Hospital, Chelsea, executed by Sebastiano Ricci while he was living in London, 1712–16. The other sketch (now in the Columbia Museum of Art, S. Carolina, U.S.A.) is slightly larger and has minor variations, both from the finished work and 195. The payments were made to Marco Ricci, Sebastiano's nephew, but this was probably because Marco had been in England for some years and was handling his uncle's business affairs.

Canvas, $34\frac{3}{4} \times 46\frac{3}{4}$in (88.3 × 118.7cm)

PROVENANCE Bourgeois Bequest, 1811

EXHIBITED NG 1947 (38); Twickenham, Marble Hill, English Baroque Sketches, 1974 (73)

LITERATURE J. von Derschau, *S. Ricci* (1922), 87; M. D. Whinney and O. Millar, *English Art, 1625–1714* (Oxford, 1957), 301, n 1; E. Croft-Murray, *Decorative Painting in England, 1537–1837* (1970), II, 267; *English Baroque Sketches* (exhibition catalogue), Marble Hill, 1974, no 73 (with earlier literature and rep.); J. Daniels, *S. Ricci* (Hove, 1976), no 177; *id, L'opera completa di S. Ricci* (Milan, 1976), no 328 (as *c* 1715 and the earlier of the two *modelli*)

Hyacinthe **RIGAUD** (1659–1743)
Rigaud won the second Prix de Rome in 1682, which entitled him to study in Italy, but did not take it up. He became the principal official Portrait Painter to Louis XIV, and, with the help of a large studio, produced an average of 35 portraits a year for 62 years.

83   *Nicolas Boileau*

Boileau (1636–1711) was the founder of French literary criticism. He was a friend of Racine and, with him, Historiographer Royal to Louis XIV. His commonsense approach to criticism was admired in England, especially by Pope and Dryden. According to Rigaud's account-book he painted a portrait of Boileau for M. Coustard in 1704. The original and a replica are at Versailles and 83 is a second replica.

Canvas, $31\frac{7}{8} \times 25\frac{5}{8}$in (81 × 65.1cm)

PROVENANCE Bourgeois Bequest, 1811

ENGRAVING Drevet (from the Versailles original)

LITERATURE J. Roman (ed.), *Le livre de raison du peintre Rigaud* (Paris, 1919), 107

Studio of **RIGAUD**

85   *Louis XIV*

Louis XIV (1638–1715), King of France. The manufacture of portraits of *le roi soleil* was a flourishing industry: this derives from the larger portraits in the Musée des Beaux-Arts, Bordeaux, and the Prado, Madrid, which can be dated *c* 1701.

Canvas on panel, $36 \times 28\frac{3}{8}$in (91.4×72.1cm)

PROVENANCE Bourgeois Bequest, 1811

93   *A Man, called Racine*

There is no reason to believe that Rigaud ever painted Racine (1639–99), since Rigaud's account-book does not mention him. James Boaden, the author of a Memoir of Kemble (1825), claimed to have given Desenfans a portrait of Racine by Rigaud 'during the French Revolution'—*ie* some 25 to 35 years earlier. If so, neither Desenfans nor Bourgeois can have believed in the identification, since this is undoubtedly 42 in the 1813 Inventory—*A Man*, and was so catalogued until the present century.

Canvas, $31\frac{1}{2} \times 25$in (80×63.5cm)

PROVENANCE Presumably a French emigrant; James Boaden; given to Desenfans 'during . . . the French Revolution'; Bourgeois Bequest, 1811

LITERATURE J. Boaden, *Memoirs of the Life of . . . Kemble* (1825), II, 437

John **RILEY** (1646–91)
Riley was the leading portrait painter in England between Lely and Kneller. He was a pupil of Soest, but nothing is known of his work before 1680 (though *see* 568). In 1688 he was appointed Principal Painter, jointly with Kneller, to William and Mary.

565   *John, Lord Somers, Lord Chancellor of England*

John Somers was a Whig lawyer who rose to fame after 1688. He was made Solicitor-General and knighted in 1689, Attorney-General in 1692 and created Baron Somers in 1697. He died in 1716. An 18th-century inscription on the back gives the history of the picture and calls it: 'Sʳ John Sommers Knight/by Mʳ Riley . . .'. Since Riley died in 1691 and Somers was knighted in October 1689, the picture was probably painted *c* 1690, when Somers was 39.

Canvas, $27\frac{3}{4} \times 25$in (70.5×63.5cm)

PROVENANCE The inscription quoted above continues: 'Given to Sir Philip Yorke by the Right/Honᵇˡᵉ Sʳ Robt. Walpole Knight of/The most noble order of yᵉ Garter'. This must have been 1726/33, when Yorke became Lord Hardwicke; passed by descent; Fairfax Murray; his Gift, 1911

568 *William Chiffinch*

William 'Backstairs' Chiffinch (*c* 1602–88) was an intriguing politician, who pimped for Charles II, ingratiated himself with the royal mistresses, and was the receiver of the secret pension paid to Charles by Louis XIV. There are several versions of this portrait, in the National Portrait Gallery, Salisbury Town Hall, and elsewhere, but this is generally agreed to be the original, dating from about 1680 or earlier. It was formerly attributed to Riley's master, Gerard Soest (*d* 1681), but has been recognised as a fine Riley since 1912.

Canvas, $29\frac{7}{8} \times 25\frac{1}{4}$in (76.1 × 64.4cm)

PROVENANCE One or other of the versions occur in several 18th- and 19th-century sales, but it is not clear which; E. A. Bulwer, Dereham, Norfolk; his Sale, Christie's, 19.xi.1910 (115: as Soest), bt Agnew; Fairfax Murray Gift, 1911 (as Soest)

LITERATURE Vertue, *Notebooks*, II, 131; V, 55; C. H. Collins-Baker, *Lely and the Stuart Portrait Painters* (1912), II, 23 (as Riley); *id* in *Onze Kunst* (1915), 106; D. T. Piper, *Catalogue of 17th Century Portraits* (NPG Catalogue, 1963), 70–71

George **ROMNEY** (1734–1802)
Romney came to London from Lancashire in 1762, visited Paris in 1764, and then went to Italy 1773–5. He returned to London to compete with Reynolds and Gainsborough as a portrait painter, and to waste much of his talent in projects for history pictures.

440 *Dr Joseph Allen*, MD, *Master of Dulwich College*

Under the original Foundation the Wardenship and Mastership of Dulwich College were reserved for men named Alleyn or Allen. Joseph Allen (1713–96), after sailing round the world with Anson, became Warden (1745–6) and Master (1746), until, in 1775, at the age of 62, he resigned in order to marry. The College Minutes record (4 September 1775) that 'he be desired to sit for his picture', but no artist is named. 'Dr Allen' occurs in Romney's sitter-book for October and November 1778, but, like many of his portraits, this seems to have remained unfinished, although valued at 36 guineas. The statue of Aesculapius, on the right, is a reference to Allen's medical training.

Canvas, $50\frac{1}{2} \times 40\frac{1}{4}$in (128.3 × 102.2cm)

PROVENANCE Commissioned by Dulwich College, 1775/8

ENGRAVING C. Townley

LITERATURE H. Ward and W. Roberts, *Romney* (1904), I, 87 (sittings in Oct–Nov 1778); II, 3

590 *William Hayley*

William Hayley (1745–1820) was a poet and biographer, but is best known as a member of the Blake–Flaxman–Romney circle of Neoclassically-minded artists. He wrote a poem on Painting, which was dedicated to Romney, as well as his *Life of Romney*, published in 1809. His *Painting* was published in 1778 and was therefore probably inspired by this portrait: he sat to Romney on several occasions in 1777, 1778, 1779, and 1788, but this was certainly painted in 1777/8 or 1778/9. He also sat to the sculptor Flaxman, as is proved by Romney's *Flaxman modelling a Bust of Hayley*, now in the Paul Mellon Collection, U.S.A.

Canvas, 30 × 25in (76.2 × 63.3cm)

PROVENANCE W. H. Mason in 1868; Colnaghi; Fairfax Murray by 1904; his Gift, 1911

EXHIBITED National Portrait Exhibition, 1868 (859), lent by W. H. Mason

ENGRAVING Johann Jacobé, 1779; T. Holloway, 1786; W. Ridley, 1798

LITERATURE W. Hayley, *George Romney* (1809), 71; H. Ward and W. Roberts, *Romney* (1904), I, 54ff. and rep.; II, 74, no 1; A. Chamberlain, *Romney* (1910), 332 and pl IV (as earliest and best of the Hayley portraits)

Salvator **ROSA** (1615–73)

Born in Naples, where he was a pupil of Fracanzano (*see* 558), Rosa worked mainly in Rome and Florence. His landscapes, especially those with battles or brigands, are the forerunners of Romanticism and were extremely popular in the 18th century, particularly in England, where 'savage Rosa' appealed to Gothick tastes. He was one of the first painters to sell his works through public exhibition rather than on commission, which would have limited his freedom. He was also active as an etcher, poet, and actor.

216   *Soldiers Gambling*

Signed: *S Rosa* (*SR* in monogram)

This was formerly regarded as a study for a picture in The Hermitage, Leningrad, which is now thought to be a copy of our picture. The standing soldier was etched, in reverse, and with some variations, by Rosa himself *c* 1656, and the painting probably dates from the same time, Rosa's second Roman period.

Canvas, $30\frac{3}{8} \times 24\frac{1}{4}$in (77.1 × 61.6cm)

PROVENANCE Desenfans 1802 Catalogue (12); Bourgeois Bequest, 1811

LITERATURE L. Salerno, *L'opera completa di S. Rosa* (Milan, 1975), no 136 and rep.

Sir Peter Paul **RUBENS** (1577–1640)

Rubens was born in Germany, but his family came from Antwerp and he became a Master in the Guild there in 1598. The decisive factor in his style was the eight years he spent in Italy (1600–8), which included a short visit to Madrid in 1603 and a period in Rome, when he received an important commission for the new Church of the Oratorians, the Chiesa Nuova. On his return to Antwerp he was made Court Painter to the Spanish Governors of The Netherlands, married his first wife, Isabella Brant, and received commissions for the altarpieces of the *Raising of the Cross* and *Descent from the Cross* (1610–14), which established him as the leading Baroque painter in Northern Europe. He created a large and productive picture-factory, with assistants of the quality of van Dyck, Jordaens and Snyders, to help him cope with the flood of grand-scale commissions, *eg* the decorations for the new Jesuit church in Antwerp, commissioned in 1620, almost all of which were burnt in 1718, but which are known from his sketches (125). In later years he continued his diplomatic activities and made a second visit to Madrid, where he was friendly with Velazquez, and, in 1629, to England as mediator between Spain and Charles I, who knighted him and commissioned the ceiling of the Banqueting House in Whitehall (1630–35, Rubens's only surviving ceiling). In 1630 he married Hélène Fourment as his second wife (131).

19   *Aeneas with the Arms of Mezentius*

The subject is taken from Virgil's *Aeneid* (XI, 1–18):

> The pious chief . . . performed a victor's vows:
> The coat of arms by proud Mezentius worn . . .

> Was hung on high, and glittered from afar,
> A trophy sacred to the god of war . . .
> Appeared his plumy crest, besmeared with blood . . .
> And on the right was placed his corselet bored;
> And to the neck was tied his unavailing sword.

It was certainly a design intended for reversal—*eg* a tapestry—since the sword is worn on Aeneas's right side. At least two other possible Aeneas subjects (in America) were identified before 1947 by Burchard as tapestry designs, all probably dating from *c* 1622/5. However, in June 1979 four large tapestry cartoons, in body-colour on paper, by Rubens and of subjects from the *Aeneid* (including the *Arms of Mezentius*) were acquired by the National Museum of Wales, Cardiff, from an anonymous Central European source. These cartoons, previously unknown, are thought to date from *c* 1630. They are all much squarer in format and the *Mezentius* varies in several details from 19—the trophy and the position of the legs are considerably altered and the landscape shows no buildings. They may well, therefore, be later revisions of the theme. It is however known that 19 was formerly much wider and more nearly approximated to the 3:2 proportion of the cartoons.

Panel, 20⅛ × 6¾in (51 × 16.8cm). The panel was formerly *c* 13½in wide, but was reduced to its present size about 1945

PROVENANCE Probably the painter G. A. Pellegrini (*d* 1741); Consul Smith, Venice (Catalogue no 39); sold by him to George III, 1762; not known how it left the Royal Collection, but Desenfans Insurance List, 1804 (26: as *Achilles* . . .); Bourgeois Bequest, 1811

EXHIBITED NG 1947 (42), identified by L. Burchard

LITERATURE F. Grossmann in *Les arts plastiques* (1948), 52 and rep.

40   *SS. Amandus and Walburga* and *SS. Catherine of Alexandria and Eligius*
40a

These two panels, until recently united, are the *modelli* for the outsides of the wings of the triptych of the *Raising of the Cross*, painted for S. Walburga's church in Antwerp, but now in the Cathedral. This very large altarpiece was the first great commission received by Rubens after his return from Italy and it shows the profound impression made upon him by Roman Baroque art. He was given the commission in 1610, after submitting these and other sketches for approval, and completed the work, for which he received the large sum of 2600 florins, about 1611. The church had a choir built above a road, so the altarpiece was seen from below, which accounts for the steep perspective. (A painting of 1661, now in S. Paul, Antwerp, shows the complete altarpiece in its original setting.) The sketch for the central part and the inner wings, once also in a British collection, is now in the Louvre, Paris.

Our two panels represent a quartet of rather unusual saints. S. Amandus of Maastricht (*d* 679) was famous as an apostle of the Low Countries, although his labours in the Antwerp area seem not to have been very successful; S. Walburga was an Englishwoman whose two brothers were also saints. She died about 776/9 and gave her name to 'Walpurgisnacht' (1 May). Although she seems to have had no connection with Flanders—she died in Germany—she was the patron of the church in Antwerp. S. Eligius was the patron saint of goldsmiths and was Bishop of Tournai, which accounts for his popularity in The Netherlands. He died in 660. The fourth saint, Catherine of Alexandria, may in fact never have existed, although she was far more popular as a female martyr supposedly of the early Christian period than any of the other three. Her usual emblem is a wheel, with or without the sword and palm shown here, but there seems no doubt that the identification is correct.

These *modelli* must have been made just before the contract was signed in June 1610, but there are several differences between them and the large picture, the most striking being the bishops' mitres, which are held in the air by cherubs in the final version. A drawing of S. Walburga (Executors of Count Seilern, London) is an intermediate stage.

Like several others in the Gallery, these *modelli* show the essential role played by the small oil-sketch in the genesis of many of Rubens's greatest works, but, like the *S. Ignatius* (148) this was, until quite recently, regarded as no more than a work of his school, or even by an imitator.

Panel, (40) 26¼ × 9⅞in (66.6 × 25cm);
    (40a) 26¼ × 9⅞in (66.6 × 25cm);

PROVENANCE Jacques de Roore Sale, The Hague, 4.ix.1747 (56); probably Desenfans Sale, Pall Mall, 8ff.iv.1786 (384)—'*An emblematical of the church*', panel, 35 × 29in including frame; Desenfans Insurance List, 1804 (101); Bourgeois Bequest, 1811

EXHIBITED NG 1947 (45); Rotterdam, 1953/4 (8, 9); Bruges 1956 (71); BM, Rubens Drawings and Sketches, 1977 (55, 56)

LITERATURE M. Rooses, *L'Oeuvre de Rubens* (Antwerp, 1886–92), II, 78; L. Burchard in National Gallery exhibition catalogue, 1947 (correct identification of the saints); J. R. Martin, *Corpus Rubenianum*, I, *The Ceiling Paintings for the Jesuit Church in Antwerp* (1968), 145, 168; id, *Rubens, The Antwerp Altarpieces* (1969), 38–43 (with reps. and comparative material); H. Vlieghe, *Corpus Rubenianum*, VIII, pt i, *Saints* (1972), 79, 96

43   *Ceres and Two Nymphs with a Cornucopia*

Ceres was the ancient Roman goddess of the harvest, and the horn of plenty is her symbol. This is a sketch for a large picture in the Prado, Madrid, in which the flowers and fruit were painted by Frans Snyders (1579–1657), who often collaborated with Rubens. A date *c* 1625/8 seems generally accepted, rather than the 1615/18 proposed by Oldenbourg.

Panel, 12¼ × 9⅝in (30.9 × 24.4cm)

PROVENANCE P. J. Snyers Sale, Antwerp, 23.v.1758 (11); Desenfans Insurance List, 1804 (123); Bourgeois Bequest, 1811

EXHIBITED NG 1947 (44: dated *c* 1625/8 by Burchard); Rotterdam, 1953/54 (70); BM, Rubens Drawings and Sketches, 1977 (185)

LITERATURE M. Rooses, *L'Oeuvre de Rubens* (Antwerp, 1886–92), III, 133, no 651 (i); R. Oldenbourg, *Rubens* (KdK, 1921), 126, 459

125   *S. Barbara fleeing from her Father*

S. Barbara was a 3rd- or 4th-century martyr, whose father, Dioscurus, shut her up in a tower to discourage suitors, and, when he discovered that she was a Christian, killed her. There is no evidence that such a martyr ever existed, but, because her father was supposed to have been struck by lightning, she was often invoked against that eventuality. Her emblem is a tower. In 1620 Rubens was commissioned to paint a series of ceiling and other decorations for the new Jesuit church in Antwerp, almost all of which—including the *S. Barbara*—were destroyed by fire in 1718. The first grisaille sketch for the S. Barbara ceiling in the south aisle is now in Oxford, but the *modello*, from which Rubens's assistants would have worked, is 125. Under the contract Rubens was permitted to retain the sketches and *modelli*, which has ensured the preservation of several.

Panel, $12\frac{7}{8} \times 18\frac{1}{8}$in ($32.6 \times 46.2$cm)

PROVENANCE Rubens; J. Sansot Sale, Brussels, 20.vii.1739 (22); A. and S. de Groot Sale, The
Hague, 20.iii.1771 (8), bt Schuller; Desenfans 1802 Catalogue (84); Bourgeois bequest, 1811

EXHIBITED NG 1947 (43); Rotterdam 1953/54 (29)

LITERATURE M. Rooses, *L'Oeuvre de Rubens* (Antwerp, 1886–92), I, 38, no 31 *bis*;
R. Oldenbourg, *Rubens* (KdK, 1921), 210, 463; J. R. Martin, *Corpus Rubenianum*, I, *The Ceiling
Paintings for the Jesuit Church in Antwerp* (1968), 37, 159–63 and pl 164 (with further literature)

131   *Hagar in the Desert*

The figure may be a portrait of Hélène Fourment, whom Rubens married, as his second
wife, in 1630. Originally, however, the figure of Ishmael at the left and of an angel in the sky,
proved that the story of Hagar was intended—*Genesis*, xxi, 14–19: 'She wandered in the
wilderness of Beersheba . . . and sat her down . . . and lifted up her voice and wept . . . and
the angel of God called to Hagar . . . and she saw a well of water; and she went, and filled the
bottle with water . . .'. The bottle is still visible, and an angel in the sky seems to have been
painted out, but the figure of Ishmael at the left is shown in an etching made *c* 1750. It seems
likely that Hagar was painted from Hélène Fourment, and the style agrees with a date after
1630 (Burchard dated it 1630/32). During the 19th century it was often wrongly called *The
Penitent Magdalen. See* colour plate VI.

Panel, $28\frac{1}{4} \times 28\frac{5}{8}$in ($71.5 \times 72.6$cm). The panel was originally about $33\frac{3}{4}$in (85.7cm) high and
also wider

PROVENANCE Augustin de Steenhaut, Brussels, v.1758, already cut down; Borremans, Brussels,
1781; Dubois, Paris, 1782; presumably Laborde Collection; in London before 1788; E. Coxe
Sale, P. Coxe, 23.iv.1807 (54: *Story of Hagar—Helena Forman*, Laborde Collection); Bourgeois
Bequest, 1811

EXHIBITED NG 1947 (41); RA, Holbein and Other Masters, 1950/51 (225); Flemish, 1953/4 (143)

VERSION A copy, reasonably attributed to Gainsborough (Mr and Mrs F. Marshall Collection,
London, 1973), proves that 131 must have reached London before 1788, when Gainsborough
died. It shows the picture in more or less its present state. An engraving by F. de Roy, in
reverse, of *c* 1750, shows it before it was cut down and includes Ishmael and the angel

LITERATURE Sm no 857 (also nos 604 and 634); M. Rooses, *L'Oeuvre de Rubens* (Antwerp,
1886–92), II, 323, no 471; and also I, 126f.; R. Oldenbourg, *Rubens* (KdK, 1921), 360; *id*,
Aufsätze (1922), 145, 147 (as portrait of Hélène Fourment); F. Grossmann in *Les arts plastiques*
(1948), 47ff.

143   *Catherine Manners, Duchess of Buckingham*(?)

Previously called *Marie de' Medici*, this portrait was identified from two drawings in the
Albertina, Vienna, one of which certainly represents the Duke and the other, certainly a
study for this portrait, presumably represents the Duchess. The painting, which is
unfinished, may well have been made from the drawing and not from life. She married the
Duke in 1620, but the black rosette she wears may refer to her widowhood—he was
murdered in 1628—and may indicate that the picture was begun in 1629 when Rubens was
in England.

Panel, $31\frac{3}{8} \times 25\frac{7}{8}$in ($79.7 \times 65.7$cm), apparently cut at the bottom. The *verso* is primed and has
several scribbles, which have been photographed by infra-red light, but which are certainly
not by Rubens

PROVENANCE Desenfans 1802 Catalogue (88: as Marie de' Medici); Bourgeois Bequest, 1811

EXHIBITED NG 1947 (40); RA, Holbein, 1950/51 (227), Paris, 1952/3 (76); RA, Flemish, 1953/4 (216); Bruges, 1956 (73: as not Duchess, but unknown French lady, *c* 1625, unfinished original)

LITERATURE Sm no 726 (School of Rubens); Glück and Haberditzl, *Die Handzeichnungen . . . Rubens* (Berlin, 1928), no 157 (identifying the sitter, but calling 143 a contemporary copy); G. Glück in *Burl.Mag.* (1940), LXXVI, 174 (by or after Rubens); F. Grossmann in *Les arts plastiques* (1948), 52ff.; *id* in *Burl.Mag.* (1957), XCIX, 56; C. Norris in *Burl.Mag.*, *ibid* 125; and F. Grossmann in *Burl.Mag.*, *ibid* 126; F. Huemer, *Corpus Rubenianum*, XIX, pt i, *Portraits*, Catalogue 6 and 6a, 110ff. and pls 57, 58 (as probably an unknown French lady, *c* 1625)

264 *The Three Graces*

A grisaille sketch, perhaps for an engraver to work from, based on the famous antique group of the Graces in Siena Cathedral or Raphael's small painting based on it (Musée Condé, Chantilly).

Panel, 15¾in (39.9cm) square

PROVENANCE John Bertels Sale, Great Room, King St., 9.v.1783 (43); Isaac Jermineau Sale, Christie's, 27.ii.1790 (16); European Museum Private Sale, 1792 (264); Bourgeois Bequest, 1811

LITERATURE M. Rooses, *L'Oeuvre de Rubens* (Antwerp, 1886–92), III, 100 (as doubtfully Rubens); J. Müller-Hofstede in *Pantheon* (1965), XXIII, 163ff. and rep. (as by Rubens and *c* 1631/2)

285 *Venus, Mars and Cupid*

Venus, though married to Vulcan, was the mother of Cupid by Mars. The same subject is shown in a sketch in Berlin, but the composition is different. A similar subject, *The Origin of the Milky Way*, was painted by Rubens for the King of Spain's hunting lodge, the Torre de la Parada, in 1636/8 and is now in the Prado, Madrid (sketch in Brussels). The figure of Venus is very close to that of Peace in the *Peace and War*, painted by Rubens for Charles I in 1629 and now in the National Gallery: both pictures show the influence of Titian, whose works Rubens had studied in Madrid in 1628. Our picture is dated by Burchard *c* 1636/8 because of resemblances to the Torre de la Parada series, but *c* 1630 has also been suggested. What may be a sketch for 285 was in the N. Fischmann Collection, London, in 1954: it shows armour on Mars's fore-arm, as is also seen in a drawing by Watteau (before 1720), and traces of the armour are still visible in the painting.

Canvas, 76⅞ × 52⅜in (195.2 × 133cm)

PROVENANCE Duc d' Orléans Collection, Paris (where seen by Watteau before 1720); Orléans Sale, iv.1793 (6); B. Vandergucht (*d* 1794); his Sale, Christie's, 11.iii.1796 (42), bt Egles; Bryan Sale, Coxe, 19.v.1798 (19); sold in Amsterdam, 27.iv.1803 (as ex-King of Poland Collection—*ie* probably ex-Desenfans, bt Josy); Bourgeois Bequest, 1811

EXHIBITED NG 1947 (39: with note by L. Burchard, dating it *c* 1636/8); RA, Holbein and Other Masters, 1950/51 (226); Flemish, 1953/4 (177); Antwerp, Rubens Exhibition, 1977 (100, as second half of the 1630s); NG 1979

ENGRAVING/VERSIONS Several copies are recorded in the Witt Library

LITERATURE Sm no 704; Dubois de Saint-Gelais, *Description des Tableaux du Palais Royal* (Paris, 1727), 414; Thiéry, *Guide des Amateurs . . . à Paris* (Paris, 1787), I, 244; W. Buchanan, *Memoirs . . .*, I, 288; M. Rooses, *L'Oeuvre de Rubens* (Antwerp, 1886–92), III, 188, 189, no 704 (as partly Rubens); R. Oldenbourg, *Rubens* (KdK, 1921), 330, 486; F. Grossmann in *Les arts plastiques* (1948), 47ff.

451 *Venus mourning Adonis*

The subject is from Ovid's *Metamorphoses*, at the end of Book X. Venus, who was deeply in love with the mortal Adonis, begged him not to go hunting, but he disregarded her pleas and was killed by a boar. Our painting is a sketch, with slight variations, for a large picture which dates from *c* 1614.

Panel, 19⅛ × 26⅛in (48.5 × 66.5cm)

PROVENANCE Perhaps the 'schetse van Rubens . . . eenen dooden Adonis' in the Inventory of Jeremias Wildens, 30.xii.1653 (649); perhaps European Museum Private Sale, London, 1792 (306: 'Death of Adonis—Venus and Cupid. Sketch for Madrid'); Bourgeois Bequest, 1811

EXHIBITED RA, Flemish, 1953/4 (195)

VERSION The 1813 Inventory describes 451 as 'the sketch for Mr Hope's picture'—*ie* the large painting owned (1977) by Messrs Duits and exhibited at Antwerp, Rubens Exhibition, 1977 (28)

LITERATURE Sm no 751; M. Rooses, *L'Oeuvre de Rubens* (Antwerp, 1886–92), III, 179, no 696; M. Jaffé in *Duits Quarterly* (1967), II, no 11 (rep. both pictures and with full literature)

Attributed to **RUBENS**

148 *S. Ignatius Loyola exorcising*

This may be the sketch for the large altarpiece by Rubens, delivered in 1620, of the *Miracles of S. Ignatius*, painted for the Jesuit church of S. Ambrogio, Genoa, and still there. There are, however, problems which make this small panel one of the most controversial pictures in the gallery. There are important differences between the *modello* and the finished altarpiece, which shows the saint looking up to heaven, not down and to the left, and there are many additional figures, principally an acolyte at the extreme left. These variations would usually be an argument in favour of the authenticity of our panel, and would permit a dating about 1619; but it has been argued that the quality of the painting is not good enough for Rubens himself, and in this connection it should be noted that the second Keeper of the Gallery recorded it as 'in a terribly damaged state; indeed all but destroyed'. The second argument against our panel is that of provenance (*see* below); Vlieghe records a sketch sold in London in 1823, many years after our panel came to Dulwich: 'Rubens. Our Saviour [*sic*] curing one possessed of an evil spirit, a sketch for the famous picture in the church of the Annunciation [*sic*] at Genoa—this celebrated study was in the possession of the Gentile family at Genoa'. This picture is now lost, and apart from the gross inaccuracy of the description, may never have had any right to the provenance claimed. The majority of modern scholars would probably accept 148 as an original *modello* by Rubens himself, but the position is analogous to that of the *modello* for the *Descent from the Cross*, now in the Courtauld Galleries, University of London.

Panel, 29 × 19¾in (73.7 × 50.2cm)

PROVENANCE Perhaps painted *c* 1619 for Niccolo Pallavicini, who commissioned the altarpiece for S. Ambrogio, Genoa; in Palazzo Gentile, Genoa, 1773; bt by J. Irvine for W. Buchanan, April/May, 1803; in Desenfans Insurance List, 1804 (21: as *S. Ignatius exorcising*); Bourgeois Bequest, 1811

LITERATURE *Description des Beautés de Gênes* (Genoa, 1773), 46; C. G. Ratti, *Istruzione di quanto puo vedersi . . . in Genova* (1780), 121; W. Buchanan, *Memoirs . . .*, II, 103, 129, 135; Sm no 347; M. Rooses, *L'Oeuvre de Rubens* (Antwerp, 1886–92), II, 293, no 455 *bis*; R. Oldenbourg, *Rubens* (KdK, 4th edn, 1921), 202; M. Jaffé, 'Rediscovered Oil Sketches by Rubens', II, in *Burl.Mag.* (1969), CXI, 529ff. and rep.; J. Müller-Hofstede, 'Neue Ölskizzen von Rubens' in *Staedel Jahrbuch* (1969), II, 190–4, 231–3 and rep.; H. Vlieghe, *Corpus Rubenianum*, VIII, pt ii, *Saints* (1973), 80ff., no 116a (with further literature, and arguing against Rubens's authorship)

165 *Venus and Cupid warming themselves (Venus frigida)*

Probably the original *modello* for the larger picture in the Akademie, Vienna. For the last century both have been regarded as studio productions, but Müller-Hofstede has recently published both as by Rubens himself, *c* 1610–20.

Panel, 14 × 18⅜in (35.5 × 46.6cm). A narrow strip at the bottom appears to have been added, but the 1813 Inventory shows the picture as an upright, 25 × 22in including the frame—*ie* about half as high again. All catalogues since 1876 give the present dimensions.

PROVENANCE Bourgeois Bequest, 1811

VERSION Apart from the Vienna picture, Rooses records one in the de Dom Collection in 1878, perhaps identical with one in the Weustenberg Collection, Berlin (59 × 82cm)

LITERATURE M. Rooses, *L'Oeuvre de Rubens* (Antwerp, 1886–92), III, 186; J. Müller-Hofstede in *Pantheon* (1967), XXV, 430ff. and rep. (with the Vienna picture)

Sir Peter Paul **RUBENS** *see* Sir Anthony van DYCK (132)

Jacob van **RUISDAEL** (1628/9–82)
Ruisdael was born in Haarlem and probably worked under his uncle Salomon van Ruysdael. About 1650 he went to the German border and saw mountains for the first time—in his later works (105) they give a more Romantic air to the scenery. He seems to have practised medicine in Amsterdam from 1676 to his death and to have painted less in these years. He was the most important painter of realistic landscape in the 17th century in Holland and his work was enormously influential on English landscape artists of the early 19th century—there is a copy by Constable of 168.

105 *A Waterfall*

Signed: *JvRuisdael* (*JvR* in monogram)

A late work.

Canvas, 38¾ × 32⅞in (98.5 × 83.4cm)

PROVENANCE Perhaps the 'upright landscape' in an undated Desenfans list of 'Pictures to be sold'; Bourgeois Bequest, 1811

EXHIBITED NG 1947 (46); RA, Dutch, 1952/3 (314)

LITERATURE Sm no 314; HdG, IV, no 247; J. Rosenberg, *Ruisdael* (Berlin, 1928), no 190

168 *Landscape with Windmills near Haarlem*

Signed: *JvR* in monogram

The church in the background is the Groote Kerk at Haarlem. Underneath the rider there are traces of a man leading a horse, but the change was probably made by the artist. There is a copy of this painting by Constable (private collection, London, in 1976), which may be the one he refers to in a letter of 4 February 1799—'I shall begin painting as soon as I have the loan of a sweet little picture by Jacob Ruysdael to copy...'. If so, the picture was in England by 1799. It is an early work, *c* 1650/52.

Panel, $12\frac{3}{8} \times 13\frac{3}{8}$in ($31.5 \times 33.9$cm)

PROVENANCE Perhaps in England by 1799; Bourgeois Bequest, 1811 (in Bourgeois Inventory as by Rembrandt)

EXHIBITED NG 1947 (47); RA, Dutch, 1952/3 (315)

LITERATURE Sm no 315; HdG, IV, no 175; J. Rosenberg, *Ruisdael* (Berlin, 1928), no 115; C. R. Leslie (ed. A. Shirley), *Memoirs of ... Constable* (1937), 12

Jacob van **RUISDAEL** *see* Jan WYNANTS (210)

Salomon van **RUYSDAEL** *see* Jakob van MOSCHER (16)

Herman **SAFTLEVEN** (1609–85)
Herman was the younger brother and pupil of Cornelis Saftleven and worked mostly in Utrecht. About the middle of the century he journeyed in the Rhineland, and his most characteristic works are views of rivers with steep banks, seen from a high viewpoint and executed with miniature-like precision.

44 *View on the Rhine*

Signed: *HSL* (in monogram)/*1656*

The monogram is easily misread, and until 1880 was thought to be that of Jan Vorsterman, Saftleven's pupil. The view is probably largely imaginary, but is very similar to other 'Rhenish' landscapes in Munich and Mainz, dated 1652 and 1653.

Panel, $16\frac{7}{8} \times 22\frac{3}{4}$in ($42.8 \times 57.8$cm)

PROVENANCE Said to have been imported into England by Moses Vanhausen, 1783; very probably Desenfans Private Sale, 8ff.iv.1786 (391: Vorsterman); Bourgeois Bequest, 1811 (as Vorsterman)

EXHIBITED NG 1947 (48)

Gerard **SANDERS** (*c* 1702–67)

Sanders was born in Wesel and died in Rotterdam, where he presumably practised. There are three decorative paintings by him in Middelburg Town Hall, of 1764, but ours seems to be the only known portrait by him, apart from the *Lady of the Hope Family* which was once its companion.

577   *Archibald Hope the Elder*

Signed and dated: *G. SANDERS/1737*

Archibald Hope (1664–1743) was a member of the far-flung Scottish family, the Hopes of Hopetoun (hence the saying, 'The world is full of blasted Hopes'). Archibald's father had sought his fortune in Holland and returned to Edinburgh; Archibald himself, christened in the Scots Church in Rotterdam in 1664, set up as a merchant there and married, in 1694, his fellow-Quaker Anna Claus. His sons founded the famous Hope Bank in Amsterdam, which was one of the great European Merchant Banks until the time of Napoleon and still exists as Bank Mees en Hope N.V. Its motto was 'At spes non fracta', which may be roughly translated: Hope not yet broke. The great art-collector and theorist of Neoclassicism, Thomas Hope of Deepdene, was his grandson.

Canvas, $34\frac{1}{8} \times 28\frac{5}{8}$in (86.6 × 72.7cm)

PROVENANCE Sale, Christie's, 27.ix.1909 (113); Fairfax Murray Gift, 1911

LITERATURE M. G. Buist, *At Spes Non Fracta: Hope & Co, 1770–1815* (Bank Mees en Hope N.V., The Hague, 1974), 4–11 and rep. 455

Daniel **SEGHERS**, SJ (1590–1661)

Seghers was the most famous exponent of the rather special form of flower-painting exemplified here—the painting of garlands round small portraits, or, more commonly, devotional images. He was a Master in Antwerp in 1611, became a Jesuit in 1614 (though brought up as a Protestant), went to Rome for a short time and then returned to Antwerp, where he was associated with Rubens. The figures in his pictures are usually by other artists, but he is said to have grown his own flowers.

322   *A Wreath of Flowers encircling a Painted Relief of the Madonna and Child with S. Anne*

Signed: *Daniel Seghers Soc^{tis} JESU*

The signature is difficult to read, and in 1854 Waagen pointed out that the picture was in fact signed, although then attributed to Jan Bruegel, Seghers's master. The figures are probably by Erasmus Quellinus (1607–78); a similar picture in the Ashmolean Museum, Oxford, has a *Madonna* by Jordaens. The flowers include hyacinths, jonquils, tulips, jasmine, roses, mallows, pinks, snowdrops, tuberoses, hellebore, ivy and iris.

Canvas, 38 × 28in (96.5 × 71cm)

PROVENANCE Bourgeois Bequest, 1811

EXHIBITED RA 1953/4 (277)

LITERATURE G. F. Waagen, *Treasures of Art in Gt Britain* (1854), II, 345

Pieter Cornelisz. van **SLINGELANDT** (1640–91)
Slingelandt was born in Leyden and was a pupil of Dou, whose style he imitated.

116   *Boy with a Flagon and a Bird's Nest*

Panel, $6\frac{3}{8} \times 4\frac{3}{4}$in (16.2 × 12.1cm)

PROVENANCE Bourgeois Bequest, 1811

EXHIBITED RA, Dutch, 1952/3 (147)

VERSION Sm no 7 (same as HdG no 127) may be identical with 116: Smith records a pedigree
from the Zaamens Collection in 1767 up to—but not beyond—1811, and much of the
description tallies (goldfinch perched on the child's finger), but other details do not agree

LITERATURE HdG, V, no 124

Gerard **SOEST** (*c* 1602–81)
Soest was a Dutch painter who settled in England in the 1640s and remained until his death.
He was never able to compete with Lely, especially as a painter of fashionable ladies.

573   *Aubrey de Vere, 20th Earl of Oxford*

Aubrey de Vere, last of the Earls of Oxford of the old creation, was born in 1626/7 and
brought up in Holland, serving as a Dutch officer until 1648. He was twice imprisoned in the
Tower under Cromwell as a Royalist, welcomed Charles II back in 1660 and turned against
the Stuarts in 1688, when he joined the Prince of Orange, later William III. He died in 1703.
This portrait was attributed to the miniaturist Samuel Cooper, but no oil-paintings by him
are known to survive. The attribution to Soest, first proposed in 1919, is now universally
accepted.

Canvas, $29 \times 24\frac{7}{8}$in (73.7 × 63.2cm)

PROVENANCE Marquess of Townshend, Raynham Hall, Norfolk; Townshend Heirlooms Sale,
Christie's, 5.iii.1904 (5: as de Vere, but unknown painter), bt Fairfax Murray; presented by
him, 1911

EXHIBITED RA 1908 (161: as by S. Cooper)

LITERATURE C. H. Collins-Baker in *Burl.Mag.* (1919), XXXV, 150ff. and rep. (as by Soest, not
Cooper); M. D. Whinney and O. Millar, *English Art, 1625–1714* (Oxford, 1957), 183

Attributed to **SOEST**

592   *Sir Harry Vane*

Sir Harry Vane (1613–62) became a Puritan and went to New England in 1635, becoming
Governor of Massachusetts, 1636–7. He returned to England and played a leading part on
the Parliamentary side during the Civil War, but later protested against Cromwell's
arbitrary government, so becoming distrusted by both sides. After the Restoration his death
was demanded by the Royalists and he was executed on Tower Hill on 14 June 1662, Pepys

being among the spectators. Pepys's diary makes it clear that the general feeling was that the government had erred in pressing for his death. This painting is probably based on the portrait by Lely, of which there are versions in Boston, Mass., and Ham House, Surrey. It was formerly attributed to Dobson, but Soest seems correct.

Canvas, $30\frac{1}{4} \times 25\frac{1}{8}$in (77.5 × 63.8cm)

PROVENANCE Fairfax Murray Gift, 1911 (as Dobson)

LITERATURE C. H. Collins-Baker in *Onze Kunst* (1915), 101ff. and rep.; *id* in *Burl.Mag.* (1919), XXXV, 150ff. and rep. (as by Soest)

Gerard **SOEST** *see* John RILEY (568)

Andrea **SOLDI** (*c* 1703–71)
Soldi was a Florentine painter who went to the Holy Land and made portraits of English residents in Aleppo which were so successful that he went to London *c* 1735. He had immediate success, but was so extravagant that he was imprisoned in the Fleet Prison for debt about 1743. George Vertue, his contemporary, recorded that he 'lived well kept house a Madam &c . . .' and was 'willing to be thought a Count or Marquis, rather than an excellent painter—Such Idle vanitys has done him no good'. He was given financial help by the Society of Artists in January 1771, and died soon afterwards, his funeral being paid for by Reynolds. His works are now rare, but they include portraits of sculptors and architects.

603   *Louis François Roubiliac*

Signed and dated: *A. Soldi/Pinx. Ao. 1751*

Roubiliac (?1705–62) was the finest sculptor working in England in the first half of the 18th century, rivalled only by Rysbrack. Rysbrack also sat to Soldi, and one version of the *Rysbrack* belonged to Fairfax Murray, who gave the *Roubiliac* to Dulwich. Roubiliac is shown here as working on the model of the figure of Charity, part of the monument to the Duke of Montagu in the church at Warkton, Northants., which is known to have been in the model stage in 1751 (there is a model in Westminster Abbey Muniment Room). The Duke's monument was erected in 1752 and was followed by one to the Duchess in 1753. Vertue records 'lately Mr Rubilliac the Statuary, his picture painted by Mr Soldi—portrait-painter—Nov. 1751 . . . he is certainly a painter of superior merit in the portrait way'. Another portrait by Soldi of Roubiliac, shown working on a bust of Garrick and dated 1758, is now in the Garrick Club, London.

Canvas, $38\frac{3}{8} \times 32\frac{3}{4}$in (97.5 × 83.2cm)

PROVENANCE One of the two versions was (with the companion *Rysbrack*) in the Sir Henry Gott Sale, Christie's, 24.ii.1810 (26); this one was in the Matthews Collection, Birmingham, 1854; Fairfax Murray Gift, 1917

EXHIBITED RA 1960 (155)

LITERATURE Vertue, *Notebooks . . .*, III, 84, 109, 120 and 132; M. D. Whinney, *Sculpture in Britain, 1530–1830* (1964), 107; R. Gunnis, *Dictionary of British Sculptors*, 2nd edn (1968), (*s.v.* Roubiliac); J. Ingamells in *Connoisseur* (1974), CLXXXVI, 178ff. and rep.

SPANISH SCHOOL, 17th century

185 *Jacob and Rachel at the Well*

The subject is from *Genesis*, xxix, 11: 'And Jacob kissed Rachel, and lifted up his voice, and wept'. Until 1880 this picture was attributed to Murillo, to whose school it clearly belongs, but it also presents Venetian elements in the landscape, reminiscent of Orrente (1580–1645), whose work recalls that of the Bassano family. Eric Young has suggested a Murcian or Cordoban painter active in the first third of the 17th century, with a knowledge of Orrente's work—Orrente was a Murcian—but Angulo Iniguez thinks it is closer to Francisco or José Antolinez.

Canvas, $36\frac{5}{8} \times 58\frac{3}{4}$in ($93 \times 149.2$cm)

PROVENANCE Perhaps B. van der Gucht Sale, Christie's, 14.iii.1788 (64: Murillo's *Jacob and Rachel* . . . ex-Prince de Conty [which seems to be a confusion with Dulwich 272, *Good Shepherd*]); his Sale, Christie's, 11.iii.1796 (49*); Earl of Bessborough Sale, Christie's, 5ff.ii.1801 (2nd day, 70); Bourgeois Bequest, 1811

LITERATURE C. B. Curtis, *Velazquez and Murillo* (London and New York, 1883), no 8a; letters from E. Young, 1977, and D. Angulo, 1977, in the Gallery archives

SPANISH SCHOOL(?)

69 *The Crucifixion of S. Peter*

Inscribed: *1660*

It is not clear whether this is a date or an inventory number—1660 seems rather late for the style of the picture. It is first recorded in the Bourgeois Inventory of 1813 (141) as by Murillo, but this attribution was clearly untenable and was dropped in favour of Spanish School (according to the 1926 Catalogue, E. Tormo suggested José Antolinez). There seems, however, no resemblance to the work of Antolinez, and no compelling reason to believe the picture Spanish. Both the style and the ultimate derivation of the composition from Michelangelo's fresco in the Cappella Paolina of the Vatican indicate a Roman-influenced Northern artist, perhaps a follower of Bartholomaeus Spranger, or a Dutch or Flemish master.

Canvas, $43\frac{1}{2} \times 33$in (110.5×83.8cm)

PROVENANCE Bourgeois Bequest, 1811

LITERATURE G. F. Waagen, *Treasures of Art in Gt Britain* (1854), II, 346 (as by Murillo and related (wrongly) to a larger picture in the Miles Collection); C. B. Curtis, *Velazquez and Murillo* (London and New York, 1883), no 379a (as Spanish School)

Abraham **STORCK** (1644–1704 or later?)
Storck worked in Amsterdam, but occasionally painted imaginary Mediterranean seaports in the manner of Weenix. He is said to have painted the reception of the Duke of Marlborough, in Holland in 1704, but this seems to be doubtful.

608 *View of Rotterdam*

Inscribed (not signed): *A.STORCK*

The town is clearly intended to be Rotterdam, and an important personage is landing. The fact that the saluting ship has a pre-1707 English flag, whereas the others are Dutch, puts this in the class of paintings by Storck associated, probably wrongly, with Marlborough. The composition is close to one called *Harbour of Amsterdam* in Dresden, signed and dated 1689. Several near-replicas are recorded in the Witt Library.

Canvas, $24\frac{1}{2} \times 31\frac{7}{8}$in (62.1 × 81cm)

PROVENANCE Gift of Dr E. Warters, 1926

LITERATURE W. Bernt, *Netherlandish Painters of the 17th Century* (1970), III, pl 1135 (for Dresden picture)

Robert **STREATER** (1624–80)
Streater was the first English history-painter and was greatly prized by his contemporaries: he was made Serjeant-Painter in 1663 and Buckeridge says of him: 'he excelled all of his time in England ... His chief excellence was in landskip ... he was the greatest and most universal Painter that ever England bred ...'. His ceiling for the Sheldonian Theatre in Oxford (1669), with an elaborate allegory of Truth and the Arts, called forth Whitehall's lines—'future Ages must confess they owe/To Streeter more than Michael Angelo'.

376 *Landscape*

The house has not been identified, and the landscape itself bears a resemblance to the works of Cuyp, but Streater is known to have painted Boscobel House, where Charles II took refuge (Royal Collection); and this may have some such significance, although it is recorded in the Cartwright Inventory (1686) merely as *A Large Landscift don by Streeker*, which makes it one of the few documented works by him.

Canvas, $40\frac{1}{4} \times 50\frac{3}{4}$in (102.2 × 129.1cm)

PROVENANCE Cartwright Bequest, 1686

EXHIBITED RA 1960/61 (303)

LITERATURE B. Buckeridge, *Essays towards an English School* in De Piles, *Art of Painting*, 3rd edn (c 1744), 420–21; Editorial in *Burl.Mag.* (1944), LXXXIV, 3f.; H. and M. Ogden, *English Taste in Landscape in the 17th Century* (1955), 115; M. D. Whinney and O. Millar, *English Art, 1625–1714* (Oxford, 1957), 265

Herman van **SWANEVELT** (1600–55)
Swanevelt was born near Utrecht, but spent most of his life in Rome and Paris; he was in Paris by 1623 and in Rome 1624–41, living in the same house as Claude, 1627–9. He and Claude developed along similar lines (*see* Claude, 174), one influencing the other. From 1644 he lived mainly in Paris, where he became Painter to the King. As his work is not always easy to distinguish from Claude's or Both's and his chronology is still confused, the three pictures in Dulwich are important.

11   *The Arch of Constantine, Rome*

Signed and dated: *VAN SWANEVELT/PARIS 1645*

The signature and date are extremely difficult to read: they are on the masonry of the arch of the Colosseum, which frames the left side. The Triumphal Arch, which is now free-standing and restored, was erected to commemorate the victory of Constantine over Maxentius at the Milvian Bridge in 312, when Constantine had a vision of the Cross. The Arch is shown in its pre-restoration state.

Canvas, 35¼ × 45¾in (89.5 × 116.2cm)

PROVENANCE Bourgeois Bequest, 1811

VERSION One in a private collection has almost identical figures, especially the artist in profile at the right

LITERATURE M. Kitson in *Revue des Arts* (1958), 219; W. Stechow, *Dutch Landscape Painting of the 17th Century* (1966), 151–2

136
219   *An Italian Landscape* and *Italian Landscape with Bridge*

Both pictures have very damaged signatures and dates, but previous catalogues have given 1675 as the date on 219. This would be impossible, and it seems that the original inscriptions were: (136) *VAN SWANEVELT/PARIS 164-* (most likely *5*, but possibly *3* or *9*); (219) fragments of *VAN SWANEVELT* and *PARIS 1645*, though the *4* is not clear. Since the two pictures are obviously pendants, it seems likely that both were originally dated 1645 (*cf* 11). The pictures may be identical with a pair of Swanevelt landscapes called *Morning* and *Evening* in 1769.

Canvas, (136) 15¼ × 21⅞in (38.7 × 55.4cm);
          (219) 15⅛ × 21⅞in (38.4 × 55.4cm)

PROVENANCE Perhaps the *Morning* and *Evening* in R. Strange Collection, 1769 (72, 73 as 19½ × 24in); probably Desenfans Sale, 8ff.vi.1786 (111, 281); Bourgeois Bequest, 1811

LITERATURE R. Strange, *Descriptive Catalogue . . .* (1769), 130–1; W. Stechow, *Dutch Landscape Painting of the 17th Century* (1966), 215, n 26 (giving 1644 as date of our 136)

David **TENIERS**

Three members of the Teniers family of painters were named David, all active in Antwerp. David I (1582–1649), his son David II (1610–90)—by far the most famous—and his son, David III (1638–85), about whom little is known except that he was a painter and tapestry designer, and probably a copyist of his father's works. Since about 1967 it has become clear that David I is a different artistic personality from the one rather arbitrarily constructed in the 1870s and 1880s and which has confused the issue: of the 23 pictures in Dulwich and 21 in the National Gallery, 15 of ours (and several in the National Gallery) were previously attributed to David I, whereas it now seems certain that only no 314 of this collection (and none of those in the National Gallery) has any claim at all to be by him.

David I was born in Antwerp in 1582 and trained by his brother Juliaan. After this he may have worked for Rubens before going to Rome, where he worked in the circle around Elsheimer (*cf* 22), between about 1600 and 1605. He became a Master in Antwerp in 1606, but from then until his death he was constantly in debt and most of his recorded works are of religious subjects held as securities. He was imprisoned for debt in 1625, and, in the last years of his life, was probably mainly active as a dealer. There are few absolutely certain works by him, none of them in British public collections. So far as can now be judged, all David I's works are close to Elsheimer in composition and handling, and bear little relation to the works of his son, although there may have been a period of mutual influence in the 1630s, for which our *Magdalen* (323), dated 1634, may be of cardinal importance. David II was the pupil of his father and became a Master in the Antwerp Guild in 1632/3 and Dean in 1645: his dated works range from 1633 to 1680. About 1651 David II moved to Brussels, where he became curator of the famous collection formed by his patron Archduke Leopold Wilhelm, Regent of The Netherlands, most of which is now in the Kunsthistorisches Museum, Vienna. Teniers made 244 copies of pictures in the Archduke's collection (39 such copies are on long loan at Kenwood, Hampstead), besides some 2000 works of his own in a bewildering variety of styles; in addition, his works were widely imitated and forged throughout the 18th and 19th centuries.

The attributions in the present Catalogue are in keeping with those in the earliest records of the collection, the Inventory of 1813 and the 1816/20 Catalogue based on it, and depart from those in the 1876 and subsequent Catalogues.

Attributed to David TENIERS I or II

314 *S. Peter in Penitence* and *S. Mary Magdalen in Penitence*

323 Signed: (314) *TINIER*; signed and dated: (323) *D. TENIER Iv 1634*

The two panels are clearly pendants, and the form of signature is not like that of David II, although the date 1634 is possible for either father or son. The influence of Brill and Mompers is evident, so that they may be considered candidates for attribution to the elder Teniers: they are recorded in the earliest catalogues of the gallery (1816–20) as by 'Teniers', but the second version specifies 'Teniers the Elder', unlike all the others in the collection. The style is also different from all the others associable with Teniers II, and it may be suggested that the discrepancy in the form of signature may be explained by reading *Tinier* as Teniers the Elder and the form *Tenier Iv*, followed by the date 1634, as meaning Teniers Junior (*ie* David II) imitating his father's work or even collaborating with him. If this hypothesis be accepted, the two panels would be the most important works from the Teniers studio in this country.

Panel, (314) $12\frac{1}{4} \times 21$in (31.1×53.5cm);
  (323) $12\frac{3}{8} \times 21$in (31.3×53.4cm)

PROVENANCE Bourgeois Bequest, 1811

EXHIBITED RA, Flemish, 1953/4 (399, 403: as Teniers I)

LITERATURE H. Gerson and E. ter Kuile, *Art and Architecture in Belgium, 1600–1800* (1960), 146; M. Waddingham in *Arte Illustra* (1970), III, 125ff.; E. Duverger and H. Vlieghe, *D. Teniers der Aeltere* (Utrecht, 1971), 7. All these authorities, specifically or by implication, attribute 314 and 323 (and all other Teniers paintings in Dulwich) exclusively to David II: the Flemish School Catalogue of the National Gallery (1970, p 275, n 8) implicitly accepts the attribution to David I of the *Magdalen* at least

David TENIERS II

31 *Gipsies in a Landscape* and *A Peasant eating Mussels*

33 Both inscribed: *DTF* in monogram

Although these pictures now form a pair it is not clear that they have always done so, as the provenance shows. Both were formerly attributed to Teniers I.

Panel, (31) 9 × 12in (23 × 30.6cm);
(33) 8¾ × 13½in (22.3 × 34.2cm)

PROVENANCE (31) Perhaps M. la Prade, 1776; 'A French Nobleman', Christie's, 19.ii.1790 (81); (31 and 33) Desenfans Sale, Skinner & Dyke, 28.ii.1795 (88: 'A pair of Landscapes, one with Gypsies telling Fortunes, the other a Man opening Muscles, of the true silver tone of colouring and a magic pencil . . .'), presumably bt in; Bourgeois Bequest, 1811

LITERATURE 31 is Sm no 169 (as la Prade Collection), but Sm no 168 describes a man and woman eating mussels and cannot be identified with our 33

---

49   *A Road near a Cottage* and *A Cottage*
52
Both inscribed: *DT.F* in monogram

Formerly attributed to Teniers I.

Panel, both originally 8⅝ × 6½in (22 × 16.6cm). Strips c¼in wide have been added to each side of both panels

PROVENANCE Desenfans Insurance List, 1804 (either nos 108, 109 or 119, 120); Bourgeois Bequest, 1811

---

54   *A Guard Room*
Signed: *D. TENIERS Fe*

One of a group of such *koortegardje* scenes, some of which are also entitled *S. Peter in Prison*. The armour on a stand, breast-plate, drums, and lantern recur in a version in the Rijksmuseum, Amsterdam, which is signed and dated 1641. The boy occurs in reverse in another picture in the Prado, Madrid. Previously catalogued as a late work, but the similarity to the Amsterdam picture makes a date in the 1640s more likely.

Canvas, 28½ × 22in (72.4 × 55.8cm). A strip, c 1¼in wide, at the right side, may be an addition

PROVENANCE Possibly Sir L. Dundas Sale, Greenwood's, 30.v.1794 (32 or 33); Desenfans Insurance List, 1804 (30); Bourgeois Bequest, 1811

EXHIBITED RA, Flemish, 1953/4 (387)

DRAWING A highly-detailed drawing of armour of a very similar type is in the Witt Collection, University of London

LITERATURE Sm nos 355, 356 are *Corps de Garde* scenes, 21 × 28in, in the Dundas Sale, but Smith describes them as on copper

---

57   *Brickmakers near Hemiksem*
Signed: *D. TENIERS F*

The church is the Cistercian abbey of S. Bernard (now destroyed) at Hemiksem, and the river is the Scheldt, some miles south of Antwerp. Teniers owned a country house at Vilvoorde in the neighbourhood, and the Hemiksem brickyard was one of the oldest in The Netherlands.

Panel, 17¼ × 26⅜in (43.8 × 67cm)

PROVENANCE Robit Collection; his Sale, Paris, 1801 (149), bt Bryan; Bourgeois Bequest, 1811

EXHIBITED RA, Flemish, 1953/4 (412)

VERSIONS A copy, dated 1781, by H. Myn, was sold in Brussels in 1929 and other versions or copies have been in trade in Holland since then

LITERATURE Sm no 379 (as *Tile Factory*, Robit Collection); H. Gerson and E. ter Kuile, *Art and Architecture in Belgium, 1600–1800* (1960), 196, n 11; letter from Dr Johanna Hollestelle, 5 February 1976, in the Gallery archives, identifying the site

76   *Peasants conversing*

Signed: *DT.F* in monogram

Attributed since 1880 to Teniers I, but before then correctly attributed to Teniers II and increased in size to serve as a pendant to 95: the 1813 Inventory showing the pictures hanging together in Bourgeois' house specifies this as a companion to *The Painter, his Wife, and a Gardener* (*ie* 95) and it was probably Bourgeois himself who added the strip at the bottom of the painting, below the monogram and the old (untraced) inventory number 116.

Canvas, $51\frac{1}{4} \times 69\frac{7}{8}$in ($130.2 \times 177.5$cm), including added strip

PROVENANCE J. Bertels (of Brussels) Sale, Walsh, London, 8.iv.1775 (55), described as *Evening—Farmer pointing to a Man*, $59 \times 85\frac{1}{2}$in including frame—*ie* about 43×70in without it; Desenfans Insurance List, 1804 (115); Bourgeois Bequest, 1811

EXHIBITED RA, Flemish, 1953/4 (409: as Teniers I)

95   *A Castle and its Proprietors*

Signed: *DTF* in monogram

Described in the 1813 Inventory as *Portraits of the Painter, his Wife and Gardener . . .* and as a companion to 76. Teniers did buy a country house in 1662, De Drij Toren (The Three Towers) at Peurck, but this seems not to represent either Teniers or his house: there is a similar problem connected with 817 in the National Gallery.

Canvas, $44\frac{1}{8} \times 66\frac{5}{8}$in ($112.2 \times 169.2$cm)

PROVENANCE Sollier Sale, Paris, 1781 (bt in); perhaps Desenfans Insurance List, 1804 (114); Bourgeois Bequest, 1811

EXHIBITED RA, Flemish, 1953/4 (405)

VERSION Desenfans owned a *Castle with Teniers and Family* in 1786, but it was 42×48in including the frame. An apparently exact replica, but only 56×82.5cm, was sold in Stockholm, Bukowski, 15–17.v.1946 (126), signed *DTF*

106   *A Peasant holding a Glass* and *An Old Woman*
110   Both inscribed: *DT.F* in monogram

Formerly attributed to Teniers I.

Copper, both $3\frac{3}{8} \times 2\frac{5}{8}$in ($8.5 \times 6.6$cm)

PROVENANCE Probably Desenfans Insurance List, 1804 (34, 35); Bourgeois Bequest, 1811

112 *Winter Scene with a Man killing a Pig*

Signed: *DTF* in monogram

Formerly attributed to Teniers I.

Canvas, $27\frac{1}{8} \times 37\frac{3}{4}$in (68.9 × 95.7cm)

PROVENANCE Probably in France; perhaps Desenfans Sale, 8ff.iv.1786 (144: *Village in Flanders, a Frost Piece*), 37 × 49in, including frame; Desenfans Insurance List, 1804 (94: *A Frost Piece*); Bourgeois Bequest, 1811

EXHIBITED RA, Flemish, 1953/4 (408)

ENGRAVING Laurent (presumably P. F. Laurent, 1739–1809)

LITERATURE Sm no 603, describing the Laurent engraving, as 25 × 35in

142 *The Chaff-cutter*

Signed: *D. TENIERS F.*

Canvas, $23 \times 33\frac{1}{8}$in (58.6 × 84.1cm)

PROVENANCE Probably Desenfans Sale, Christie's, 8.iv.1786 (74); Charles James Fox; Richard Walker; his Sale, Christie's, 5.iii.1803 (7); Desenfans Insurance List, 1804 (90); Bourgeois Bequest, 1811

EXHIBITED RA, Flemish, 1953/4 (406)

LITERATURE Sm no 402 (wrongly as on panel and about 22 × 26in)

146 *A Sow and her Litter*

Signed: *D. TENIERS. FEC*

Panel, $9\frac{5}{8} \times 13\frac{1}{2}$in (24.4 × 34.3cm)

PROVENANCE C. A. de Calonne Collection, but not in his Sale, London, Skinner & Dyke, 23ff.iii.1795; Desenfans Insurance List, 1804 (39); Bourgeois Bequest, 1811

EXHIBITED NG 1947 (49)

LITERATURE Sm no 300 (as Calonne, 1788)

Attributed to **TENIERS**

35 *Cottage with Peasants playing Cards*

Formerly attributed to Teniers I, but probably an 18th-century pastiche.

Canvas, $10\frac{7}{8} \times 14\frac{3}{4}$in (27.5 × 37.5cm)

PROVENANCE Bourgeois Bequest, 1811

David **TENNIERS I** *see* FLEMISH SCHOOL(?) (14)

Attributed to David **TENIERS II**

299   *Sunset Landscape with a Shepherd and his Flock*

If this is by Teniers himself, it is a poor example of his work. It was formerly attributed to Teniers I.

Canvas, $22\frac{1}{2} \times 32\frac{3}{4}$in ($57.2 \times 83$cm). A strip at the bottom about 2in deep appears to be an addition

PROVENANCE Probably the *Sun behind Clouds—Shepherds [sic] with Flock*, sold by a 'French Nobleman', Christie's, 19.ii.1790 (84); Desenfans Insurance List, 1804 (64); Bourgeois Bequest, 1811

Studio of David **TENIERS II**

614   *The Seven Corporal Works of Mercy*

The seven corporal—as distinct from spiritual—works of mercy are: 1. to feed the hungry; 2. to give drink to the thirsty; 3. to clothe the naked; 4. to give shelter to travellers; 5. to visit the sick; 6. to visit the imprisoned; 7. to bury the dead. This is a version of a composition by Teniers, of which the original is probably that in the collection of Sir J. Dunnington-Jefferson, on copper, lent to the Royal Academy Flemish Exhibition in 1953/4 (404). Our painting was formerly monogrammed *DT*, but this was removed during cleaning in 1947, and it seems that 614 is the work of a good pupil of Teniers, copying one or more of his original pictures. David Ryckaert is a possibility.

Panel, $25\frac{1}{2} \times 34\frac{7}{8}$in ($64.8 \times 88.5$cm)

PROVENANCE T. C. Avery; his step-nephew, Professor C. D. Broad (*b* 1887); presented by him, 1946

EXHIBITED NG 1947 (50)

VERSIONS Smith lists five, including one in the Louvre, but the prime original appears to be that in the Dunnington-Jefferson Collection, mentioned above

LITERATURE Sm nos 1–5 for the various versions (excluding 614)

Giovanni Battista **TIEPOLO** (1696–1770)
Giovanni Domenico **TIEPOLO** (1727–1804)
The elder Tiepolo, the last of the great Venetian decorators, was influenced by Veronese, Sebastiano Ricci and Piazzetta, and his early style is relatively heavy and dark. He executed an enormous number of decorative frescoes, usually mythological and allegorical, mostly in North Italy, but he also decorated the Palace of the Prince-Bishop of Würzburg (1750–53) and the Royal Palace in Madrid, where he died. His principal assistant was his son Domenico, who is first recorded as a painter in 1744. His own style, more down-to-earth than his father's, is first traceable in the Villa Valmarana in 1757, but throughout his life he continued to imitate and copy his father's works. After his father's death Domenico returned to Venice, where he became President of the Academy in 1780 and died in 1804.

158   *Joseph receiving Pharaoh's Ring*

The subject is from *Genesis*, xli: 'And Pharaoh said unto Joseph, See, I have set thee over all the land of Egypt. And Pharaoh took off his ring from his hand, and put it upon Joseph's hand, and arrayed him in vestures of fine linen, and put a gold chain about his neck'. Until 1880 this painting was attributed to Giovanni Battista Tiepolo, but Richter, in his Catalogue, gave it to Domenico. In 1955 it was re-attributed to G. B. Tiepolo by Morassi, at about the same time as a *Madonna and Saints*—(National Gallery, 2513) which belonged to Desenfans in 1802—was also returned to G. B. Tiepolo after passing for years as the work of Domenico. Both pictures are now often regarded as the work of the elder Tiepolo—the National Gallery *Madonna* as *c* 1733 and our 158 as *c* 1734/5. Although Morassi's attribution has won some acceptance, it seems prudent to regard the question as still open—especially as Morassi also regarded 186 and 189 as works by G. B. Tiepolo of about the same date. If *Joseph* were by Domenico, working in his father's style, it might date from the 1750s or later.

Canvas, $41\frac{3}{4} \times 70\frac{3}{4}$in (106.1 × 179.7cm)

PROVENANCE Bourgeois Bequest, 1811

LITERATURE A. Morassi in *Burl.Mag.* (1955), XCVII, 11 (as by G.B.); *id, Complete Catalogue of . . . Tiepolo* (1962), 17; G. Piovene and A. Pallucchini, *L'opera completa di . . . Tiepolo* (Milan, 1968), no 107 (accepting Morassi's attribution)

Giovanni Battista **TIEPOLO**

186
189   *Diana, Apollo, and another Goddess*

These two paintings originally formed a single *modello* for a ceiling decoration. There are three main candidates for the actual ceiling, all showing affinities with the rather generalised gods-and-goddesses patterns used by Tiepolo for such commissions. In chronological order they are: 1. Villa Cornaro, Merlengo, Treviso, *c* 1735/6; 2. a rejected design for Villa Cordellina, Montecchio Maggiore, Vicenza, 1743; 3. Villa Valmarana, Vicenza, 1757. If the *modello* were for the Villa Cornaro it would, according to Morassi and others, be contemporary with our *Joseph* (158), which seems stylistically impossible; if it were for the Villa Cordellina it would be exactly contemporary with 278, which is certainly a *modello* for that villa; and if it were for the Villa Valmarana it would be much later in date, yet it is painted on a reddish ground (instead of the sandy colour more usual in the 1750s), and for an unknown subject, since nothing now in the villa corresponds at all closely. It may be observed that Morassi first (1955) identified 186 and 189 as *modelletti* for the Villa Cordellina (*c* 1743), and then later (1962) re-identified them as for the Villa Cornaro at Merlengo, accepting a date *c* 1735—*ie* the date he had himself proposed for the *Joseph*.

     In the present state of knowledge the safest guess is probably the Villa Cordellina, on account of the affinity with 278.

Canvas, (186) $13\frac{1}{8} \times 13$in (33.3 × 33cm);
          (189) 13in (33cm) square

PROVENANCE Anon. Sale, Christie's, 29.v.1802 (16: probably then uncut), bt Sir F. Bourgeois; Bourgeois Bequest 1811 (in the 1813 Inventory as two pictures, 292, 293)

EXHIBITED NG 1947 (51, 52); RA 1954/5 (490, 495); 1960 (413, 418: as for Villa Valmarana)

LITERATURE E. Sack, *Tiepolo* (Hamburg, 1910), 225; G. Knox in *Connoisseur* (1955), CXXXV, 34 (as for Valmarana); A. Morassi in *Burl.Mag.* (1955), XCVII, 11, n 23 (as Cordellina—*ie* an earlier version of Dulwich 278); *id, Complete Catalogue of . . . Tiepolo* (1962), 17, 23 (both formed *modello* for Villa Cornaro, Merlengo, and perhaps connected with one in Patino Collection, Paris—but later refers Patino sketch to V. Valmarana); G. Knox in *Burl.Mag.* (1963), CV, 328 (retracting Valmarana connection and agreeing Cornaro); G. Piovene and A. Pallucchini, *L'opera completa di . . . Tiepolo* (Milan, 1968), no 112 (as for V. Cornaro at Merlengo)

278   *Fortitude and Wisdom* or *Wisdom putting Ignorance to Flight*

A *modello* for a ceiling in the Villa Cordellina at Montecchio Maggiore, near Vicenza. The ceiling was formerly in the Museum of Vicenza, but was replaced in the villa in 1956. The progress of the work was described in a letter from Tiepolo to his friend Count Algarotti of 26 October 1743: '. . . I have finished almost half of the ceiling, which, I flatter myself—indeed, I am sure—I shall finish by the 10th or 12th of next month . . . I can do nothing because there are too many visitors'.

Canvas, $25\frac{1}{2} \times 14$in (64.2 × 35.6cm)

PROVENANCE   Presumably from the Villa Cordellina; Bourgeois Bequest, 1811

EXHIBITED   NG 1947 (53); RA 1954/5 (485); 1960 (420)

LITERATURE   E. Sack, *Tiepolo* (Hamburg, 1910), 86, 225 and rep. p 91 (first suggesting the Villa Cordellina); P. Molmenti, *Tiepolo* (French) (Milan, 1911), 202, 264; A. Morassi, *Tiepolo* (1955), 20–21; *id, Complete Catalogue of . . . Tiepolo* (1962), 17, 29 and 64, and rep. fig 346 (347 shows the Vicenza ceiling); G. Piovene and A. Pallucchini, *L'opera completa di . . . Tiepolo* (Milan, 1968), no 147a

John **VANDERBANK** (*c* 1694–1739)
Vanderbank, like Hudson, was one of the leading portrait painters in England between the death of Kneller in 1723 and the rise of Reynolds. According to Vertue he had great promise, but wasted it in dissipation 'according to the fashion of the Age'.

581   *Lady in White*

Signed and dated: *Jn° Vanderbank Fecit 1736*

The white satin dress and wreath of flowers probably indicate that it is a marriage portrait, or, rather, betrothal portrait, since she wears no ring.

Canvas, $50 \times 40\frac{1}{8}$in (127 × 101.9cm)

PROVENANCE   Anon. Sale, Christie's, 31.v.1902 (106), bt Murray; Fairfax Murray Gift, 1911

Diego de Silva y **VELAZQUEZ** (1599–1660)
Velazquez was born in Seville and became the leading Spanish painter of the 17th century, and one of the greatest of portrait painters. He was Court Painter from 1623 and became the friend of his King, Philip IV, whom he painted throughout his reign.

Studio of **VELAZQUEZ**

249   *Philip IV, King of Spain*

A contemporary copy, perhaps by Juan Bautista del Mazo (*see* 277). Velazquez painted a portrait of Philip (1605–65) at Fraga in June 1644, during the campaign against the French: a detailed contemporary description of the dress worn by the King corresponds with this portrait. Until 1911 it was generally accepted that this was the 'Fraga Portrait', although it was known that copies were already being made in the summer of 1644. Since 1911, however, it has been generally agreed that the version then bought in Italy by Henry Frick (now in the Frick Collection, New York) is the original, and ours is one of the contemporary copies. Another copy was in a private collection in New York in 1936. The Frick picture was in London for a short time in 1911 and Roger Fry, who saw it then and was able to compare it directly with 249, accepted that it was the autograph version.

Canvas, $51\frac{1}{4} \times 38\frac{1}{2}$in ($130.2 \times 97.8$cm)
(The Frick picture is 133×98cm)

PROVENANCE The French sculptor, E. Bouchardon; his Sale, ix.1762; F. Tronchin, Geneva, by 1765; his Sale, Paris, 1801 (2 Germinal, an IX); Desenfans by 1804 (1804 Insurance List, 32); Bourgeois Bequest, 1811

EXHIBITED BI 1828 (111); NG 1947 (54); Madrid, Velazquez Exhibition, 1960/61 (68: perhaps by Mazo)

LITERATURE W. Stirling-Maxwell, *Annals of the Artists of Spain* (1848), 745ff.; C. B. Curtis, *Velazquez and Murillo* (London and New York, 1883), no 120 (details of provenance); C. Justi, *Velazquez and his Times* (1889), 305, 311; R. Fry in *Burl.Mag.* (1911), XIX, 5; A. L. Mayer, *Velazquez, a Catalogue Raisonné* (1936), no 229 (as Mazo); E. Trapier, *Velazquez* (New York, 1948), 271ff. (contemporary description of costume); M. Asturias and P. Bardi, *L'opera completa di Velazquez* (Milan, 1969), no 91a

Adriaen van de **VELDE** (1636–72)
Adriaen was the son of Willem the Elder and brother of Willem the Younger van de Velde. As well as learning from his father he studied under Wynants and Wouwerman. His earlier animal pictures, such as 51, are closer to Wouwerman, while his later works are Italianate landscapes in the style of Wynants.

51   *Cows and Sheep in a Wood*

Panel, $7\frac{1}{4} \times 8\frac{7}{8}$in ($18.4 \times 22.5$cm)

PROVENANCE Desenfans Insurance List, 1804 (105); Bourgeois Bequest, 1811

LITERATURE HdG, IV, no 192

Willem van de **VELDE II** (1633–1707)
Willem II was the son of the painter and marine draughtsman Willem and the elder brother of Adriaen. He was born in Leyden and his best works were done in Holland between 1653 and 1672, when he settled in England. In 1674 he and his father were employed by Charles II

as marine artists, working mostly at Greenwich and recording many battles of the sea war with the Dutch. He died in London.

103   *A Brisk Breeze*

Signed: *WVV* in monogram

Also called *A View off the Texel*. According to Michael Robinson, a work of the early 1660s.

Canvas, $20\frac{1}{2} \times 25\frac{5}{8}$in ($52.1 \times 65$cm)

PROVENANCE Bourgeois Bequest, 1811

LITERATURE Sm no 40; G. F. Waagen, *Treasures of Art in Gt Britain* (1854), II, 345 (as one of his most charming pictures); HdG, VII, no 493; M. Robinson (orally), 1978

197   *A Calm*

Signed and dated: *WVV 1663*

Canvas on panel, $13\frac{3}{8} \times 14\frac{3}{4}$in ($34 \times 37.5$cm)

PROVENANCE Earl of Bute Collection; Bryan Sale, Coxe, 18.v.1798 (17: as ex-Bute); Anon. (Nesbitt) Sale, Coxe, 25.v.1802 (58), bt FB (*ie* Bourgeois); Bourgeois Bequest, 1811

LITERATURE HdG, VII, no 201

VENETIAN SCHOOL *see* Circle of MOLA (75)

Adriaen **VERBOOM** (*c* 1628–*c* 1670)
Verboom, whose name was Adriaen and not Abraham, was a landscape painter influenced by J. van Ruisdael. He worked in Rotterdam, Haarlem and Amsterdam.

9   *Landscape with a Church*

The 1813 Inventory of the Gallery attributes this picture to Hobbema, but Richter, in his Catalogue of 1880, gave it to Verboom and this is confirmed by the likeness to signed examples.

Panel, $17\frac{1}{4} \times 21\frac{1}{4}$in ($43.7 \times 53.9$cm)

PROVENANCE Bourgeois Bequest, 1811

LITERATURE W. Bernt, *Die Niederlaendischen Maler des 17. Jahrhunderts* (Munich, 1948), III, pl 900 (for similar signed picture in trade)

Claude-Joseph **VERNET** (1714–89)
Vernet was the founder of a dynasty of French painters. He went to Rome in 1734 and was influenced by Claude and Gaspard Poussin, a combination of landscape which, with a dash of Salvator Rosa's melodrama, appealed greatly to British patrons. He remained in Rome until

1753 when he returned to France and spent a decade working on the great series of the *Ports of France* commissioned by Louis XV. His early works, such as 328, are reckoned his best.

319 *An Italianate Harbour Scene*

Signed and dated: *Joseph Vernet/f Romae/1749*

Formerly catalogued as *Genoa Harbour* and attributed to the School of Vernet. The signature and date were revealed by cleaning in 1952. There seems to be no reason to identify the harbour as Genoa.

Canvas, $41\frac{1}{8} \times 46\frac{3}{8}$in (104.4 × 117.8cm)

PROVENANCE Possibly commissioned by M. Sauvan in January 1749; sold 12.iii.1782 (138) and 8.iv.1783 (85), both presumably in Paris; Bourgeois Bequest, 1811

LITERATURE F. Ingersoll-Smouse, *Vernet* (Paris, 1926), I, 55, no 237; P. Conisbee (letter in Gallery archives) identifies 319 with Smouse 237, but does not think it is the picture commissioned by M. Sauvan

328 *Italian Landscape*

Signed and dated: *Fait à Rome par J Vernet/1738*

The signature has always been known, but the date was first read by P. Conisbee in 1973. The landscape is probably imaginary, but the temple on the cliff led the Calonne Sale Catalogue of 1795 to identify it as Tivoli. This is an excellent example of Vernet's early style.

Canvas, $48\frac{3}{4} \times 68\frac{1}{2}$in (123.8 × 174cm)

PROVENANCE C. A. de Calonne; his Sale, Skinner & Dyke, 23ff.iii.1795 (72, of the 4th day's sale); bt privately by Desenfans (1804 Insurance List, 73); Bourgeois Bequest, 1811

EXHIBITED Kenwood, Vernet Exhibition, 1976 (4) and Paris, Musée de la Marine, 1976/7

LITERATURE F. Ingersoll-Smouse, *Vernet* (Paris, 1926), I, 69, no 466 and fig 113; P. Conisbee in *Burl.Mag.* (1973), CXV, 789ff. and fig 15; *id, Vernet* (exhibition catalogue), Kenwood, 1976

School of **VERNET**

300 *Seaport at Sunrise*

Inscribed: *J. Vernet 17--*

The date is usually read *1767* and the signature is probably not autograph. A copy of the original picture now in Chicago Art Institute: our 306 is a companion copy of a *Seaport at Sunset*, formerly in the Noël Collection, Paris.   A set of four pictures, commissioned by M. Journu of Bordeaux in 1759, probably included the Chicago and Noël paintings as well as a *Storm at Midday* and a *Fire at Night*. The Chicago *Sunrise* is signed and dated 1760.

Canvas, $26\frac{5}{8} \times 39\frac{1}{4}$in (67.6 × 99.7cm)

PROVENANCE Probably Desenfans Sale, Skinner & Dyke, 28.ii.1795 (61, 62: *Italian Sea Port* and the Companion); Bourgeois Bequest, 1811

VERSIONS Several other versions of the Chicago original are known

LITERATURE F. Ingersoll-Smouse, *Vernet* (Paris, 1926), I, no 732

VERONESE (*c* 1528–88)

Paolo Caliari, called Veronese from his native Verona, was the pre-eminent Venetian decorator of the High Renaissance, specialising in large scenes of Biblical, allegorical, or mythological inspiration, largely filled with beautiful Venetian women in magnificent dresses, set against festal Venetian architecture. He had a brush with the Inquisition in 1573 over the appropriateness of his setting of the Last Supper, but after agreeing to rename it the *Feast in the House of Levi*, Veronese seems to have carried his point that he had a lot of space to fill and he filled it to the best of his artistic judgement.

270   *S. Jerome and a Donor*

A fragment of a very large altarpiece—at least 15 × 10ft—two other parts of which are in the National Galleries of Scotland and Canada. When the Dulwich picture was cleaned in the late 1940s, and the Edinburgh one in 1958, not only was S. Jerome's lion revealed (though very damaged), but enough indications appeared to show that the gap between the Edinburgh and Dulwich sections, some two feet wide, once contained a figure of the Archangel Michael. He stood on a vanquished demon and held the scales for weighing souls in his left hand. The *Dead Christ supported by Angels*, now in Ottawa, occupied the top half of the picture. From the Ionic columns and the indications of S. Michael it has been possible to reconstruct the original appearance of this major altarpiece and to make some tentative deductions. The physical similarity between the two donors makes it likely that they were related, probably brothers. The Edinburgh patron saint is S. Antony Abbot, and, from the T-cross on his *mozzetta*, he probably appears in his capacity as patron of the Antonites, or Hospitallers of S. Antony, an order devoted mainly to the care of contagious diseases, often in isolation hospitals. The presence of S. Michael as the central figure allows the hypothesis that the brothers were Antonio and Girolamo Sanmicheli, Sanmicheli being a Veronese name. The most famous member of the family, the architect Michele Sanmicheli (*d* 1559), is known to have had a brother, Don Girolamo, who became Superior of the Augustinian Canons, but, although it is tempting to try to identify him with the donor in 270, it is chronologically improbable, since the style of the altarpiece is generally agreed to be late— around 1580—and Don Girolamo must have been born around 1480/90.

The fact that so large an altarpiece does not appear to be recorded in any Veronese or Venetian sources may, perhaps, be explained on the assumption that it was painted for the chapel of an Antonite hospital, which would not be visited in the usual way. This hypothesis receives some support from the fact that the Order was suppressed at the French Revolution, and the earliest date we have for any of the fragments is 1795 (when Desenfans owned 270), which was already separated from the others, although all three seem to have been in England very soon after that date. There is a strong probability that the S. Michael was damaged and the remainder cut into more saleable sizes for export to England. It was once believed that a fourth part was in the collection at Castle Howard, but there was never any foundation for this, and the traces of S. Michael now visible on 270 and the Edinburgh fragment prove that the figure did not survive intact (*see* reconstruction in monochrome plates).

Canvas, $90\frac{5}{8} \times 49\frac{1}{2}$in (230.2 × 125.6cm)
(Edinburgh: $76\frac{1}{4} \times 46\frac{1}{2}$in; Ottawa: $85 \times 95\frac{5}{8}$in)

PROVENANCE Desenfans Sale, Skinner & Dyke, 28.11.1795 (108: as *Cardinal blessing the Founder of Lorretto* (*ie* perhaps Lazzaretto?)); Insurance List, 1804 (7); Bourgeois Bequest, 1811

EXHIBITED BI 1816 (333), 1823 (168); RA, Italian, 1930 (180); Holbein and Other Masters, 1950/51 (232)

LITERATURE F. Ingersoll-Smouse in *Gazette des Beaux-Arts,* V^e per. (1926), XIV, 23; B. Berenson, *Italian Pictures . . . Venetian School* (1957), I, 131; G. Piovene and R. Marini, *L'opera completa . . . di Veronese* (Milan, 1968), no 156c, L. Crosato Larcher in *Arte Veneta* (1968), XII, 222 (as not Veronese and *c* 1588); I Pignatti, *Veronese* (Venice, 1976), I, 89 and no 337; II, fig 709 (as after 1577 and before 1584)

Studio of **VERONESE**

239   *The Mystic Marriage of S. Catherine*

Inscribed: *PAVLO CALL(E)ARI* [*sic*]/*VERONESE*

The subject was very popular in 16th-century Venice and there are several other versions of it by Veronese, including a very large one in the Accademia, Venice, and a fine one in the Royal Collection. This is not a copy of any known version, but it is (in spite of the inscription) not by Veronese himself. It was formerly identified with a picture of the same subject by Veronese in the Desenfans 1802 Catalogue (40), but the description differs considerably. The condition of 239 also makes any judgement difficult.

Canvas, 39 × 34⅛in (99.1 × 86.6cm)

PROVENANCE Bourgeois Bequest, 1811

Roelof van **VRIES** (1630/31–after 1681)

Van Vries was admitted to the Leyden Guild in 1653. Mostly he imitated the works of Jacob Ruisdael, and his own monogram *VR* lends itself to alteration into Ruisdael's *JvR*. The figures in van Vries's pictures (particularly good in 7) were sometimes added by A. van de Velde or Lingelbach.

7   *Landscape with a Tower*

This landscape was attributed to Wynants in the earliest catalogues of the Gallery, but since 1880 it has been given to the Dutch School: the present attribution is based on the peculiar treatment of the bricks and stones by small blobs of paint. A very similar picture in the National Gallery (134) and several signed examples (*eg* in Munich) exhibit this characteristic.

Panel, 19⅝ × 16⅛in (49.8 × 41.1cm)

PROVENANCE Bourgeois Bequest, 1811

LITERATURE Sm no 167 (as by Wynants); not in HdG; W. Bernt, *Netherlandish Painters of the 17th Century* (1970), III, rep. 1355 (the signed picture in Munich)

Antoine **WATTEAU** (1684–1721)

Watteau was a painter of Flemish descent who became the greatest of the French followers of Rubens, whose works he studied in Paris. In 1717 he became a member of the Académie royale, the first to be received as a painter of pastoral subjects—*fêtes galantes*. His diploma work, the *Embarkation for Cythera* (or *from Cythera*, as it is now sometimes called), epitomises his melancholy Romanticism. Because of his habit of working from drawings and using them over and over again, many of the figures in his paintings have a family likeness. He visited London in 1719 to consult the famous Dr Mead, physician and collector, about the consumption which killed him at 37.

156 *Les Plaisirs du Bal* (*'Le Bal Champêtre'*)

Several of the figures are to be found in other pictures by Watteau, and his drawings for them are in the Louvre and the Ecole des Beaux-Arts, Paris, the Teyler Museum, Haarlem, and elsewhere. X-rays made in 1949, when the picture was cleaned, show that the original background architecture was more Italianate in character (it is still faintly visible), whereas the present ringed columns derive from the work of Salomon de Brosse at the Tuileries. The general character of the setting, however, owes much to Hieronymus Janssens's *Court Ball*, of 1658, in the Museum at Lille.

Constable wrote to his friend C. R. Leslie, who copied our picture in 1831: 'Your Watteau looked colder than the original, which seems as if painted in honey; so mellow, so tender, so soft, so delicious . . . be satisfied if you touch but the hem of his garment, for this inscrutable and exquisite thing would vulgarise even Rubens and Paul Veronese . . .'. (In fact, the negro page leaning over the balustrade is derived from Veronese and there are several references to Rubens.) Anita Brookner dates the picture 1714/15, but others have put it at 1717 or even as late as 1719: the years between 1715 and 1717 seem most likely, especially by comparison with *Les charmes de la vie* in the Wallace Collection (which probably also belonged to Claude Glucq).

Canvas, $20\frac{3}{4} \times 25\frac{7}{8}$in ($52.6 \times 65.4$cm), probably slightly cut all round

PROVENANCE Claude Glucq, Conseiller du Parlement (who had bought Watteau's *Enseigne de Gersaint* a few weeks after the artist's death), by 1731; Louis Pasquier by 1752, and bequeathed by him to V. de Gournay in 1754; Jean de Jullienne before 1756; Montullé Sale, Paris, 22.xii.1783 (55); Vaudreuil Sale, Paris, 26.xi.1787 (60) sold privately; Montesquiou in 1788; J. P. B. Lebrun Sale, Paris, 11ff.iv.1791 (197) unsold and passed to his friend and partner, Desenfans; Sir Abraham Hume in 1792, who exchanged it with Desenfans for another picture; again exchanged with Hume, 1797; Desenfans 1802 Catalogue (68) and perhaps sold, but back with Desenfans again in 1803; Insurance List, 1804 (46); Bourgeois Bequest, 1811

EXHIBITED RA 1896 (78); French, 1932 (166); Landscape in French Art, 1949/50 (90); Eighteenth Century, 1954/5 (241); French, 1968 (724)

ENGRAVING G. Scotin, in reverse, *c* 1730/31, when in the Glucq Collection

VERSIONS There are about a dozen recorded (two by Pater in the 1791 Lebrun Sale Catalogue), and doubts had been expressed about the autograph quality of 156 until the X-rays revealed the changes in the course of execution. One version, attributed to Pater, is Wallace Collection 420. A passage in Caylus's *Life of Watteau* (1748) suggests that Watteau himself made a replica for Boyer de Bandol

LITERATURE E. de Goncourt, *Catalogue raisonné de l'oeuvre . . . de Watteau* (Paris, 1875), no 155; E. Dacier and A. Vuaflart, *J. de Jullienne et les graveurs . . .* (Paris, 1922–9), no 114; W. T. Whitley, *Art in England, 1800–20* (Cambridge, 1928), 33–4; L. Dimier, *Les peintres français du XVIIIe siècle* (Paris, 1928), I, no 113; K. T. Parker, *The Drawings of Watteau* (1931), 34 and fig 10; *id* in *Old Master Drawings* (1932), VII, 7 n (as based on Janssens); H. Adhémar, *Watteau* (Paris, 1950), no 196 and rep. (as 1719); F. J. B. Watson in *Burl.Mag.* (1953), XCV, 238 (the basic article, with X-rays); A. Brookner, *Watteau* (1967), 35, 37 (as 1714/15); J. Sunderland and E. Camesasca, *Complete Paintings of Watteau* (1971), no 164 and pls LII–LV (as *c* 1717)

Circle of **WATTEAU**

167 *Fête Champêtre*

This picture, attributed in the older catalogues to Watteau himself, is so close to such works as the *Halt during the Chase* in the Wallace Collection that it must derive from his immediate circle. It has been attributed to Lancret, and, more convincingly, Pater.

Canvas, $21\frac{1}{4} \times 25\frac{7}{8}$in ($54 \times 65.7$cm)

PROVENANCE Probably Desenfans Private Sale, 8ff.iv.1786 (361) and 8ff.vi.1786 (157) both as 29×34in framed; perhaps Insurance List, 1804 (47); Bourgeois Bequest, 1811

EXHIBITED RA 1896 (80: as Watteau); Landscape in French Art, 1949/50 (82: as attributed to Lancret); French 18th century, 1968 (540: as Pater)

LITERATURE F. Ingersoll-Smouse, *Pater* (Paris, 1928), no 191 and rep. (as Pater)

Jan **WEENIX** (?1642–1719)
Weenix was the son and pupil of Jan Baptist Weenix, who, after his Italian years (*c* 1642/6), painted Italianate scenes and signed them Giovanni Battista Weenix. In later years Jan painted extremely detailed still-life pictures, being especially famous for his dead hares—there are 16 such paintings in the Wallace Collection—but in his early works he is extremely close to his father, as is evident in our example.

47 *Landscape with Shepherd Boy*

Signed and dated: *JWeenix. 1664/*

This is an early work by Jan Weenix, very similar in style to such works by his father as the *Boy* of 1656 belonging to Lord Allendale. In 1664 Jan was recorded as a member of the Utrecht Painters' Guild, so, if he ever went to Italy, it must have been painted immediately after his return.

Canvas, $32\frac{1}{8} \times 39\frac{1}{4}$in ($81.6 \times 99.6$cm)

PROVENANCE Desenfans Insurance List, 1804 (79); Bourgeois Bequest, 1811

EXHIBITED NG 1976 (122)

LITERATURE W. Bernt, *Netherlandish Painters of the 17th Century* (1970), III, rep. pl 1376

Adriaen van der **WERFF** (1659–1722)
Van der Werff was born near Rotterdam and worked there for most of his life, although his main patron was the Elector Palatine at Düsseldorf who took most of his output and ennobled him in 1703. His career was highly successful—Houbraken called him the greatest Dutch painter—and he represented the end of the *fijnschilder* tradition (*see* Dou, 56), with a mixture of French Classicism.

147 *The Judgement of Paris*

Signed and dated: *Chev^r van d^r/Werff fec/an 1716*

In Greek mythology Paris, the most handsome of men and the son of King Priam, was called upon to award the golden apple inscribed 'to the fairest' to one of the three goddesses Minerva, Juno, and Venus. Minerva offered him dominion, Juno victory in war, and Venus the most beautiful woman on earth: Paris sensibly chose the last, and Venus is shown reaching for the apple. Just behind Paris, now somewhat obscured, is the figure of Mercury. Cleaning has revealed the signature and date, and two seals on the back are also connected with van der Werff. The picture, dated 1716, was purchased from the artist by the Duc d' Orléans, Regent of France, in 1718 for a very large sum.

Panel, $24\frac{7}{8} \times 18$in (63.3×45.7cm)

PROVENANCE Bought by the Duc d' Orléans, 1718; imported with the Orléans Collection to London, 1793; B. van der Gucht Sale, Christie's, 11.iii.1796 (80), bt Desenfans; Desenfans 1802 Catalogue (169) and Insurance List, 1804 (100); Bourgeois Bequest, 1811

ENGRAVING Blot, in the Orleans Gallery (the figure of Mercury is more prominent than it now is in the painting)

LITERATURE A. Houbraken, *De Groote Schouburgh* (Amsterdam, 1721), III, 403; W. Buchanan, *Memoirs . . .*, I, 208; Sm no 83; HdG, X, no 117

Benjamin **WEST**, PRA (1738–1820)
West was an American Loyalist from Pennsylvania who became George III's favourite painter. He was trained in America and Italy and settled in London where he succeeded Reynolds as President of the Royal Academy, refusing a knighthood because of his Quaker principles. He was principally a history painter, but is now more regarded as a portrait painter, especially of intimate family groups such as 586.

586   *Mother and Child*

Signed and dated: *B. West 1805*

Formerly called *Mrs West and Daughter* (*ie* the painter's daughter-in-law and granddaughter), but it is clear from the sale catalogue that it does not represent a member of West's family, nor is it related to the portrait of his two sons, now in Kansas City, which was formerly said to be a pendant.

Canvas, 36×28in (91.4×71.1cm)

PROVENANCE West family; B. West Sale, Christie's, 19.iii.1898 (146: as *Lady with Child on her Lap*), bt Murray; Fairfax Murray Gift, 1911

Benjamin **WILSON** (1721–88)
Wilson's works are often confused with those of the much greater Richard Wilson, since both are known to have painted portraits in the mid-18th century. Benjamin succeeded Hogarth as Serjeant-Painter in 1764, but from about 1770 increasingly devoted himself to science, becoming a gold medallist of the Royal Society.

561   *The Earl of Egremont*

This portrait was sold in 1911, as by Richard Wilson and of the Earl of Egremont: the identification with the 2nd Earl (1710–63) seems reasonable and would give a date for the painting in the 1750s. Richard Wilson was in Italy by 1750 and spent about seven years there. Benjamin Wilson painted Lord Chesterfield in 1752 (signed and dated picture in Leeds Gallery) and the two portraits in the Foundling Hospital (*Lord Macclesfield*, *c* 1760, and *Faquier*, 1750s) once attributed to Richard Wilson are now given to Benjamin. The similarities are such that 561 can also be attributed to Benjamin, especially as 593 (not exhibited, *Unknown Lady*) is signed and dated 1753 by him.

Canvas, 50 × 40¼in (127 × 102.2cm)

PROVENANCE Anon. Sale, Christie's, 25.xi.1911 (121: as R. Wilson), bt Agnew; Fairfax Murray Gift, 1911

EXHIBITED Tate Gallery 1925 (32)

LITERATURE W. Constable, *R. Wilson* (1953), 46, 232 and pl 133b (doubtfully R. Wilson); B. Nicolson, *Treasures of the Foundling Hospital* (Oxford, 1972), 81 and pls 77, 80

Richard **WILSON**, RA (1713/14–82)

Wilson was the greatest landscape painter of the Classical tradition in England in the 18th century. His style was formed on those of Claude, Gaspar Poussin and Cuyp, as well as Poussin himself. He went to Italy *c* 1749–*c* 1757, and decided to devote himself to landscape painting (perhaps on the advice of Zuccarelli, *see* 175), although he had previously also painted portraits (*cf* B. Wilson, 561). He was a Founder-Member of the Royal Academy in 1768, but never obtained the fame he deserved.

171 *Tivoli, the Cascatelle and the 'Villa of Maecenas'*

It was at Tivoli that Wilson is supposed to have exclaimed 'Well done water, by God!'; and certainly he represented the Cascatelle several times. Joseph Farington, RA, in his Diary for 3 May 1809, records a visit to Sir P. Bourgeois: 'He shewed me a beautiful picture of Tivoli by Wilson, for which Desenfans gave Hill the picture dealer 150 guineas. Wilson had 25 or 30 for it. In it He represented himself with an Easel painting'.

Canvas, 28⅞ × 38¼in (73.3 × 97.2cm)

PROVENANCE Dr Monro, perhaps 1796; Mr Norris of Manchester; his Sale, Wright, Liverpool, 14.iii.1804 (49); presumably Hill; Desenfans before 1807; Bourgeois Bequest, 1811

EXHIBITED BI 1817 (92)

VERSION A smaller one in the National Gallery, Dublin. Others exist, including one in the Tate Gallery (5538) once attributed to Turner

LITERATURE J. Farington, *Diary* (ed. J. Grieg, 1922–8), 3 May 1809 entry; T. Wright, *Some Account . . . Wilson* (1824) (Winstanley's copy contains details of Mr Norris: information from Mr F. Simpson); W. G. Constable, *Wilson* (1953), 84, 225 and pl 117a

Richard **WILSON** *see* Benjamin WILSON (561)

Philips **WOUWERMAN** (1619–68)

Wouwerman (or Wouwermans), a Haarlem painter, was a pupil of Frans Hals, but his style was quite different, since he specialised in landscapes with riders, hunting scenes, and battle pieces. He was noted for introducing a white horse into many of his compositions to serve as a light spot. Most of his pictures represent aristocratic pursuits such as hawking or warfare, in mountainous scenery, all of which were removed from the experience of his clientele in Haarlem. Most of his paintings (which are well represented in Dulwich) are signed with a monogram: those made up of *PHW* are said to be early works and those made up of *PHILS W* are said to be later. His work was much imitated, both by his brother Pieter (34, 36) and later artists (18).

67 *The Coast near Scheveningen*

Signed: *PHLSW* in monogram

Probably an early work.

Canvas, $19\frac{5}{8} \times 31\frac{1}{8}$in (49.6 × 79cm)

PROVENANCE Perhaps Jacomo de Wit Sale, Amsterdam, 14.v.1741 (22); Desenfans Private Sale, 8ff.iv.1786 (70); Bourgeois Bequest, 1811

LITERATURE Sm no 310; HdG, II no 978

77 *Halt of Cavaliers at an Inn*

Signed: *PHW* in monogram (the so-called 'early' monogram)

Apparently a pendant to 79.

Panel, $17\frac{1}{4} \times 24$in (43.8 × 61cm)

PROVENANCE Possibly Desenfans Sale, Skinner & Dyke, 27.ii.1795 (63); Bourgeois Bequest, 1811

EXHIBITED RA, Dutch, 1952/3 (279)

VERSION According to HdG (no 819) the main group is exactly repeated in a picture then in a private collection

LITERATURE Sm no 309: HdG, II, no 425 (as pendant to our 79)

78 *Halt of a Hunting Party*

Signed: *PHLSW* (or ?*PHW*) in monogram

Canvas, $21\frac{7}{8} \times 32\frac{5}{8}$in (55.6 × 82.9cm)

PROVENANCE Orléans Collection, Paris, in 1739; I. Hoogenbergh Sale, Amsterdam, 10.iv.1743 (10); J. Danser Nijman Sale, Amsterdam, 16.viii.1797 (303), bt Desenfans; Bourgeois Bequest, 1811

ENGRAVING J. Moyreau, *Œuvres de P. Wouwerman*, Paris, 1737–62 (no 38)

LITERATURE Sm no 215; HdG, II, no 659; J. Rosenberg, S. Slive and E. ter Kuile, *Dutch Art and Architecture* . . . (1966), rep. pl 141A

79 *Two Horsemen near a Fountain*

Signed: *PHLW* in monogram

Apparently a pendant to 77.

Panel, $17\frac{3}{8} \times 24\frac{1}{8}$in ($44.1 \times 61.3$cm)

PROVENANCE Possibly Desenfans Sale, Skinner & Dyke, 27.ii.1795 (39); Bourgeois Bequest, 1811

EXHIBITED RA, Dutch, 1952/3 (205)

LITERATURE Sm no 308; HdG, II, no 293 (as pendant to our 77)

91 *The Return from Hawking*

Signed: *PHLSW* in monogram

Probably a late work.

Panel, $18\frac{5}{8} \times 25\frac{1}{2}$in ($47.3 \times 64.8$cm)

PROVENANCE Desenfans Sale, Skinner & Dyke, 28.ii.1795 (17); Desenfans Insurance List, 1804 (84); Bourgeois Bequest, 1811

EXHIBITED RA, Dutch, 1952/3 (283)

ENGRAVING J. Moyreau

LITERATURE HdG, II, no 705

92 *Courtyard with a Farrier shoeing a Horse*

Signed: *PHLSW* in monogram

Canvas, $18\frac{1}{4} \times 21\frac{7}{8}$in ($46.3 \times 55.6$cm)

PROVENANCE D'Argenville Collection, Paris, 1766; J. B. Horion, Brussels, Sale, 11.ix.1788 (71), bt Walkiers; Desenfans by 1802; Bourgeois Bequest, 1811

EXHIBITED RA, Dutch, 1952/3 (294)

ENGRAVING J. Moyreau, *Œuvres de P. Wouwerman*, Paris, 1737–62 (no 26)

LITERATURE Sm no 69; HdG, II, no 131

97 *Halt of Travellers*

Signed: *PHLSW* in monogram

Because of its resemblance to the work of I. van Ostade this has been thought to be an early work.

Panel, $17\frac{3}{4} \times 16\frac{3}{8}$in ($45.1 \times 41.6$cm)

PROVENANCE Desenfans 1802 Catalogue (perhaps 114); Bourgeois Bequest, 1811

EXHIBITED Probably not BI 1815 (71); RA, Dutch, 1952/3 (596)

LITERATURE Sm no 232; HdG, II, no 317 (both, probably wrongly, as exhibited at the British Institution in 1815)

182 *Peasants in the Fields: Hay Harvest*

Signed: *PHLW* in monogram

Panel, $16\frac{1}{4} \times 14\frac{1}{8}$in ($41.3 \times 35.9$cm)

PROVENANCE J. Van Bergen van der Grijp and others, Sale, Soeterwoude, 25.vi.1784 (134), bt

Fouquet; very probably Desenfans Insurance List, 1804 (83: *A Cart and figures . . .*);
Bourgeois Bequest, 1811

EXHIBITED RA, Dutch, 1952/3 (289)

LITERATURE Sm no 311; HdG, II, no 941

193 *Halt of Sportsmen*

The 1880 Catalogue records a monogram, perhaps *PHLW*, and this is repeated in the 1926
Catalogue, although Hofstede de Groot had referred to it as 'doubtful': no trace is now
visible.

Panel, $12\frac{1}{8} \times 14\frac{3}{8}$in (30.8 × 36.5cm)

PROVENANCE Possibly Paillet Collection, 1777; Bourgeois Bequest, 1811

EXHIBITED Perhaps BI 1843 (75); RA 1952/3 (450)

LITERATURE Sm no 137 describes the Paillet picture, which may be identical with 193; HdG,
II, no 660, which may be identical with no 677d

Imitator of Philips **WOUWERMAN**

18 *Hay Harvest*

An old copy of a Wouwerman in the Royal Collection.

Canvas on panel, $18\frac{1}{8} \times 23\frac{3}{4}$in (46 × 60.4cm)

PROVENANCE Bourgeois Bequest, 1811

EXHIBITED RA, Dutch, 1952/3 (291)

LITERATURE HdG, II, no 940 (as a copy of the Royal Collection picture)

Pieter **WOUWERMAN** (1623–82)

Pieter was the younger brother of Philips, who was probably his teacher. Pieter seems to
have imitated his brother's work, perhaps meeting the demand after his brother's death in
1668.

34 *Sandhills with Figures* and *Sandbank with Travellers*
36

Signed: (36) *PW* in monogram

These pictures are obviously intended as a pair, and the attribution to Pieter Wouwerman
depends partly on the form of monogram on 36 and partly on the fact that they are coarser in
handling than genuine works by Philips Wouwerman (*cf* 182). There are similar pictures by
Pieter in the Fitzwilliam Museum, Cambridge.

Canvas, both $9\frac{1}{2} \times 14\frac{1}{8}$in (24.1 × 36cm)

PROVENANCE (34 may well be Desenfans Sale, Skinner & Dyke, 28.ii.1795 (93: Wouwermans,
A Landscape with a Traveller giving Charity to poor Peasants)); both were in the Bourgeois
Bequest, 1811

LITERATURE Richter in the 1880 Catalogue first made the attribution to Pieter Wouwerman

After John Michael **WRIGHT** (?1617–1700)

424 *Charles II*

Charles Stuart (1630–85) became Charles II at the Restoration of the Monarchy, 1660. This portrait, formerly attributed to Greenhill, is a version of the portrait by J. M. Wright, of which another early copy or studio replica is in the National Portrait Gallery (531).

Canvas, 30 × 25in (76.2 × 63.5cm)

PROVENANCE Cartwright Bequest, 1686 (76: without attribution)

EXHIBITED National Portrait Exhibition, 1866 (874: as by Greenhill)

LITERATURE D. T. Piper, *Catalogue of 17th Century Portraits* (NPG catalogue, 1963), 67, no 531 and pl 9b

Jan **WYNANTS** (active 1643–84)
Wynants was a Haarlem landscape painter and inn-keeper. He painted landscapes exclusively, the figures being supplied by others, such as Wouwerman, Lingelbach, and his own pupil Adriaen van de Velde. The landscapes often feature a dead tree in the foreground, with dunes and a winding road: they greatly influenced English landscape painters such as Gainsborough (*cf* 588).

114 *Landscape with Cow drinking* and *Landscape*
117
Signed: (114) *J Wynants*

Panel, (114) 6⅛ × 7⅜in (15.6 × 18.7cm);
    (117) 6¼ × 7⅜in (15.8 × 18.8cm)

PROVENANCE Desenfans Insurance List, 1804 (23, 24); Bourgeois Bequest, 1811

LITERATURE Sm nos 165, 166; HdG, VIII, nos 312 (114: as signed in full) and 590

210 *A Wood near The Hague, with a View of the Huis ten Bosch*

The Huis ten Bosch ('House in the Wood') is about 1½ miles east of The Hague. It was built for the Stadhouder (Provincial Governor) between 1645 and 1652. The attribution of this picture oscillates between J. van Ruisdael and Wynants: the 1880 Catalogue reproduces a *JVR* monogram and accordingly attributes the picture to Ruisdael, but this is no longer visible, and, in any case, Smith attributed it to Wynants in 1835.

Canvas, 46¾ × 61in (118.7 × 154.9cm)

PROVENANCE Bourgeois Bequest, 1811 (as 'Ruysdael')

EXHIBITED RA 1952/3 (316: as by Wynants)

LITERATURE Dulwich Catalogue, 1816 (as Ruisdael); Sm no 168 (as Wynants); HdG, IV, no 761 (as Ruisdael); H. Gerson in *Burl.Mag.* (1953), XCV, 34, 51 n 17 (as Wynants and van Kessel)

Jan **WYNANTS** *see* Roelof van VRIES (7)

Francesco **ZUCCARELLI**, RA (1702–88)
Zuccarelli was born near Florence but was trained in Venice and worked with the architect
Visentini on architectural fantasies (some in the Royal Collection). He arrived in London in
1752 and stayed ten years, with great success, returning in 1765. He was patronised by
George III and became a Founder-Member of the Royal Academy (1768), before retiring to
Italy in 1772. His rather sweet Rococo landscapes were generally preferred to those by his
friend Richard Wilson.

175   *Landscape with a Fountain, Figures and Cattle*

A characteristically idealised Italian landscape in the pinkish tones employed by Zuccarelli.

Canvas, $39\frac{1}{4} \times 49\frac{1}{8}$in (99.7 × 124.8cm)

PROVENANCE Bourgeois Bequest, 1811

Antwerp Master (second quarter of the 16th century)
250 *The Crucifixion*

Ludolf Bakhuizen (1631–1708)
327 *Boats in a Storm*

Mary Beale (1633–99)
574 *Young Man, perhaps one of the Painter's Sons*

Lower left
Sir William Beechey, RA (1753–1839)
17 *Sir Peter Francis Bourgeois, RA*

Lower right
Copy after Sir William Beechey, RA
by Sir Peter Francis Bourgeois, RA (1756–1811)
466 *Sir Peter Francis Bourgeois, RA*

Sir William Beechey, RA (1753–1839)
111 *John Philip Kemble*

Sir William Beechey, RA (1753–1839)
169 *Charles Small Pybus*, MP

Nicolaes Berchem (1620–83)
88 *A Farrier and Peasants near
Roman Ruins*

Nicolaes Berchem (1620–83)
122 *A Road Through a Wood*

Nicolaes Berchem (1620–83)   157 *Travelling Peasants ('Le Soir')*

Nicolaes Berchem (1620–83)   166 *Roman Fountain with Cattle and Figures ('Le Midi')*

Nicolaes Berchem (1620–83)
196 *Peasants at a Ford*

Simon Du Bois (Dubois) (1632–1708)
584 *Sir William Jones*

Cornelis Bol (?1589–1666 or later?)
360 *Westminster and the Thames*

Simon Du Bois (Dubois) (1632–1708)
585 *Lady Jones*

Jan Both (c 1618–52)
12 *Banks of a Brook*

Jan Both (c 1618–52)
10 *Italian Landscape with an Ox-cart*

Jan Both (c 1618–52)
15 *Road by the Edge of a Lake*

Jan Both (c 1618–52)
208 *A Mountain Path*

Sébastien Bourdon (1616–71)
557 *A Brawl in a Guard-room*

Bartholomeus Breenbergh (1599/1600–57)   23   *A Ruined Temple*

Bartholomeus Breenbergh (1599/1600–57)   26   *Landscape with a Roman Ruin*

Bartholomeus Breenbergh (1599/1600–57)
338 *Valley with Ruins and Figures*

Henry Perronet Briggs, RA (1791–1844)
291 *Charles Kemble*

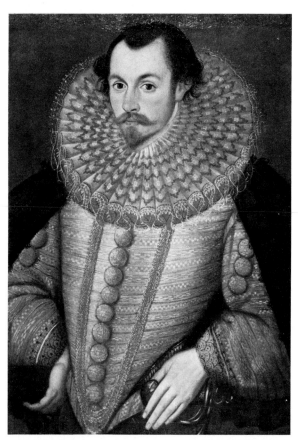

British School
375 *Called Sir Martin Frobisher*

British School
385 *Nathan Field*

British School
390 *Tom Bond*

British School
391 *Head of a Man, called William Sly*

British School
395 *Richard Burbage*

British School
400 *'Old Mr Cartwright'*

British School
411 *'Young Mr Cartwright'*

Lower left
British School
423 *Richard Perkins*

Lower right
British School
430 *Michael Drayton*

British School
443 *Edward Alleyn, Founder of the
College of God's Gift at Dulwich*

British School
444 *Joan Alleyn*

British School
445 *Francis Bacon, 1st Baron Verulam
and Viscount St Alban*

British School
569 *Nathaniel Lee*

British School
604 *John Dive*

Adriaen Brouwer (1605/6–38)   108 *Interior of a Tavern*

Abraham van Calraet (1642–1722)   65 *White Horse in a Riding School*

Abraham van Calraet (1642–1722)   71 *Two Horses*

Abraham van Calraet (1642–1722)   181 *Fishing on the Ice*

Abraham van Calraet (1642–1722)   296 *A Riding School in the Open Air*

Govaert Camphuysen (1623/4–72)   64 *Two Peasants with Cows*

Canaletto (1697–1768)
599 *The Bucentaur at the Molo on Ascension Day*

Canaletto (1697–1768)
600 *Old Walton Bridge over the Thames*

Agostino Carracci (1557–1602)
255 *The Last Communion of S. Francis*

After Annibale Carracci (1560–1609)
265 *The Entombment of Christ*

Attributed to Lodovico Carracci (1555–1619)
232 *SS. Peter and Francis of Assisi*

Studio of Lodovico Carracci
269 *S. Francis in Meditation*

L. A. Castro
(active last quarter of the 17th century)
359 *Seapiece*

L. A. Castro
(active last quarter of the 17th century)
361 *Seapiece*

L. A. Castro (active last quarter of the 17th century)
436 *Seapiece*

L. A. Castro (active last quarter of the 17th century)
428 *Seapiece*

L. A. Castro
(active last quarter of the 17th century)
437 *Seapiece*

L. A. Castro
(active last quarter of the 17th century)
517 *Seapiece*

Claude Lorrain (1600–82)
205 *Jacob with Laban and his Daughters*

Circle of Claude   174 *The Campo Vaccino, Rome*

Imitator of Claude   215 *Classical Seaport at Sunset*

School of Claude   53 *Landscape with a Column and Figures*

Copy after Claude
312 *The Rest on the Flight into Egypt*

Attributed to John Baptist Closterman
(*c* 1660–1711)
611 *A Physician, formerly called Boerhaave, but perhaps Blackmore*

Adam Colonia (1634–85)
371 *Sheep Shearing*

Adam Colonia (1634–85)
431 *The Flight into Egypt*

John De Critz(?) (1555–1641)
548 *James I and VI*

Aelbert Cuyp (1620–91)
4 *View on a Plain*

Aelbert Cuyp (1620–91)   96 *An Evening Ride near a River*

Aelbert Cuyp (1620–91)
124 *A Road near a River*

Aelbert Cuyp (1620–91) 128 *Herdsmen with Cows*

Aelbert Cuyp (1620–91) 144 *Cattle near the Maas, with Dordrecht in the distance*

Aelbert Cuyp (1620–91)
348 *Landscape with Cattle and Figures*

Michael Dahl (1656/9–1743)
575 *Unknown Man*

Michael Dahl (1656/9–1743)
576 *Unknown Woman*

Dirck van Delen
(1604/5–71)
470 *The Entrance to
a Palace*

Carlo Dolci (1616–86)
242 *S. Catherine of Siena*

Stephen Poyntz Denning (*c* 1787–1864)
304 *Queen Victoria, aged Four*

Gerrit (Gerard) Dou (1613–75)
56 *A Lady playing a Clavichord*

Gaspar Dughet (1615–75)
70 *Landscape in the Roman Campagna*

Karel Du Jardin (Dujardin) (?1621/2–78)
72 *Peasants with a White Horse*

Karel Du Jardin (Dujardin) (?1621/2–78)
82 *A Smith shoeing an Ox*

Cornelis Dusart (1660–1704)
39 *Figures in the Courtyard of an old Building*

Sir Anthony van Dyck (1599–1641)
90 *The Madonna and Child*

Sir Anthony van Dyck (1599–1641)
132 *Sunset Landscape with a Shepherd and his Flock*

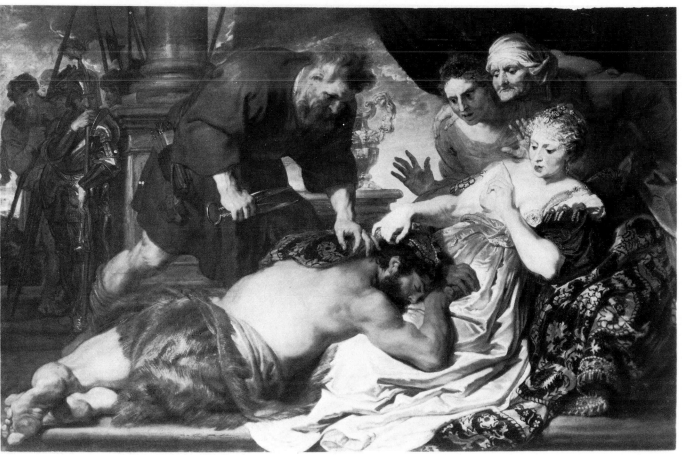

Sir Anthony van Dyck (1599–1641)
127 *Samson and Delilah*

Sir Anthony van Dyck
(1599–1641)
170 *A Young Man, perhaps the
Earl of Bristol*

Sir Anthony van Dyck
(1599–1641)
194 *Venetia Stanley, Lady
Digby, on her Death-bed*

Sir Anthony van Dyck (1599–1641)
173 *Emmanuel Philibert of Savoy,
Prince of Oneglia*

Studio of van Dyck
81 *Charity*

Circle of Adam Elsheimer (1578–1610)
22 *Susanna and the Elders*

Flemish School(?)
14 *A Village on Fire*

Francesco Fracanzano (1612–c 1656)
558 *The Prodigal Son*

Thomas Gainsborough, RA (1727–88)
66 *Philipp Jakob de Loutherbourg*, RA

Thomas Gainsborough, RA (1727–88)
140 *Thomas Linley the Elder*

Thomas Gainsborough, RA (1727–88)
302 *Samuel Linley*, RN

Thomas Gainsborough, RA (1727–88)
316 *Mrs Moody and two of her Children*

Thomas Gainsborough, RA (1727–88)
320 *The Linley Sisters (Mrs Sheridan and Mrs Tickell)*

Thomas Gainsborough, RA (1727–88)
588 *An Unknown Couple in a Landscape*

Thomas Gainsborough, RA (1727–88)
331 *Thomas Linley the Younger*

Aert de Gelder (1645–1727)
126 *Jacob's Dream*

John Greenhill (*c* 1640/45–76)
374 *Unknown Man, perhaps an Actor*

John Greenhill (*c* 1640/45)–76)
387 *Jane Cartwright*

John Greenhill (*c* 1640/45–76)   393   *William Cartwright*

John Greenhill (*c* 1640/45–76)
399 *Elisabeth Cartwright*

John Greenhill (*c* 1640/45–76)
416 *James, Duke of York, later James II*

John Greenhill (*c* 1640/45–76)
418 *Self-portrait*

Jean-Alexis Grimou (1678–1733)
74 *Young Woman*

Guercino (1591–1666)   282 *The Woman taken in Adultery*

Adriaen Hanneman (*c* 1601–71)
572 *Unknown Man*

Guilliam van Herp I (*c* 1614–77)
332 *Figures and Sheep at a Well*

Jan van der Heyden (1637–1712)   155 *Two Churches and a Town Wall*

Meindert Hobbema (1638–1709)
87 *Wooded Landscape with Water-mill*

Gerard Hoet (1648–1733)
176 *Apollo and Daphne*

Gerard Hoet (1648–1733)
179 *Pan and Syrinx*

William Hogarth (1697–1764)
562 *A Fishing Party ('The Fair Angler')*

William Hogarth (1697–1764)
580 *Unknown Man*

Gerard van Honthorst (1590–1656)
571 *A Lady aged 40*

Attributed to John Hoppner, RA (1758–1810)
589 *Unknown Man*

Gerrit Willemsz. Horst (*c* 1612–52)
214 *Isaac Blessing Jacob*

Thomas Hudson (1701–79)
578 *Unknown Lady*

Jan van Huysum (1682–1749)
42 *A Delft Bowl with Fruit*

Thomas Hudson (1701–79)
579 *Unknown Gentleman*

Jan van Huysum (1682–1749) 61 *A Delft Vase with Flowers*

Jan van Huysum (1682–1749)
139 *Vase with Flowers*

Jan van Huysum (1682–1749)
120 *Vase with Flowers*

Charles Jervas (?1675–1739)
567 *Dorothy, Lady Townshend*

Cornelius Johnson (1593–1661)
564 *A Dutch Gentleman*

George Knapton (1698–1778)   606 *Lucy Ebberton*

Sir Godfrey Kneller (1646/9–1723)
570 *Two Children, perhaps of the
Howard Family*

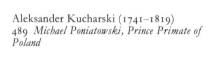

Aleksander Kucharski (1741–1819)
489 *Michael Poniatowski, Prince Primate of
Poland*

Aleksander Kucharski (1741–1819)
490 *Stanislas Augustus Poniatowski, King of Poland*

Samuel Lane (1780–1859)
449 *George Bartley*

Jan Lapp (active 1627–70)
330 *An Italian Landscape with Figures and Cattle*

Filippo Lauri (1623–94)
164 *Apollo and Marsyas*

Sir Thomas Lawrence, PRA (1769–1830)
178 *William Linley*

Sir Thomas Lawrence, PRA (1769–1830)
474 *The Rev. Ozias Thurstan Linley, as a Boy*

Sir Thomas Lawrence, PRA (1769–1830)
475 *Maria Linley*

Charles Lebrun (1619–90) 202 *The Massacre of the Innocents*

School of Lebrun
188 *A Man, called Molière*

Charles Lebrun (1619–90) 244 *Horatius Cocles defending the Bridge*

Sir Peter Lely (1618–80)   555 *Nymphs by a Fountain*

Sir Peter Lely (1618–80)
559 *Lady in Blue*

Sir Peter Lely (1618–80)
560 *Lady in Blue holding a Flower*

Sir Peter Lely (1618–80)
563 *Young Man as a Shepherd*

Johannes Lingelbach (1622–74)
326 *An Italian Seaport*

James Lonsdale (1777–1839)
456 *Mrs Thomas Linley*

Philipp Jakob de Loutherbourg, RA
(1740–1812)
297 *Landscape with Cattle*

Philipp Jakob de Loutherbourg, RA
(1740–1812)
339 *Landscape with Cattle and Figures*

Circle of Mabuse (active 1503–32)
505 *The Fall of Man*

Alessandro Magnasco (1677–1749)
279 *The Entombment of Christ*

Attributed to Carlo Maratta (1625–1713)
274 *The Holy Family with S. Anne,
the Baptist and Zacharias*

Juan Bautista del Mazo (*c* 1612–67)
277 *One of the Painter's Sons*

Attributed to Jan Miel (1599–1663)
20 *Landscape with Figures*

Circle of Pier Francesco Mola (1612–66)
75 *Pluto and Proserpine*

Jakob van Moscher (active 1635–55)
16 *A Road near Cottages*

Robert Muller (active 1789–1800)
587 *Mrs George Morland*

Bartolomé Estéban Murillo (1617/18–82)
199 *The Flower Girl*

Bartolomé Estéban Murillo (1617/18–82)
222 *Two Peasant Boys and a Negro Boy*

Bartolomé Estéban Murillo (1617/18–82)
224 *Two Peasant Boys*

Opposite
Bartolomé Estéban Murillo (1617/18–82)   281 *The Madonna of the Rosary*

Pieter Nason (*c* 1612–*c* 1689)
556 *Unknown Man*

Peeter Neeffs I (active 1605–*d* in or after 1656)
141 *Interior of a Gothic Church*

James Northcote, RA (1746–1831)
28 *Noel Joseph Desenfans*

Archer James Oliver (1774–1842)
476 *A Man of the Linley Family,
probably the Rev. Ozias*

Adriaen van Ostade (1610–85)
45 *Interior of a Cottage*

Opposite
James Northcote, RA (1746–1831)
172 *Sir Peter Francis Bourgeois, RA*

Above left
Adriaen van Ostade (1610–85)
98 *A Woman with a Beer-jug*

Above right
Adriaen van Ostade (1610–85)
113 *A Man Smoking*

Adriaen van Ostade (1610–85)
115 *Boors making Merry*

Imitator of Jean-Baptiste Pater
(1695–1736)
620 *Encampment of Soldiers*

Piero di Cosimo (*c* 1462–?1521)
258 *A Young Man*

Pietro da Cortona (1595–1669)
121 *The Age of Bronze*

Opposite
Cornelis van Poelenburgh (*c* 1586–1667)
25 *Nymphs and Satyr*

After Pietro da Cortona
226 *Sta Martina calling down Lightning on the Idols*

Opposite
Nicolas Poussin (1594–1665)
203 *A Roman Road*

Nicolas Poussin (1594–1665)   234 *The Nurture of Jupiter*

Nicolas Poussin (1594–1665)
236 *The Triumph of David*

Nicolas Poussin (1594–1665)   238 *Rinaldo and Armida*

Nicolas Poussin (1594–1665)   240 *The Return of the Holy Family from Egypt*

Nicolas Poussin (1594–1665)
263 *Sta Rita of Cascia*

Nicolas Poussin (1594–1665)
481 *Venus and Mercury*

Copy after Poussin
227 *The Adoration of the Magi*

Cornelis Pronk (1691–1759)
615 *Unknown Man*

Adam Pynacker (1622–73)
86 *Landscape with Sportsmen and Game*

Adam Pynacker (1622–73)
183 *Bridge in an Italian Landscape*

Attributed to Allan Ramsay (1713–84)
596 *Unknown Man*

Below left
Raphael (1483–1520)
241 *S. Francis of Assisi* from the *Colonna Altarpiece*

Below right
Raphael (1483–1520)
243 *S. Anthony of Padua* from the *Colonna Altarpiece*

Copy after Raphael   507   *The Transfiguration*

Rembrandt van Ryn (1606–69) 99 *Jacob III de Gheyn*

Rembrandt van Ryn (1606–69)   163 *Girl leaning on a Window-sill*

Rembrandt van Ryn (1606–69)
221 *A Young Man, perhaps the Artist's Son Titus*

Guido Reni (1575–1642)
262 *S. John the Baptist in the Wilderness*

Attributed to Reni
204 *Lucretia*

Sir Joshua Reynolds, PRA (1723–92)
17a *A Girl with a Baby*

Sir Joshua Reynolds, PRA
(1723–92)
102 *Recovery from Sickness, an Allegory*

Sir Joshua Reynolds, PRA
(1723–92)
104 *Self-portrait*

Sir Joshua Reynolds, PRA (1723–92)
223 *The Infant Samuel*

Sir Joshua Reynolds, PRA (1723–92)
318 *Mrs Siddons as the Tragic Muse*

Left
Sir Joshua Reynolds, PRA (1723–92)
333 *A General on Horseback*

Right
Copy after Reynolds
627 *Margaret Desenfans*

Sir Joshua Reynolds, PRA (1723–92)
598 *Robert Dodsley*

Neapolitan Follower of Jusepe Ribera
(?1591–1652)
233 *The Locksmith*

Sebastiano Ricci (1659–1734)
134 *The Fall of the Rebel Angels*

Sebastiano Ricci (1659–1734)   195 *The Resurrection*

Hyacinthe Rigaud (1659–1743)
83 *Nicolas Boileau*

Studio of Rigaud
85 *Louis XIV*

Studio of Rigaud
93 *A Man, called Racine*

John Riley (1646–91)
565 *John, Lord Somers, Lord Chancellor*
of England

John Riley (1646–91)
568 *William Chiffinch*

George Romney (1734–1802)
440 *Dr Joseph Allen*, MD, *Master of Dulwich College*

George Romney (1734–1802)
590 *William Hayley*

Sir Peter Paul Rubens (1577–1640)
19 *Aeneas with the Arms of Mezentius*

Salvator Rosa (1615–73)
216 *Soldiers Gambling*

Sir Peter Paul Rubens (1577–1640)   40 *SS. Amandus and Walburga*   40a *SS. Catherine of Alexandria and Eligius*

Sir Peter Paul Rubens (1577–1640)
43 *Ceres and Two Nymphs with a Cornucopia*

Sir Peter Paul Rubens
(1577–1640)
125 *S. Barbara fleeing from her Father*

Sir Peter Paul Rubens (1577–1640)
131 *Hagar in the Desert*

Sir Peter Paul Rubens (1577–1640)
143 *Catherine Manners, Duchess of
Buckingham*(?)

Sir Peter Paul Rubens (1577–1640)
264 *The Three Graces*

Opposite
Sir Peter Paul Rubens (1577–1640)
285 *Venus, Mars and Cupid*

Sir Peter Paul Rubens (1577–1640)
451 *Venus mourning Adonis*

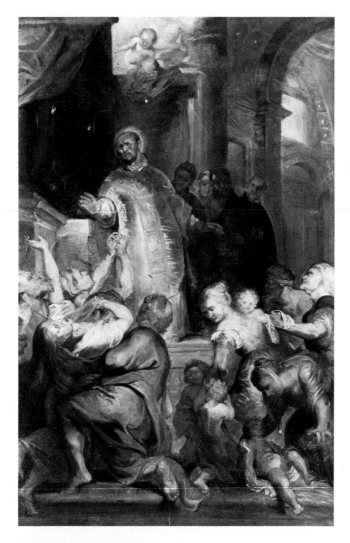

Attributed to Rubens
148 *S. Ignatius Loyola exorcising*

Attributed to Rubens
165 *Venus and Cupid warming themselves
(Venus frigida)*

Jacob van Ruisdael (1628/9–82)
105   *A Waterfall*

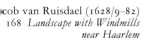

cob van Ruisdael (1628/9–82)
168   *Landscape with Windmills*
near Haarlem

Herman Saftleven (1609–85)
44 *View on the Rhine*

Gerard Sanders (*c* 1702–67)
577 *Archibald Hope the Elder*

Daniel Seghers, SJ (1590–1661)
322 *A Wreath of Flowers encircling a Painted Relief of the Madonna and Child with S. Anne*

Pieter Cornelisz. van Slingelandt (1640–91)
116 *Boy with a Flagon and a Bird's Nest*

SOEST

Gerard Soest (c 1602–81)
573 *Aubrey de Vere, 20th Earl of Oxford*

Attributed to Soest
592 *Sir Harry Vane*

Andrea Soldi (c 1703–71)
603 *Louis François Roubiliac*

Spanish School, 17th century
185 *Jacob and Rachel at the Well*

Spanish School(?)
69 *The Crucifixion of S. Peter*

Abraham Storck (1644–1704 or later?)
608 *View of Rotterdam*

Robert Streater
(1624–80)
376 *Landscape*

Herman van
Swanevelt
(1600–55)
11 *The Arch of
Constantine, Rome*

Herman van Swanevelt (1600–55)   136 *An Italian Landscape*

Herman van Swanevelt (1600–55)   219 *Italian Landscape with Bridge*

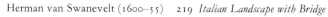

Attributed to David Teniers I (1582–1649) or II (1610–90)   314 *S. Peter In Penitence*

Attributed to David Teniers I (1582–1649) or II (1610–90)   323 *S. Mary Magdalen in Penitence*

David Teniers II (1610–90)   31 *Gipsies in a Landscape*

David Teniers II (1610–90)   33 *A Peasant eating Mussels*

David Teniers II (1610–90)
49 *A Road near a Cottage*

David Teniers II (1610–90)
52 *A Cottage*

David Teniers II (1610–90)
54 *A Guard Room*

David Teniers II (1610–90)
57 *Brickmakers near Hemiksem*

David Teniers II (1610–90)　76　*Peasants conversing*

David Teniers II (1610–90)　95　*A Castle and its Proprietors*

David Teniers II (1610–90)
106 *A Peasant holding a Glass*

David Teniers II (1610–90)
110 *An Old Woman*

David Teniers II (1610–90)   112 *Winter Scene with a Man killing a Pig*

David Teniers II (1610–90)　142　*The Chaff-cutter*

David Teniers II (1610–90)　146　*A Sow and her Litter*

Attributed to Teniers
35 *Cottage with Peasants playing Cards*

Attributed to David Teniers I
299 *Sunset Landscape with a Shepherd and his Flock*

Studio of David Teniers II   614 *The Seven Corporal Works of Mercy*

Giovanni Battista Tiepolo (1696–1700) or Giovanni Domenico Tiepolo (1727–1804)
158 *Joseph receiving Pharoah's Ring*

Giovanni Battista Tiepolo (1696–1700)
186, 189 *Diana, Apollo, and another Goddess*

Giovanni Battista Tiepolo (1696–1700)
278 *Fortitude and Wisdom* or *Wisdom putting Ignorance to Flight*

John Vanderbank (*c* 1694–1739)
581 *Lady in White*

Studio of Diego de Silva y Velazquez
(1599–1660)
249 *Philip IV, King of Spain*

Adriaen van de Velde (1636–72)
51 *Cows and Sheep in a Wood*

Willem van de Velde II (1633–1707)
103 *A Brisk Breeze*

Willem van de Velde II (1633–1707)
197 *A Calm*

VERBOOM

Adriaen Verboom (*c* 1628–*c* 1670)
9 *Landscape with a Church*

Claude-Joseph Vernet (1714–89)
319 *An Italianate Harbour Scene*

Claude-Joseph Vernet (1714–89)   328 *Italian Landscape*

School of Vernet
300 *Seaport at Sunrise*

Reconstruction of Veronese altarpiece
see 270 *opposite*

Paolo Veronese (*c* 1528–88)
270 *S. Jerome and a Donor*

Studio of Veronese
239 *The Mystic Marriage of S. Catherine*

Roelof van Vries (1630/31–after 1681)
7 *Landscape with a Tower*

Antoine Watteau (1684–1721)   156 *Les Plaisirs du Bal ('Le Bal Champêtre')*

Circle of Watteau   167 *Fête Champêtre*

Jan Weenix (?1642–1719)   47 *Landscape with Shepherd Boy*

Adriaen van der Werff (1659–1722)
147 *The Judgement of Paris*

Benjamin West, PRA (1738–1820)
586 *Mother and Child*

Benjamin Wilson (1721–88)
561 *The Earl of Egremont*

Richard Wilson, RA (1713/14–82)
171 *Tivoli, the Cascatelle and the*
'Villa of Maecenas'

Philips Wouwerman (1619–68)   67 *The Coast near Scheveningen*

Philips Wouwerman (1619–68)   77 *Halt of Cavaliers at an Inn*

Philips Wouwerman (1619–68) 78 *Halt of a Hunting Party*

Philips Wouwerman (1619–68) 79 *Two Horsemen near a Fountain*

Philips Wouwerman (1619–68)   91 *The Return from Hawking*

Philips Wouwerman (1619–68)   92 *Courtyard with a Farrier shoeing a Horse*

Philips Wouwerman (1619–68)
97 *Halt of Travellers*

Philips Wouwerman (1619–68)
182 *Peasants in the Fields: Hay Harvest*

Philips Wouwerman (1619–68)   193 *Halt of Sportsmen*

Imitator of Philips Wouwerman   18 *Hay Harvest*

Pieter Wouwerman (1623–82)   34 *Sandhills with Figures*

Pieter Wouwerman (1623–82)
36 *Sandbank with Travellers*

After John Michael Wright (?1617–1700)
424 *Charles II*

Jan Wynants (active 1643–84) 114 *Landscape with Cow drinking*

Jan Wynants (active 1643–84)
117 *Landscape*

Jan Wynants (active 1643–84) 210 *A Wood near The Hague, with a View of the Huis ten Bosch*

Francesco Zuccarelli, RA (1702–88)   175 *Landscape, with a Fountain, Figures and Cattle*

Numerical Index of Exhibited Paintings

For numbers not in this list, *see* below.

Numerical Index of Non-Exhibited Paintings

Most of the following pictures are in the Gallery store. Exceptions, including those destroyed in the Second World War, are noted in the list. Some paintings, mainly portraits, are in the various College buildings, not the Gallery.

The attributions given here should not be regarded as definitive: they derive mainly from the 1926 and 1953 Catalogues and are subject to revision as work on a new catalogue of the reserve pictures proceeds.

283 Domenichino
Adoration of the Shepherds
Now in the National Gallery, Edinburgh

284 School of Reni
Mater Dolorosa
Canvas (circular), $19\frac{7}{8} \times 19\frac{1}{16}$in
$(50.5 \times 48.4$cm)

286 Italian School(?)
Old Man
Canvas, $15\frac{1}{2} \times 11$in $(39.4 \times 27.9$cm)

287 Turchi
*The Madonna with S. Lorenzo Giustiniani
and a Venetian Nobleman*
Marble (arched top), $19\frac{1}{2} \times 10\frac{1}{4}$in
$(49.5 \times 26$cm)

288 School of van Dyck
The Deposition
Panel, $23\frac{3}{16} \times 17\frac{3}{16}$in $(58.8 \times 43.7$cm)

289 Bugiardini
Holy Family with S. John
Panel, $32\frac{7}{8} \times 26\frac{1}{2}$in $(83.5 \times 67.3$cm)

290 C. de Vos
Old Lady
Canvas, $67\frac{5}{8} \times 41\frac{7}{8}$in $(171.8 \times 106.4$cm)

292 Dolci
Female Saint (?Veronica)
Canvas (oval), $29\frac{3}{8} \times 24\frac{1}{4}$in
$(74.6 \times 61.6$cm)

293 After Jordaens
Satyr and Peasants
Canvas, $18\frac{5}{8} \times 22$in $(47.3 \times 55.9$cm)

294 Bourgeois
Landscape with Cattle
Canvas, $36\frac{1}{8} \times 57\frac{1}{8}$in $(91.7 \times 145.1$cm)

295 Venetian School
Artist Drawing
Canvas, $35\frac{7}{8} \times 27\frac{7}{8}$in $(91.1 \times 70.7$cm)

298 Monamy
A Calm
Canvas, $24\frac{1}{4} \times 29\frac{7}{8}$in $(61.5 \times 75.9$cm)

301 Bourgeois
Funeral Procession
Canvas, $51\frac{1}{4} \times 81\frac{1}{8}$in $(131.5 \times 206.1$cm)

303 Italian School(?)
Landscape with Aqueduct
Canvas, $18\frac{3}{8} \times 13\frac{3}{4}$in $(46.6 \times 34.9$cm)

305 Italian School(?)
Castle and Waterfall
Canvas, $18\frac{3}{8} \times 13\frac{3}{4}$in $(46.6 \times 34.9$cm)

306 Vernet
Seaport, Sunset
Canvas, $26\frac{5}{8} \times 39$in $(67.6 \times 99$cm)

307 P. Longhi
Girls Sewing
Canvas, $22 \times 28\frac{7}{8}$in $(56 \times 73.3$cm)

308 Bourgeois
Seashore
Canvas, $36\frac{1}{8} \times 57\frac{3}{4}$in $(91.7 \times 146.7$cm)

309 Claude
Gathering Grapes
Canvas, $20 \times 26\frac{1}{2}$in $(50.8 \times 67.3$cm)

310 Bourgeois
Friar in Prayer
Panel (arched top), $6\frac{1}{2} \times 4\frac{11}{16}$in
$(16.5 \times 12$cm)

311 Bourgeois
Soldiers
Panel (arched top), $6\frac{1}{2} \times 4\frac{11}{16}$in
$(16.5 \times 12$cm)

313 Franceschini
Guardian Angel
Canvas, $39\frac{1}{2} \times 29\frac{5}{8}$in $(100.3 \times 75.3$cm)

315 After Cuyp
View on the Maas
Canvas, $25 \times 31\frac{7}{8}$in $(63.5 \times 81$cm)

317 Lost

321 Teniers
Winter
Canvas, $25\frac{3}{8} \times 16\frac{7}{8}$in $(67 \times 42.9$cm)

324 After Potter
Cattle
Panel, $7\frac{3}{8} \times 9\frac{1}{8}$in $(18.7 \times 23.2$cm)

325 Bourgeois
Landscape with Cattle
Canvas, $40\frac{1}{8} \times 50\frac{3}{16}$in $(101.9 \times 127.5$cm)

329 Dutch School
Hawk and Sparrows
Canvas, $29\frac{1}{8} \times 20\frac{3}{4}$in $(73.9 \times 52.7$cm)

334 After Potter
Cattle and Sheep
Panel, $15\frac{1}{8} \times 20\frac{7}{8}$in $(38.4 \times 53$cm)

335 Bourgeois
Seashore
Canvas, $39\frac{3}{4} \times 49\frac{3}{4}$in $(101 \times 106.3$cm)

336 School of Claude
Mercury and Argus
Panel, $12\frac{13}{16} \times 14\frac{3}{8}$in $(32.5 \times 36.5$cm)

337 Berchem
Washerwomen
Panel, $14\frac{7}{16} \times 17\frac{1}{4}$in $(36.8 \times 43.8$cm)

340 Copy after A. van der Neer
River Scene by Moonlight
Canvas, $22\frac{5}{8} \times 29\frac{1}{8}$in $(57.5 \times 74$cm)

341 Teniers
Autumn
Canvas, $26\frac{3}{8} \times 16\frac{7}{8}$in $(67 \times 42.9$cm)

342 Bourgeois
Man holding a Horse
Canvas, $8\frac{3}{8} \times 6\frac{3}{16}$in $(21 \times 15.8$cm)

343 Dutch School
A Cow
Panel, $7\frac{13}{16} \times 5\frac{3}{8}$in $(19.8 \times 13.6$cm)

344 Bourgeois
Tobias and the Angel
Panel (circular), $8 \times 8\frac{3}{16}$in $(20.3 \times 20.8$cm)

345 French School
Girl with a Hurdy-Gurdy
Canvas on panel?, $9\frac{5}{8} \times 8$in $(24.3 \times 20.3$cm)

346 Wood
Stothard
Canvas, $50\frac{1}{16} \times 40\frac{1}{8}$in $(127.2 \times 101.9$cm)

347 Snayers
Cavalry Skirmish
Canvas, $29\frac{1}{8} \times 43$in $(74 \times 109.2$cm)

349 After J. van Ruisdael
Canal with Bridge
Panel, $15\frac{15}{16} \times 20\frac{7}{8}$in $(40.5 \times 53$cm)

350 Unknown (?Dutch)
Fruit with Squirrel
Canvas, $20\frac{3}{8} \times 42\frac{3}{4}$in $(51.7 \times 108.6$cm)

351 Destroyed 1939/45

352 After van Dyck
Christ and S. John as Children
Canvas, $29\frac{5}{8} \times 24\frac{5}{8}$in $(75.3 \times 62.6$cm)

353 Unknown (?Flemish)
Marine Deities
Panel, $24\frac{3}{4} \times 31$in $(62.8 \times 78.8$cm)

354 British School
The Judd Memorial
Panel, $31\frac{1}{2} \times 40\frac{1}{4}$in $(80 \times 102.2$cm)

355 Unknown
Still-life
Panel, $14\frac{3}{4} \times 11\frac{5}{8}$in $(37.5 \times 29.5$cm)

356 Flemish School
Company of Cavalry
Panel, $20\frac{5}{8} \times 15\frac{7}{8}$in $(52.4 \times 40.3$cm)

357 Unknown (?Dutch)
Dead Game
Canvas, $32\frac{3}{8} \times 23\frac{7}{8}$in $(82.2 \times 60.6$cm)

358 Unknown (?Dutch)
Bagpiper and Girl
Panel, $25\frac{1}{2} \times 31$in $(64.8 \times 78.8$cm)

362 Huysmans
Woman
Canvas, $29\frac{1}{2} \times 24\frac{5}{8}$in $(74.9 \times 62.5$cm)

363 British School
Colonel R. Lovelace
Canvas, $29\frac{1}{2} \times 25$in $(74.9 \times 63.5$cm)

364 British School
Thomas Lovelace
Panel, $30\frac{1}{4} \times 23\frac{7}{16}$in $(76.8 \times 59.5$cm)

365 British School
Sir William Lovelace
Panel, $25\frac{1}{2} \times 21\frac{1}{2}$in $(64.7 \times 54.6$cm)

366 Destroyed 1939/45

367 British School
Sir William Lovelace
Panel, $42 \times 31\frac{3}{4}$in $(106.7 \times 80.6$cm)

452 Zuccarelli
Bacchanal
Canvas, $13\frac{1}{2} \times 18\frac{1}{8}$in ($34.3 \times 46$cm)

453 Wood
Diana and Endymion
Canvas, 50×40in (127×101.5cm)

454 Wood
The Orphans
Canvas, $56\frac{3}{8} \times 41\frac{1}{2}$in ($143.2 \times 105.4$cm)

455 Flemish School
Abraham, Sarah and Hagar
Panel, $11\frac{3}{8} \times 7\frac{7}{16}$in ($28.9 \times 18.9$cm)

457 School of Rosa
Mountainous Landscape
Canvas, $19\frac{1}{4} \times 26$in (48.9×66cm)

458 After Albani
Salmacis and Hermaphrodite
Canvas, $23\frac{7}{8} \times 29\frac{1}{8}$in ($60.6 \times 74$cm)

459 Destroyed 1939/45

460 Bourgeois
Landscape with Soldiers
Canvas, $25\frac{1}{8} \times 29\frac{7}{8}$in ($63.8 \times 75.8$cm)

461 Bourgeois
Figures in a Landscape
Canvas, 17×30in (43.2×76.2cm)

462 Bourgeois
Landscape with Cattle
Canvas, $16\frac{7}{8} \times 20\frac{7}{8}$in ($42.9 \times 53$cm)

463 Bourgeois
Cavalry in a Landscape
Canvas, $15\frac{3}{4} \times 26\frac{3}{4}$in ($40 \times 67.9$cm)

464 Bourgeois
Self-portrait
Canvas, 24×20in (61×50.8cm)

465 Bourgeois after Beechey
Bourgeois
Canvas, 30×24in (76.2×60.9cm)
—badly damaged 1939/45

467 Bourgeois
William Tell
Canvas, $30\frac{1}{4} \times 43\frac{3}{8}$in ($76.8 \times 110.2$cm)

468 Copy after Correggio
Venus and Cupid
Canvas, $19\frac{1}{2} \times 10\frac{3}{4}$in ($49.5 \times 27.3$cm)

469 Unknown
Landscape with Shepherds
Panel, $18\frac{3}{4} \times 29$in (47.6×73.6cm)

471 Houbraken
Landscape with Sportsman
Canvas, $19\frac{5}{8} \times 17\frac{3}{16}$in ($49.8 \times 43.6$cm)

472 Dutch School(?)
A Light Breeze
Panel, $16\frac{1}{16} \times 27\frac{5}{16}$in ($40.7 \times 69.3$cm)

473 Unknown
Infant S. John
Canvas, $24 \times 32\frac{1}{8}$in (61×81.5cm)

477 Copy after Poussin
The Nurture of Bacchus
Canvas, $29 \times 39\frac{1}{8}$in (73.6×99.4cm)

478 After Poussin
Abraham and the Angels
Canvas, $27\frac{1}{8} \times 36\frac{3}{8}$in ($69.9 \times 92.4$cm)

479 After Poussin
Mountainous Landscape
Canvas, $19\frac{3}{4} \times 25\frac{3}{4}$in ($50.2 \times 65.4$cm)

480 After Poussin
Fishermen near a Rocky Gateway
Canvas $19\frac{1}{2} \times 25\frac{7}{8}$in ($49.5 \times 65.7$cm)

482 After Poussin
Jupiter and Antiope
Canvas, $26\frac{5}{8} \times 19\frac{3}{4}$in ($67.7 \times 50.2$cm)

483 Destroyed 1939/45

484 After Titian
Sleeping Venus
Canvas, $39\frac{7}{8} \times 73\frac{1}{4}$in ($101.3 \times 186$cm)

485 Verwilt
Jupiter and Antiope
Panel, $14\frac{7}{8} \times 18\frac{5}{8}$in ($37.8 \times 47.3$cm)

486 British School
Landscape with Horses
Canvas, $14\frac{5}{8} \times 19\frac{3}{8}$in ($37.2 \times 49.2$cm)

487 Unknown
Massacre of the Innocents(?)
Canvas on panel, $25\frac{1}{4} \times 24\frac{3}{4}$in
(64.1×62.8cm)

488 Bourgeois(?)
N. Desenfans
Canvas, $47\frac{1}{8} \times 39\frac{3}{4}$in ($119.7 \times 101$cm)

491 Destroyed 1939/45

492 Hodgkins
Samson and the Lion
Panel, $12\frac{1}{2} \times 39\frac{3}{4}$in ($31.7 \times 101$cm)

493 Hodgkins
Samson and the Philistines
Panel, $12\frac{5}{8} \times 39\frac{3}{4}$in ($31.7 \times 101$cm)

494 British School
'Duke of Marlborough'
Canvas, $29\frac{3}{4} \times 24\frac{7}{8}$in ($75.5 \times 63.1$cm)

495 British School
James Allen
Canvas, $40\frac{1}{4} \times 49\frac{1}{2}$in ($102.2 \times 125.7$cm)
—not kept in the Gallery

496 C. Stoppelaer(?)
James Allen
Canvas, 93×58in (236.1×147.2cm)
—not kept in the Gallery

497 Fisher
Rev. Dr A. J. Carver
Canvas, $59\frac{5}{8} \times 37$in (151.4×93.9cm)
—not kept in the Gallery

498 British School
Lady Falkland
Canvas, $50\frac{1}{8} \times 40\frac{5}{8}$in ($127.3 \times 102.9$cm)

499 Briggs
Charles Druce
Canvas, $93\frac{7}{8} \times 57\frac{3}{4}$in ($238.4 \times 146.7$cm)

500 Lane
Mrs Bartley
Canvas, $53\frac{3}{4} \times 40\frac{1}{4}$in ($136.5 \times 102.2$cm)

501 Unknown
Head of a Woman
Canvas, $18\frac{7}{8} \times 16$in (47.9×40.6cm)

502 Lost

503 French School(?)
N. Desenfans
Canvas, $18\frac{5}{8} \times 14\frac{15}{16}$in ($47.3 \times 38$cm)

504 Unknown
Head of a Man
Canvas, $29\frac{7}{8} \times 24\frac{3}{4}$in ($75.9 \times 62.9$cm)

506 Unknown
The Holy Family
Canvas, $12\frac{1}{8} \times 8\frac{7}{8}$in ($30.8 \times 22.5$cm)

508 Lost

509 Unknown
Winged Figure
Panel, $17\frac{3}{8} \times 22\frac{5}{8}$in ($44.2 \times 57.5$cm)

510 Destroyed

511 Unknown
Venus and Adonis
Panel, $13\frac{3}{4} \times 9\frac{1}{8}$in ($35 \times 23.2$cm)

512 Unknown
A Jester
Canvas, $19\frac{1}{8} \times 13\frac{3}{4}$in ($48.6 \times 34.9$cm)

513 Unknown
Time and Truth
Panel, $15\frac{1}{4} \times 19$in (38.7×48.3cm)

514 Dutch School
Ice Scene
Panel, $11\frac{3}{4} \times 22\frac{15}{16}$in ($29.8 \times 58.3$cm)

515 Dutch School
Interior
Canvas, $20\frac{1}{2} \times 25\frac{5}{8}$in ($52 \times 65.1$cm)

516 Dutch School
Interior
Canvas, $20\frac{5}{8} \times 25\frac{1}{2}$in ($52.4 \times 64.8$cm)

518 Unknown
Seapiece
Canvas, $13 \times 20\frac{1}{2}$in (33×52cm)

519 Unknown
Ducks on a Pond
Canvas, $17\frac{7}{8} \times 21\frac{3}{4}$in ($45.4 \times 55.3$cm)

520 Lost

521 British School
William the Conqueror
Panel, $22\frac{1}{2} \times 16\frac{3}{4}$in ($57.2 \times 42.5$cm)

522 British School
William Rufus
Panel, 22½ × 16¹¹⁄₁₆in (57.2 × 42.4cm)

523 British School
Henry I
Panel, 22⅜ × 16¾in (56.8 × 42.5cm)

524 British School
Henry II
Panel, 22⅝ × 16½in (57.5 × 41.9cm)

525 British School
Richard I
Panel, 22⅝ × 16½in (57.5 × 41.9cm)

526 British School
King John
Panel, 22⅝ × 16½in (57.5 × 41.9cm)

527 British School
Edward I
Panel, 22⅝ × 16½in (57.5 × 41.9cm)

528 British School
Henry IV
Panel, 22⅞ × 17⅞in (58.1 × 45.4cm)

529 British School
Henry VI
Panel, 22½ × 17¼in (57.2 × 43.8cm)

530 British School
Edward V (ie VI)
Panel, 22⅞ × 17¹⁵⁄₁₆in (58.1 × 45.6cm)

531 British School
Richard III
Panel, 22¾ × 17⅝in (57.8 × 44.8cm)

532 British School
Henry VII
Panel, 21¾ × 16¼in (55.2 × 41.3cm)

533 British School
Henry VIII
Panel, 23 × 18in (58.4 × 45.7cm)

534 British School
Queen Anne Boleyn
Panel, 22⅜ × 16⅝in (56.8 × 42.2cm)

535 British School
Henry V (wrongly called Edward VI)
Panel, 22½ × 17¾in (57.2 × 45.1cm)

536 British School
Queen Mary
Panel, 22⅞ × 16½in (58.1 × 41.9cm)

537 Unknown
Egyptian Sibyl
Canvas, 24 × 17½in (61 × 44.4cm)

538 Unknown
Samian Sibyl
Canvas, 23⅛ × 17⅜in (58.7 × 44.1cm)

539 Unknown
Cumaean Sibyl
Panel, 22½ × 16⅛in (57.2 × 40.9cm)

540 Unknown
'Sibilla Cumea'
Canvas, 25 × 17¾in (63.5 × 45.1cm)

541 Unknown
Delphic Sibyl
Panel, 22½ × 16⅛in (57.2 × 41cm)

542 Unknown
European Sibyl
Panel, 22½ × 16⅛in (57.2 × 41cm)

543 Unknown
Hellespontic Sibyl
Panel, 22½ × 16¹¹⁄₁₆in (57.2 × 42.4cm)

544 Unknown
Persian Sibyl
Panel, 22½ × 16⅝in (57.2 × 42.3cm)

545 Unknown
Tiburtine Sibyl
Canvas, 22½ × 16¾in (57.2 × 42.5cm)

546, 547 Unknown
Piety and *Liberality*
Panel (arched tops), both 60 × 24in
(152.3 × 61cm)—not kept
in the Gallery

549 Morris after van Somer
Francis Bacon, Lord Verulam
Canvas, 55 × 38in (139.6 × 96.5cm)
—not kept in the Gallery

550 Lost?

551 Unknown
Edward Alleyn
Canvas, 55 × 38in (139.6 × 96.5cm)
—not kept in the Gallery

552 White
Rev. J. Smith
Canvas, 44 × 33in (111.7 × 83.8cm)
—not kept in the Gallery

553 Hastain
Rev. A. Carver
Canvas, 32 × 26in (81.3 × 66cm)

554 Beechey
Sir P. F. Bourgeois
Ivory, 6 × 4⅜in (15.3 × 11.1cm)

566 Highmore
Lady in Blue
Canvas, 36 × 29in (91.4 × 73.6cm)

582 T. Kettle
E. and M. Davidson
Canvas, 50 × 40⅛in (127 × 101.9cm)

583 T. Kettle
Lady
Canvas, 29⅞ × 24⅞in (75.9 × 63.2cm)

591 Beach
Gentleman
Canvas, 30⅛ × 25in (76.5 × 63.5cm)

593 B. Wilson
Lady
Canvas, 36⅛ × 27⅞in (91.7 × 70.7cm)

594 Dutch School(?)
Hound
Canvas, 10¹⁵⁄₁₆ × 13⅞in (27.8 × 35.2cm)

595 Grignon
Haines Jr
Canvas, 24 × 19¾in (61 × 50.1cm)

597 Flemish School(?)
Fox and Poultry
Canvas, 45½ × 66⅞in (115.5 × 169.9cm)

601 Russell
Samuel Moody
Pastel on paper, 23¾ × 17⅝in
(60.3 × 44.8cm)

602 Copy after Raphael
Madonna and Child with SS. Elizabeth and John
Panel, 58⅜ × 46⅛in (148.3 × 117.2cm)

605 Lievens
Self-portrait
Panel, 24½ × 19¼in (62.2 × 48.9cm)

607 Horsley
Old-time Tuition at Dulwich College
Canvas, 33⅛ × 42¼in (84.1 × 107.3cm)
—not kept in the Gallery

609 After Hanneman
Gentleman
Canvas, 22⅛ × 18⅜in (56.2 × 45.7cm)

610 Vernet
Seapiece
Canvas, 17⅜ × 24½in (44.1 × 62.2cm)

612 Murray
King's Daughters
Panel, 10⅛ × 14⅜in (25.8 × 36.5cm)

613 Highmore
Lady
Canvas, 50¼ × 40in (127.6 × 101.6cm)

616 After Wynants
Landscape
Canvas, 23¼ × 31in (59.1 × 78.8cm)

617 Dutch School(?)
Landscape
Panel, 24¼ × 29⅜in (61.6 × 74.6cm)

618 M. Green
Self-portrait
Paper? on canvas, 16 × 10in (40.6 × 25.4cm)

619 A. van Ostade
Peasants Drinking
Panel, 16⅛ × 19¼in (41 × 49cm)

621 Brakenburgh
Peasants Celebrating
Panel, 15⅞ × 21⅝in (40.3 × 54.9cm)

622 Mahu
Scullery Maid
Panel, 22 × 30⅞in (55.8 × 78.4cm)

623 Vernet
Coastal View
Canvas, 21¼ × 32¼in (54.1 × 82cm)

624 After van der Neer
River Scene, Moonlight
Canvas, 27¼ × 36¼in (69.2 × 92.3cm)

625 After Jordaens
Bacchanal
Canvas, 49⅞ × 59⅛in (126.5 × 150cm)

626 Belgian School
A Well at Antwerp
Canvas, 20¾ × 15⅛in (52.5 × 28.4cm)

628 Copy after Rembrandt
Man in Armour
Panel, 15¾ × 11⅞in (40 × 30.1cm)

629 Franceschini
Lot and his Daughters
Canvas, 41¾ × 35¼in (106.3 × 89.7cm)

630 Copy after Rubens
Judgement of Paris
Canvas, 37⅜ × 50in (95 × 127cm)

631 Ward
Bay Hunter
Panel, 27½ × 36⅞in (69.8 × 93.7cm)

632 Brodie
Landscape
Canvas, 36 × 24in (91.4 × 60.9cm)

633 Heusch
Landscape
Canvas, 31 × 24in (78.8 × 60.9cm)

634 Pickersgill
Two Children
Canvas, 35¾ × 28in (91 × 71cm)

635 Owen
Man
Canvas, 30⅛ × 24⅝in (76.5 × 62.6cm)

636 Unknown
Woman
Canvas, 29¾ × 24¾in (75.6 × 62.8cm)

637 Smart
Miss Planner
Canvas, 30 × 24¼in (76.2 × 61.6cm)

638 Unknown
Woman
Canvas, 30 × 24¾in (76.2 × 62.8cm)

639 Unknown
Man
Canvas, 23¾ × 19⅞in (60.3 × 50.5cm)

640 After Lawrence
Girl
Panel, 8⅝ × 7in (22 × 17.8cm)

641 Spanton
Nude
Canvas, 14 × 12in (35.5 × 30.5cm)

642 Unknown
Woman
Canvas, 46⅛ × 26in (117 × 66cm)

643 Durck
Woman
Canvas, 29⅞ × 24¾in (75.8 × 62.8cm)

644 After Stanzione
Woman
Canvas, 34¼ × 28⅛in (86.9 × 71.4cm)

645 Sandby
Desenfans and Bourgeois
Watercolour on card, 5⅝ × 6in (14.3 × 15.3cm)

646 Montanini
Landscape
Canvas, 17⅛ × 13in (43.5 × 33cm)

647 Shayer
Seapiece with Cliffs and Lighthouse
Canvas, 11⅞ × 15⅞in (30.2 × 40.4cm)

648 Unknown
F. Lane(?)
Canvas, 30 × 25in (76.2 × 63.5cm)

649 After Reynolds
Girl with Cat
Watercolour on card, 8 × 6½in (20.3 × 16.5cm)

650 J. Wood
Susan Jay and her Dog
Canvas, 27 × 22¼in (68.5 × 56.5cm)

651 Flemish School
Woodland Landscape
Canvas, 52⅝ × 56⅜in (133.6 × 143.1cm)

Index of Exhibited Portraits

Concordance of Changed or Rejected Attributions

Old or rejected attribution	Attribution in this Catalogue
Anonymous 505	Circle of MABUSE
Badalocchio, Sisto 265	After Annibale CARRACCI
Bergen, Dirk van 330	Jan LAPP
Burbage, Richard 395	BRITISH SCHOOL
Cooper, Samuel 573	Gerard SOEST
Dobson, William 592	Gerard SOEST, Attributed to
Dutch School 7	Roelof van VRIES
Flemish School 250	ANTWERP MASTER
Floris, Manner of Frans 250	ANTWERP MASTER
Fragonard, Jean Honoré 74	Jean-Alexis GRIMOU
French School 188	School of LEBRUN
French School 489	Aleksander KUCHARSKI
Gheeraerts, Marcus the Younger 548	John De CRITZ(?)
Greenhill, John 424	After John Michael WRIGHT
Hagelstein, J. T. 22	Circle of ELSHEIMER
Humphrey, Ozias 456	James LONSDALE
Kneller, Godfrey 611	John Baptist CLOSTERMAN, Attributed to
Lairesse, Gerard de 176, 179	Gerard HOET
Lancret, Nicolas 167	Circle of WATTEAU
Neapolitan School 558	Francesco FRACANZANO
Owen, William 476	Archer James OLIVER
Pareja, Juan de 277	Juan Bautista del MAZO
Pater, Jean-Baptiste 167	Circle of WATTEAU
Ribera, Jusepe 558	Francesco FRACANZANO
Rubens, Peter Paul 132	Sir Anthony van DYCK
Ruisdael, Jacob van 210	Jan WYNANTS
Ruysdael, Salomon van 16	Jakob van MOSCHER
Soest, Gerard 568	John RILEY
Teniers, David I 14	FLEMISH SCHOOL(?)

(For all other paintings previously attributed to Teniers I, *see* TENIERS)

Venetian School 75	Circle of Pier Francesco MOLA
Wynants, Jan 7	Roelof van VRIES
Wilson, Richard 561	Benjamin WILSON

Index of Former Owners

Listed below are the names of all persons known or reasonably believed to have owned the paintings in this Catalogue, except for Alleyn, Cartwright, Desenfans, Bourgeois and Fairfax Murray, who are listed separately. Modern dealers—Agnew, Colnaghi, Lesser—have also been excluded, but 18th- and 19th-century ones such as Lebrun or Buchanan are included.

	Cat No
Acworth	445
Amory, David	127
Andrew	445
Avery, T. C.	614
Backer, C.	86
Bacon, Francis	445
Balbi di Piovera	262
Barberini	263
Barnard, J.	96
Bartley, George	188, 291, 449
Basan	199, 481
Beechey, Sir William	17, 17a
Bergen van der Grijp see Grijp	
Bertels, John	76, 132, 264
Bessborough, Earl of	185, 233
Boaden, James	93
Boisset, Randon de	199
Borremans	131
Bouchardon, E.	249
Braamcamp	42, 61
Bracciano, Duca di	241, 243
Brand, T.	600
Briggs, H. P.	291
Broad, Professor C. D.	614, 615
Bryan	57, 128, 197, 285
Buchanan, W.	148
Bulwer, E. A.	568
Burch	240
Bute, Earl of	197
Bye, de	56
Calonne, C. A. de	146, 183, 199, 221, 236, 328
Campbell	234
Carysfort, Lord	236
Champernowne	269, 282
Charles	598
Christina, Queen of Sweden	241, 243
Cologne, Elector of	481
Conti, Prince de	56, 185
Cordellina, Villa	278
Coxe, E.	131
Crawford	82
Crozat	274
Cuff	598
D'Argenville	92
Delfos	86
Delme	575, 576

	Cat No
Denison	600
Desmarets	173
Digby, Sir Kenelm	194
Dillen	126
Disney	600
Dodsley	598
Doherty, John	588
Donjeux, V.	173
Dubarry, Comte de	56
Dubois	131
Dundas, Sir L.	54
Dyce, William	572
Egles	285
Erba, Odescalchi-	241, 243
European Museum	264, 451
Fouquet	42, 61, 182
Fox, Charles James	142
Gagny, Blondel de	199, 234
Gaignat	157, 166
Geldermeester (?Gildemeester)	82 (56)
Gentile, Palazzo	148
George III, King	19
Gersaint	90
Gheyn, J. de	99
Gibbs	620
Gildemeester (?Geldermeester)	56 (82)
Glucq, Claude	156
Gott, Sir Henry	603
Gournay, V. de	156
Grijp, J. Van Bergen van der	182
Groot, de	125
Gruyter	296
Gucht, B. van der	147, 185, 236, 285, 507
Guiche, Comte de la	199
Halifax, Earl of	205
Hardwicke, Lord	565
Heemskirk	82
Herbert, Alleyne Fitz	281
Hill	171
Hollis, T.	600
Hollond, Robert	578, 579
Hoogenbergh, I.	78
Horion, J. B.	92
Howard, Hon. Mary	570
Hume, Sir Abraham	156
Huygens	99

Major Bequests—exhibited

The following numbers are those of pictures given to the Gallery by Edward Alleyn, William Cartwright, Noel Desenfans–Sir P. F. Bourgeois, RA, and Charles Fairfax Murray (including 611, which seems to have been in his possession at one time: it was actually given by Miss H. M. Spanton in 1934, probably in fulfilment of his wishes).

ALLEYN:

443, 444

CARTWRIGHT:

359, 360(?), 361, 371, 374, 375, 376, 385, 387, 390, 391, 393, 395, 399, 400, 411, 416, 418, 423, 424, 428, 430, 431, 436, 437, 517

DESENFANS–BOURGEOIS:

4, 7, 9, 10, 11, 12, 14, 15, 16, 18, 19, 20, 22, 23, 25, 26, 28, 31, 33, 34, 35, 36, 39, 40, 40a, 42, 43, 44, 45, 47, 49, 51, 52, 53, 54, 56, 57, 61, 64, 65, 66, 67, 69, 70, 71, 72, 74, 75, 76, 77, 78, 79, 81, 82, 83, 85, 86, 87, 88, 90, 91, 92, 93, 95, 96, 97, 98, 99, 102, 103, 104, 105, 106, 108, 110, 111, 112, 113, 114, 115, 116, 117, 120, 121, 122, 124, 125, 126, 127, 128, 131, 132, 134, 136, 139, 141, 142, 143, 144, 146, 147, 148, 155, 156, 157, 158, 163, 164, 165, 166, 167, 168, 169, 170, 171, 172, 173, 174, 175, 176, 179, 181, 182, 183, 185, 186, 189, 193, 194, 195, 196, 197, 199, 202, 203, 204, 205, 208, 210, 214, 215, 216, 219, 221, 222, 223, 224, 226, 227, 232, 233, 234, 236, 238, 239, 240, 241, 242, 243, 244, 249, 255, 258, 262, 263, 264, 265, 269, 270, 274, 277, 278, 279, 281, 282, 285, 296, 297, 299, 300, 312, 314, 318, 319, 322, 323, 326, 327, 328, 330, 332, 333, 338, 339, 348, 451, 466, 470, 481, 489, 490

FAIRFAX MURRAY:

555, 556, 557, 558, 559, 560, 561, 562, 563, 564, 565, 567, 568, 569, 570, 571, 572, 573, 574, 575, 576, 577, 578, 579, 580, 581, 584, 585, 586, 587, 588, 589, 590, 592, 596, 603, 604, 606, 611(?)

Major Bequests—non-exhibited

The following numbers refer to pictures in the Gallery, but not included in the Catalogue of Exhibited Pictures, given by Alleyn, Cartwright, Desenfans or Bourgeois, and Fairfax Murray.

ALLEYN:

160(?), 354(?), 368, 369, 370, 384, 392, 417, 419, 421, 521, 522, 523, 524, 526, 527, 528, 529, 530, 531, 532, 533, 534, 535, 536, 537, 538, 539, 540, 541, 542, 543, 544, 545, 546, 547

CARTWRIGHT:

160(?), 350, 351, 352, 353, 354(?), 356, 357, 358, 362, 363, 364, 365, 367, 372, 373, 377, 378, 379, 380, 381, 386, 388, 389, 394, 396, 397, 398, 401, 404, 406, 407, 408, 409, 410, 412, 413, 414, 420, 422, 425, 426, 429, 432, 433, 434, 435, 506, 509, 511, 513, 514, 515, 516, 520

DESENFANS—BOURGEOIS:

1, 2, 3, 5, 6, 8, 13, 21, 24, 27, 29, 30, 32, 37, 38, 41, 48, 50, 55, 58, 59, 60, 62, 63, 68, 73, 80, 84, 89, 94, 100, 101, 107, 109, 118, 119, 123, 129, 130, 133, 135, 137, 138, 149, 150, 151, 152, 153, 154, 159, 160(?), 161, 162, 177, 180, 184, 187, 190, 191, 192, 198, 200, 201, 206, 207, 209, 211, 212, 213, 217, 218, 220, 225, 228, 229, 230, 231, 237, 245, 246, 247, 248, 251, 252, 253, 254, 256, 257, 259, 260, 261, 266, 267, 268, 271, 272, 273, 275, 276, 280, (283), 284, 286, 287, 288, 289, 290, 292, 293, 294, 295, 298, 301, 303, 305, 306, 307, 308, 309, 310, 311, 313, 315, 317, 321, 324, 325, 329, 334, 335, 336, 337, 340, 341, 342, 343, 344, 345, 347, 349, 350, 351, 352, 353, 354(?), 450, 452, 457, 458, 459, 460, 461, 462, 463, 465, 467, 468, 469, 471, 472, 473, 477, 478, 479, 480, 482, 483, 484, 485, 486, 487, 488, 503

FAIRFAX MURRAY:

566, 582, 583, 591, 593, 595, 602, 605